MEDIA AND PRESS

MEDIA AND PRESS

N. Afaque Shamsi

ANMOL PUBLICATIONS PVT. LTD.
NEW DELHI - 110 002 (INDIA)

ANMOL PUBLICATIONS PVT. LTD.
H.O.: 4374/4B, Ansari Road, Darya Ganj,
New Delhi-110 002 (India)
Ph.: 23261597, 23278000
B.O.: No. 1015, Ist Main Road, BSK IIIrd Stage
IIIrd Phase, IIIrd Block,
Bangalore - 560 085 (India)
Visit us at: www.anmolpublications.com

Media and Press

First Published, 2006

ISBN 81-261-2669-8

PRINTED IN INDIA

Published by J.L. Kumar for Anmol Publications Pvt. Ltd., New Delhi - 110 002 and Printed at Mehra Offset Press, Delhi.

Contents

Preface

Media is the plural of 'Medium' and 'mass' means a large number. Thus, by mass-media, what is meant is 'the main means of communication at a large number' i.e., all those means, which are used to communicate with people on a vast level or at a great number, as, newspapers, magazines, radio and television, etc.

Though communication has always been an important need of life, it assumed the status of the most essential and one of the basics of life in the later half of the 20th century. As a result, a number of different and diverse forms of media emerged and institutions imparting their thorough knowledge mushroomed throughout the width and length of the country and world.

In this battle of survival and cut-throat comptetion, the one which won the greatest appreciation and applaud of the masses is the Electronic Media by virtue of its being capable of communicating to people, live and pulsating coverage of news and events occurring in every nook and corner of the world and in all the strata of the society ranging from the laymen to the top brass of Government, Semi-Government and non-Government administrations.

Given the above-discussed situation, there was an urgent demand for such an Encyclopaedia, which may cater to the maximum requirements of the seekers of knowledge in this regard. This series has been prepared with a view to encapsulating most of the stuff required by a media-lover.

Should we succeed in our attempt and get a favouring feedback excluding unnecessary brickbats, we would put a more enlightening, informative and comprehensive ocean of knowledge in the hold of your hands.

Editor

1

Technology of Printing

A printing unit is the part and parcel of print media and journalism. Normally most of the journal editors inherit a printer, unless the journal is a new one. Book editors looking for a publisher are influenced to some extent by the quality of printing and production of the publisher's other books; that is, by the typeface, quality of illustrations, layout-whether the pages looked cramped or spacious, easy or difficult to read-and strength and quality of the binding. Most publishers use several printers and can influence many of these variables according to an editor's requirements, though only within the limits of the printer's capabilities and the publisher's own financial constraints.

Finding or changing printers is not a step to take in a huffy. Any editor faced with this task should visit several printers and ask them to set some material to show the range and quality of their work. It is important to know what facilities the printer can offer (copy-marketing, proof-reading, binding in-house, distribution to subscribers, invoicing), proof-reading, binding in-house, distribution to subscribers, invoicing), what form quality control takes, and how large the printing team is. Other points to note are the error rate in proofs (ask to see some proofs) and whether the agreement includes penalty clauses for errors or for late delivery. Most publishers of any size will employ experts to deal with these matters but will expect editors to take an interest and become involved in the production processes.

Here, we deal first with the general question of design, mainly as it applies to journals, and then with the specification and style sheet that the editor and copy editor should agree with the printer, either directly or via the publisher. And since editors need at least a theoretical knowledge of the main procedures, ancient or modern, that go towards the making of books and journals, the rest of the chapter discusses typesetting, printing, artwork, proofing, paper and binding, with a final note on offprints and reprints.

Arrangement and Presentation Skill : New editors often feel they should change the design and format of the journals or book series they have taken on, and scientist-editors sometimes think they now more about the design of scientific publications than any professional book designer. As consumers they are sometimes right: but major changes in design raise complicated issues and the arguments for and against a new look should be carefully weighed. A distinctly obsolete appearance, for example may seem to be a dis-advantage, yet it may turn out to be a selling-point for a journal because it emphasizes that the journal is long-established. The important issue is whether the format or design impedes legibility or comprehension. If necessary, the editor or publisher should call in a designer, whether free-lance or employed by the publisher or printer, and explain what problems need to be solved.

Cover Designing

The cover design of a journals is one candidate for change. Here the designer must take into account both the essential and the desirable items for the cover. The editor should provide at the outset as much information as possible about what is wanted, so that the designer does not have to produce innumerable mock-ups of possible covers.

A change in a journal's page size is rarely popular with librarians and should never be made in the middle of a volume. An increased page size may, however, allow tables or figures to be printed where readers most want to see them—on or opposite the pages where they are discussed, If the increase in size entails a change from single to double-column layout, the editors should make sure that the new layout is appropriate for the journal: where there are many complex equations or large tables a single column is preferable.

The designer and the printer can advise the editor which standard page size (economically available in the type of paper required) would best suit the needs of the journal. The printer should at the same time advise the editor whether a new mailing wrapper or envelope can be provided easily and economically.

In the text itself, the editor will want headings and abstracts to stand out boldly. Typefaces should be chosen to marry happily (and economically) with the type used in the text, and here a typographer's help is particularly valuable. In principle many typefaces are available but not every printer carries every fount. Some founts are more suitable than others for particular kinds of work, for example mathematics. The typographer can suggest which typefaces should be used, after making sure what the printer has to offer.

If type size is reduced, more words can be printed on a page, saving paper and mailing costs. The 10-point type still used in some scientific publications can with advantage be reduced to 9-point, but any further reduction in type size would be bad for readers' eyesight. (A 'point' as used by British and American printers is about 1/72 of an inch, or 0.3515 nun; a point in the Didot system, widely used in Europe, measures 0.376 nun.) The 10/12 setting (i.e. 10-point characters on a 12-point body, giving a 2-point space between the lines), formerly widely used, is now often replaced by 9/11 or 9/10. Subsidiary matter such as acknowledgments, footnotes, appendixes and references can be reduced to 8/10. To save space, some journals reduce the type size for references to 6/8; this is the lowest permissible limit, even for material that is not read continuously but only referred to. Computer typesetting can provide many gradations in point size, giving 9.2 on 10.5 and so on. This flexibility is useful if there are short or long pages.

In spite of the general need to save space, wide inner margins, i.e. those forming the 'gutter' of a double-page spread, should be specified so that the reader can make satisfactory photocopies from the bound book or journal volume. Publishers may resists this (because they wish to discourage photo-copying); so my designers (because they will say that the double-page spread falls apart visually); and so may printers (who will think it is untraditional). They should all be overruled: photo-copying of single items for individual users is legitimate and desirable for the progress of science, and this is what counts.

A well-designed book or journal has a unified appearance throughout, with all the chapters or articles styled in the same way, and with the cover, prelims and indexes fitting in with that style. If, for example, all chapter or article titles, legends, headings and sub-headings in the text are printed flush with the left-hand margin (which saves typing and typesetting time and is therefore more economical than having them all centered), the jacket or cover looks best if it matches this style.

The tables and illustrations should then in theory also be set to the left instead of being centered, although to many eyes this looks peculiar. In this style, if there are more than three levels of subheading which should not often be necessary a variety of type sizes and typefaces will be called for if the reader is to understand the structure immediately. "The flush-left style then presents its own impediments to the achievements of a unified appearance. One solution is to centre all main headings as well as all tables and illustrates but otherwise keep to the flush-left style, making sure that third-order headings are clearly subordinated to second-order headings. The important principle is that aesthetic considerations, important though they are, must be secondary to the reader's rapid grasp of structure.

Layout is in the printer's domain, but some printers are overfond of the notion that each page or double-page spread should look balanced, with (for example) two illustrations always placed at diagonally opposite corners of a page or spread. This idea should be forgotten: Illustrations must be printed as close to the relevant text as possible, and if the balanced look conflicts with this principle it will have to be abandoned it is not a work of art that is being created but a carrier for a piece of scientific information.

Manuscripts with a high ratio of illustrations to text present other, layout problems. Editors can help to minimize these problems by asking authors to supply clear and simple illustrations that can be reduced as far as is consistent with legibility; or pairs or triplets of illustrations can be combined; or photographs can be cropped so that only the strictly relevant parts are shown-at full magnification but taking up only as much room as is strictly necessary.

Copy Style

The designer and the printer's typographer will be concerned not only with overall design but also with the detailed printing specification. This should be agreed between the editor, copy editor and publisher or printer at an early stage. A well-thought-out specification is a powerful time saver for the editorial office. It may take weeks or months to get it right but the effort is worth it. The editor (or publisher) should be guided, but not bullied, by the printer in discussions of the specification. The printer knows what is routine in the printing plant, what is easily arranged, and what will lead to difficulties and mistakes. On the other hand, if the publication has special requirements that the printer cannot meet, another printer will have to be found.

The specification will include some or all the following:

(a) size of page and size, quality and weight of paper;
(b) type of binding;
(c) approximate number of pages in the book or in each issue of a journal;
(d) type founts for all parts of the publication, including prelims, indexes, running heads, headings, references, legends, tables and footnotes (if any) for the text;
(e) type size and body for the different parts;
(f) type areas or imposition size; that is, the length of the lines and the number of lines on each page—or, put the other way round, the size of margins;
(g) style or arrangements of legends, table titles and columns headings;
(h) use of horizontal lines and their relative weights in tables, and use of vertical lines, if allowed (these should be used rarely, if at all: they are expensive to set);
(i) symbols for linking footnotes to tables (Superscript letters, Superscript numbers, or other symbols, such as ?)
(j) typeface, size and placement of acknowledgments
(k) style for reference lists;
(l) method of identifying mathematical symbols or Cyrillic or Greek letters in the margins of typescripts (either spelt out, e.g. 'Gk mu' or by means of a code referring to the type found, e.g. 'Gk no. 34');
(m) spacing above and below illustrations and on the title page of chapters and articles;
(n) placement of page numbers;
(o) typeface, size and number of indexes.

Once the specification has been agreed, specimen pages showing chapter openings, sub-headings and so on are usually prepared and shown to the editor. When the details have been approved, a style sheet can be prepared for printer's copy-maker, showing what has to be done in marking up typescripts. The editor and printer (or publisher) also discuss whether typescripts will be fully copy-edited, partially copy-edited, or perhaps no copy-edited at all. It is important for both the editorial office and the printer to know how much marking should be down, and by whom: there is, for example, no point in copy editors marking every Greek mu in a paper full of measurements in micrometers. With a well-prepared style sheet which lists the relevant points from the specification, copy marking becomes almost automatic; with modern typesetting methods it can even be partly computerized.

This brings us to the basic process of 'printing,' which in fact consists of several processes, the two main ones being composition (type-setting or key-boarding), and the actual printing (presswork, machining) during which recognizable patterns appear on the paper. For information about these two processes I have relied heavily on Jennett, Varley, Dessauer and Seybold. Plate-making, which takes place between the main two processes, is not described here.

Different Elements

Three are four main methods of composition:

(1) hot-metal or hot-lead composition on Linotype, Monotype or similar machines;

(2) handsetting, which is used as little as possible;

(3) typewriter (strike-on) composition, including IBM Composer composition; and

(4) filmsetting and photo-composition, usually computer-assisted.

Typewriter composition and photo-composition are also known as 'cold composition'. Editors who want to mark and arrange typescripts intelligently, with the smallest probability of causing misunderstanding and costly mistakes, should visit their printers and see the processes in action.

With Linotype composition whole list of type are cast from a reservoir of molten metal after the compositor has keyboarded the copy. Monotype casters produce single characters from a similar hot metal alloy. The keyboards on Linotype and Monotype composing machines look like large typewriter keyboards, except that on the Linotype machine the characters are arranged in a different order.

The Monotype compositor has seven alphabets, Plus numbers and extra characters, to choose from. For book work (including journals) the alphabets might be upper-and lower-case roman, italics and bold face, and small capitals. The monotype machine produces a punched paper tape which is used to drive a separate casting machine. Some Linotype machines are type-driven too, but they have a built-in caster.

Compositors using either Monotype or Linotype machines must judge, when they get near the end of a line, how many more characters can be fitted in, since books and journals are conventionally justified (aligned) on the right as well as on the left. The compositor may decide that word should be split at the end of a line, according to well-defined hyphenating rules, or that the spacing between words already on the line should be increased in order to extend the line to the full measure. On the Monotype machine a measuring device shows how much space is left and the compositor presses justifying keys which punch spacing instructions in the tape at the end of each line. Since the tape is fed into the casting machine backwards from the end of the last line of the piece of copy being set, the spacing instructions reach the machine first and spaces of the correct width are set in each line.

The Monotype casting machine holds an exchangeable Matrix case containing 255 characters in one type found and size. The punched tape instructs the casting machine to centre the required character in the matrix case over a mould, Molten metal is pumped into the mould, the character is stamped out and the resulting piece of rectangular type is quickly cooled and ejected. The character on the piece of type is reversed left-right so that it comes out the right way round when printed on the page. The size, or body, or the rectangular piece of metal in relation to the size of the character determines the width between lines of text (e.g. a 9-point letter on an 11-point body).

As the type comes out a Linotype machine or monotype caster, the metal slugs (Linotype) or separate pieces of type (Monotype) slide into long metal trays called galleys. When enough galleys are fully, the type is inked and proofs are pulled of checking by the printer's reader. Who marks obvious errors on these pages. Corrections are made almost immediately. With Monotype setting, in correct letters can be picked out with a pair of tweezers-, the correct letter is then substituted from a tray of ready-cast spares and the line re-justified. With Linotype machines, the whole slug has to be reset on the machine if a line contains a single mistake. With either Linotype or Monotype setting, a damaged or dirty matrix will produce a defective letter every time that matrix is used. This is why sections of proof are sometimes found in which almost every 't', for example, seems to be broken. The printer's proof-reader usually sees this and replaces the 'broken' letters.

The speed of the Monotype caster is limited to about 11000 characters an hour by the stop-start mechanism and the time the metal takes to cool. Another limitation is that a matrix case contains only one typeface in one size of type, so the matrix has to be replaced each time a different typeface or size is needed; alternatively, sections of the copy may be set separately on different machines. Linotype composition can be a little faster than Monotype and it was, for a long time, the machine used for setting newspapers. However, its slugs of type make it less flexible for book or journal work than Monotype and it has not been used so often for these purposes in Europe as it has in the USA.

Both Monotype and Linotype are labour-intensive-and they are both rapidly being superseded by cold composition. But where hot metal composition is still available, it may for various reasons cost less than photo-composition, and some printers may be using it for many years to come. The vocabulary of printing is largely based on this method.

Setting Procedure

Handsetting may still be used for display work in which unusual type sizes are needed, for lettering that runs diagonally or vertically, and for complex tables, mathematical equations or chemical formulae. With this method ready-cast Monotype characters are inserted by hand between blanks (for spaces) in a pattern as close as possible to the author's or designer's requirements. The process is, of course, expensive. This is why editors should instruct authors to translate terms such as a/b, which usually has to be handset, into a/b, which can be set mechanically. Authors (or editors) should also transform exponential functions with superscripts and super-superscripts into logarithmic functions, and simplify the construction of tables as much as possible-for example so that column headings can be set straight, not sideways, and so that vertical lines are not necessary.

The cost of conventional printing can be cut drastically if perfectly typed material is provided which is suitable either for photographing and printing by offset lithography or for feeding though a scanner which produces a drive tape for a photocomposer (see next section). Typescripts ready to be photographed ('camera-ready copy') may be supplied by the author or prepared by the editorial office, the publisher's staff, specialist outside firms or the printing firm itself (Printing unions often object to the first three of these, and editors thinking of changing to this system should enquire first about the local attitude.) The copy mug-fit within stated limits and special typing paper with limiting rectangles and lines printed in blue is sometimes provided by publishers or required by printers who use this method. The luxury of justified typing is usually abandoned in favour of the more economical (and possibly more legible) ragged right-hand edge. Although justifying typewriters exist, most people consider that the slightly improved appearance does not warrant the expense. Typewriter composition may be done on anything from an ordinary typewriter with a fresh ribbon, or an electric typewriter with a one time carbon or plastic ribbon, to an IBM Composer or a word processor. The IBM and other typewriters that offer a choice of typefaces an sets of symbols on exchangeable 'golf ball' heads can produce results which on the printed page compare well with the appearance obtained with hot-metal systems.

With typewriter setting, authors know exactly how the finished pages will look and can insert diagrams and figures just where they want them. They see their work in print quickly too, since the production process is fast and proof-reading for typesetting errors is not necessary. The editor will, however, have to do some checking of proofs for other kinds of mechanical faults. Publishers may agree to publish material produced in this way even when they expect sales to be small, because their production costs are much lower than usual (although marketing costs are unchanged).

The disadvantages of the method are that typed characters take up more space than typeset characters, so that more pages are needed for the same amount of material, and that some readers (and authors) dislike the look of the product, although this prejudice is disappearing as typewriter setting becomes more widespread and techniques improve.

Composing, Film and Plates : Mechanical filmsetting led composition out of the age of hot metal towards the era of electronics. The Monophoto filmsetter, for example, is based on the Monotype caster but uses a case of photographic images instead of a metal matrix case. The filmsetter contains a lamp, lenses, prisms, mirrors and a drum of film and is driven by punched paper tape produced on a slightly modified Monotype keyboard. The punched tape causes the required characters to be projected in turn by the lamp through the system of lenses, Prisms and angled mirrors onto the film. The mirrors move as each line is being set. Reflecting the characters to their place on the film. At the end of each line the film moves on, ready for the next line. A major advance over hot-metal systems is that different sizes of 'type' can be produced from one matrix by adjusting the lenses and prisms. Mechanized filmsetters are still in use but they work at only about the same speed as the hot metal caster around 11000 characters an hour.

Electromechanical photo-composing machines work 20 to 30 times faster than film-setters, although they operate on a similar principle. Photo-matrix (transparent) characters are held on a spinning disc, a drum or a grid, and the machine operates with a light source and a system of lenses and mirrors or prisms. The light source, often a xenon flash, projects each character onto a photosensitive medium (film or paper) in response to instructions from a punched paper or magnetic tape, or direct from a keyboard operator. Many type sizes and founts are available on these machines, and changes from one size or found to another can be made automatically.

Cathode-ray tube (CRT) photo-composers operate even faster than the 'second-generation' electromechanical machines, producing up to a million characters an hour. In CRT photo-composers, characters stored either on a photographic master or in digital form are generated on the CRT by an electron beam and then photographed. Photo-composers are highly flexible devices which can be instructed not only to change the type size and fount but to expander condense letters horizontally, change them from roman to italic or bold, and compose complete pages, dealing with line-end hyphenation and justification and all the other problems of page make-up.

The paper or magnetic tapes, cassettes or floppy disks that drive second-and third-generation photo-composers are usually produced by computer-linked keyboards. Some keyboards produce a paper copy ('hard copy') as well as computer-input tape; others are linked to a video display which shows the operator what has just been keyed, and the tape can be corrected immediately, if necessary; a third kind of keyboard produces only tape or, disks, though many machines of this kind now display the last 16 or 32 characters keyed by the operator.

The keyboarding step may be eliminated if the original manuscript' was typed, with or without coded printed instructions, in an optical character recognition (OCR)-readable typeface. Perry, Courier-12, OCR-A and OCR-B typefaces can be 'read' by a scanning machine such as the Compusan Alpha. Scanners produced paper or magnetic type for driving a photo-composer or they may be linked directly to a photo-composer.

Direct-entry photo-composers: are now available which are technologically somewhere between the first-and second-generation machines and are much cheaper than the more advanced photo-composers. They have small memories and set one line at a time. They produce good quality work and are easy to use-as the name implies, the copy is entered directly from a typewriter-like keyboard that has extra type-setting commands to control founds held on film or on a glass disk.

With all kinds of photo-composition, the images captured on film or photo-sensitive paper are transferred to metal, plastic or rubber plates for the printing process described in the next section. Once the film has been made corrections are often expensive, as pieces of corrected film may have to be stripped in carefully by hand. Authors should therefore be encouraged more strongly than ever to avoid making trivial changes in proof.

The main advantages of photo-composition over other methods are speed, flexibility of type size and form, and the degree of automation which can be achieved with the help of computers. Not all photo-composers now in use are linked to computers, but future developments will undoubtedly depend on such links.

In spite of the great speeding-up of this part of book or journal production, photo-composed text is at present still being printed by the mainly mechanical processes described next.

Technical Knowhow

The three printing processes in widest use until now have been letter press, offset lithography and photogravure. Printing is done either direct from metal type (letter-press) or from plates (all three methods). Only letter-press and lithography are mentioned here, as photogravure is rarely used for books or journals.

Letter-press, used mainly in conjunction with bot-metal composition, is the long-established method in which sheets of paper are pressed directly against the inked surface of type held on a flat bed press, or in which sheets or rolls (webs) of paper are pressed against inked plates.

The printing plates are moulded from the metal type and they may be flat or curved, and made of metal, plastic or rubber. Curved plates are made for rotary presses, which work much faster than flatbed presses. 'Perfecter' presses are rotary presses which print both sides of the paper in one pass through, the machine. Another development is the Belt Press, in which the printing plates for one or more books fit on a continuous belt, which prints in sequence on a web of paper. The machine also slits, folds and collates the pages ready for binding, and may bind them too, which greatly speeds up the production processes.

In offset lithography the film produced by the composition process is photographically reproduced on printing plates. Each plate is wrapped round a cylinder on the printing press and then moistened and inked. A chemical process allows image areas to accept ink but not water, while the non-image areas accept water but not ink. When the cylinder rotates, the image is transferred-that is, offset-onto a rubber blanket on another cylinder, and from that blanket onto the paper.

The only difference in quality between good offset printing and letter-press is that letter-press may give a slightly sharper effect. Illustrations (see the section on Artwork below) are easier and cheaper to print by lithography, and cheaper paper can often be used than for letter-press. Offset lithography is therefore likely to be the method of choice until new methods are discovered and developed.

For printing by letter press, line drawings are first photographed and then transferred to a plate from which the non-printing areas are etched or hand-tooled away, leaving a raised surface to be inked. For offset plates the image is transferred to the plate surface photographically, as for the text.

For half-tone illustrations, the original prints are photographed through a screen of two sets of fine lines crossing each other at right angles, each set being regularly spaced at (usually) 100, 133, 150 or even 200 lines to the inch. The finer the detail required, the more lines to the inch are needed, i.e. the finer the screen. For a photograph of a piece of equipment, the print might use a 100-mesh screen; for a light micrograph. 150-mesh with offset printing; and for an electron micrograph, possibly 200-mesh will be used. The finer the screen, the more care has to be used to prevent the ink from smudging, and the better the quality of paper needed. In letter-press printing, 200-mesh is about the finest screen that can satisfactorily be used, even on coated paper and with careful engraving; when screens finer than 200-mesh are used there is a loss of contrast. With offset lithography, screens of 133 or 150 lines to the inch are quite common.

The principle of the half-tone process is that light reflected from the photograph through each square in the mesh impinges on the photo-sensitive plate, and the greater the degree of blackness in the original print, the smaller the area Within that minute square that is affected. A white area on the original print will produce a series of discrete exposed ('black') squares on the plate. For letter press printing the plate is then dipped in an etching fluid which dissolves away the 'black' areas, leaving the unexposed areas-corresponding to black in the original—raised above the exposed ones. When the plate is inked these areas will print black. Grey areas in the original give rise to exposed squares of varying size according to the depth of grey. The purpose of these hundreds of tiny squares is to break the picture into dots, with areas of white between the inked areas. The printed picture then looks as if it had various shades of grey.

In letter-press printing the half-tone process, with its metal plats mounted on wooden or metal blocks, is expensive and authors are usually asked to keep the number of illustrations to a minimum. The original photographs must be of the best possible quality, since some quality is lost in even the best reproductions. If the high quality paper needed for 200-mesh reproductions is too expensive for a journal, the editor should warn authors and settle for medium quality semi-gloss paper and 1000-mesh screens.

To reduce costs without sacrificing the scientific evidence, the editor may select portions of photographs supplies by the author and reproduce them at full magnification rather than reduce whole photographs. Authors' photographs should never be cult instead they should be cropped or masked. That is, the margins of the photograph are marked to show which part is to be reproduced; or a rectangle of the appropriate size is marked on an overlay fixed to one edge of the print.

In letter-press printing the process known as 'routing out, can be used to remove any small blemishes from a plate, and this is cheaper than having a new photo-engraving made. Nothing can be added to, or altered in the engraving at this stage, which explains why photographs must be sent to the printer in the best possible condition, having been well protected throughout the editorial process. Paperclips must never be used on photographs and only the softest pencil should be used to identify them on the back. A completely flat surface, to be pressed against the screen, is essential, though slight bending or rolling is not armful. Several small photographs may be mounted together on white card if this is carefully done but, in general, authors should be asked not to mount individual photographs; some glues produce a bumpy surface, and if each photograph is mounted, mailing costs soar. A piece of thin cardboard on either side of each set of photographs protects them adequately during mailing and the editorial process.

The editor, or printer, may chose to reduce costs by grouping several photographs together to make a large plate, which is latter cut up as necessary. It is not a good idea to combine photographs and line drawings if an engraving is being made, first because it is twice as expensive as an ordinary block, and secondly because the screen needed for the half-tones will maker the line drawing look grey.

Most illustrations are reduced in size during printing. The editor may have to decide which illustrations can be reduced to one-column width and which should run right across the page or occupy a full page, turned sideways if necessary. The larger the page size, the greater the choice in this regard. The degree of reduction can be stated simply as 'Reduce width to 50 nun', or expressed as percentage: (desired width of the illustration) divided by (actual width of the original) x 100%.

Colour reproduction costs too much for most scientific journals and books. If colour is wanted, the editor will either have to persuade the publisher that colour is essential for scientific or commercial reasons or ask the author to cover the extra costs-which are amazingly high.

The principles of 'process' colour printing are the same as for black and white, except that four different plates are usually made for each photograph. Three plates are made by photographing the original through coloured filters (red, blue and green, for printing in blue, yellow and red respectively): the fourth plate is made for printing in black, to give richer shading and contrast. The final reproduction is made by printing from each of the four plates in turn. The skill and expense lie in getting the four plates exactly aligned, or 'in register.'

Two-colour printing (for line drawings, diagrams, etc.) is less expensive than four-colour, process printing. It can be by prior separation of the colours, that is by getting an artist to prepare two separate versions of the picture, each showing where one of the colours is to go.

An inexpensive alternative to two-colour printing for book-jackets or journal covers is the use of screens of different mesh sizes to produce shades of colour with a single ink.

Strictly speaking, galley proofs are produced only in letter-press printing, where metal type is collected in long trays (galleys) as described earlier. But the term is widely used for the first set of proofs, which usually go to authors as well as to the editor for correction. The first proofs may be 'page on galley', already measured into numbered or unnumbered pages on the long galley sheets, or they may be actual page proofs.

The paste-up process varies with each printer's practice. In the most orderly, and leisurely, procedure it goes as follows for hot-metal composition. Galley proofs are pulled by hand from the type standing in galleys. When corrected galley proofs are received, corrections are made in the type accordingly. Another proof is made, and this is cut up and pasted onto pages ruled to the size of the book or journal. Illustrations are placed appropriately, and the paste-up artist deals with problems like headings that land at the very bottom of page, or single word lines ('widows') that land at the top of one.

The paste-up person does this usually by instructing the printer to adjust the amount of space between line's or around headings, sometimes by directing that the type on several lines should be squeezed closer together or that a tightly set line should be opened up to make an extra line. This set of planning may have to take several pages into consideration.

When the paste-up is satisfactory the type is moved from the galleys and arranged, together with the blocks for the illustrations, in page 'formes' (metal frames) in accordance with the paste-up. Page numbers and running heads are added before the forms are locked tip ready for carrying to the press. These forms hold 16, 32 or other multiples of four pages, and the pages are so arranged that they will come out in the right order (and the right way up) when the printed press sheet is eventually folded into signatures (a portion of a publication containing however many pages are printed on each sheet).

To speed up publication, the total process has been streamlined by modern printers. Paste-up may be done while the authors are correcting proofs. Then, when authors' corrections result in an increase or decrease in the number of lines ' of text, the paste-up has to be adjusted before the type is placed in forms. Some printers do not only the paste up but also the page make-up before sending out the first proofs. For either of these procedures it is evidently highly disruptive if the author makes changes in proof which alter the number of lines, or the number or sequence of illustrations, and this is why such changes are so strongly discouraged. Sometimes the editor or other proof-reader can make a judicious further change that shortens or lengthens a sentence slightly and brings it back to its original length without changing its meaning.

Direct photography of typescript and photo-composition are easier for the printer to work with than hot metal, as there is no heavy type to be moved around in the late stages, with the attendant risks of small pieces of type being lost or getting out of alignment. On the other hand adjustment of vertical or horizontal spacing by cutting and stripping in small pieces of film is difficult to do well. Re-setting a whole page by computer may be done in a moment, but it can be an expensive moment. Alterations in any system are troublesome; that is why it is important first to find a printer who makes few typesetting errors and then to provide well-prepared thoroughly edited copy.

Final page proofs usually go to the editor only, unless an author insists on receiving a set too. Corrections must be kept to the absolute minimum at this stage. When final ad ustments-for example inserting page numbers in the contents list or index—have been made, the book or journal is ready for printing by one of the methods already described.

Use of Paper

The editor should ask the printer's or publisher's advice before specifying a particular quality of paper for a book or journal. Printers can work more economically with some papers than others, depending on the machines they use and other factors. Economy usually has to be balanced against the quality desired. For textual material, near-opaqueness, lightness of weight and a matt surface giving good contrast without glare are the desirable properties. If the book or journal has many illustrations calling for first-rate reproduction (e.g. electron micrographs), a glossy paper may have to be used throughout. Where there are only a few photographs in one or two places, the heavier paper can be inserted in four-page sections but this makes printing and binding much more expensive than usual.

Articles with electron micrographs, or the electron micrographs alone, are sometimes grouped on glossy paper at the end of a journal so that cheaper paper can be used for the rest of the issue. Another method is to have single sheets of glossy paper tipped in or 'hooked in' glued to the following page or 'wrapped round'-wrapped round the first and last page of a section. With all these method machinery has to be stopped for manual processes, at exorbitant expense, so that if superb reproduction is essential it is sometimes cheaper to use glossy paper throughout. Because of the manual work involved, fold-out pages are expensive too.

Paper may be either 'free sheet' (wood free) or groundwork stock. 'Free' means that the wood pulp has been chemically treated to remove the impurities and reduce the acidity of ground wood. Woodfree paper is the kind mainly used for scientific books and journals, though coated groundwood stocks with a reasonably long life are now available.

The weight of a paper is quoted in grams per square metre (g/m, sometimes written as 'gsm') or as pounds per ream (500 sheets). Papers weighing 75-100 g/m are commonly used for books and journals. Papers of the same weight may differing bulk (measured in pages per centimetre or inch), depending on how much air has been whipped into the pulp during milling, on how much fibre content there is, and on the method of milling. Except in North America (for the present), paper is usually supplied in 'A' sizes or the book sizes (Demy, Royal, Crown) and a press sheet may hold 16, 24, 32, 48, 64 or more printed pages, depending on the size of the press and the size of the book being printed.

The opacity and finish of appear are important. It is distracting to read a page if the text from the next page shows through clearly. Substances such as titanium oxide are added to increase opacity. The 'finish' refers to the final treatment in the manufacturing process, when a paper may be coated with china clay, to give it a glossy appearance, or 'super calendred'-pressed between metal rollers to make it very smooth. 'Machine-finished' papers are the kind most commonly used when a glossy finish is not needed.

The colour of the paper ('white' is not a precise term), and whether it has a high or a low glare, are other important qualities to take into consideration. Some coated papers now have a low glare, which makes for easier reading.

Binding Quality

Binding may be done either in the printing plant or in a separate bindery. Journals and paper-back books are usually bound in the printing plant, and binding may follow printing without any interruption. The processes involved are folding, gathering, sewing and/or gluing, trimming and attaching a cover. A book may be given a dustjacket, and books and journals may also be protectively wrapped for mailing, all in one series of mechanized processes.

The printed sheets that come off the press are folded into signatures, each signature representing one press sheet. The uncut signatures are gathered or collated to make up complete books or journal issues, and they are then saddle-wired (stapled at the back, for publications of up to 64 pages), side-wired (stronger than saddle-wiring and taking more pages), sewn (with the pages in each signature swwn together and sewn to the next signature), 'or glued direct to the spine without any stitching (so-called 'perfect' binding). Perfect binding is probably the most widely used method for binding both journals and paper-back books.

For books that are to have hard covers, 'endpapers' are attached at the beginning and end before the paper is trimmed, and the backs ands, (spines) are ten rounded. Reinforced gauze ('crash') and 'headbands' and Tootbands' are attached to the spines and these are glued to accept the covers ('cases'). Cases usually consists of 'boards' of various materials to which cloth, plastic or certain kinds of treated papers have been glued. Covers are usually prepared in advance, with wording and design as agreed in the specification.

. The title and other lettering are stamped on the front cover or spine, or both, with ink or through coloured foil. The books are then either pressed between heavy boards until the glue has died and the characteristic crease along the spine has taken shape, or they are seasoned to this stage in a few seconds in 'building-in' machines. Dustjackets, if used, go on last of all.

Finally, binding practices for journal volumes should be mentioned. In the USA, UK and some other countries-though not in Scandinavia, it seem-binders customarily remove advertisements and other 'extraneous matter', as well as covers and contents pages, from journal issues before volumes are bound. Where pages are removed in this way the editor should arrange to have at least one copy of each volume bound exactly as the issues were published, complete with covers, and stored in the editorial office. Queries of various kinds including legal problems, may arise in later years and a reference copy is essential.

Here I need only mention the methods the printer uses to produce extra copies of chapters or journal articles. Authors are often given 25, 50, or sometimes more, free copies of their chapters in a book, and sometimes of articles in journals, in partial recompense for writing the chapter or article. They can usually order further copies at a price slightly higher than the cost of producing them.

The printer makes the extra copies either by printing more sheets than are needed for the print run of the book or journal issue, or by reprinting copies by photo-offset from the finished book or journal issue in accordance with the numbers of copies ordered. The offprint or run-on method provides authors with their copies as soon as, if not before, the book or journal is published (which authors like); however, orders can be accepted only until the time that the relevant signatures go on the press. The second, or reprint, method, is more flexible in that reprints can be made at any time, however late the order is received; and no paper is wasted since only the required pages (and not unwanted ones in the same signature) are printed.

The relative costs of the two methods depend on many factors, including the variability in size of reprint orders for different articles the size of the printing plant, and the way it is organized. The editor's main object when negotiating reprint or offprint arrangements with the printer should be to ensure that the copies, especially of journal articles, are reliable available within a few weeks of publication.

System of Offset

Among the metals used for offset plates, zinc is a bluish white metal, heavier than aluminium, extracted from natural ores, chiefly zinc blende and carbonate calamine, melts at 800° F (301° C) and is soluble in hydrochloric, nitric and sulphuric acids. Zinc plates are melted down, cast into suitable sizes, passed between heavy rolls and transformed into sheets.

With specific gravity of 7. 18 when rolled and tensile strength of 10 tons per square inch parallel to grain and 3 tons per square inch across grain, zinc stands about 13 foldings crosswise and 6 foldings in the direction of rolling and stretches more than aluminium. When etched with muriatic acid, it becomes water repellant. In damp atmosphere, it becomes coated with basic carbonate.

Zinc is more grease receptive which makes it easier to add work with tuche emulsified ink with pen or brush but difficult to correct without leaving a tint.

Aluminium occurs combined with oxygen and associated with iron oxide in mineral bauxite. In its extraction by electricity, bauxite is decomposed by previously mixing it with cryolite, into oxygen and aluminium. It is a white metal capable of being polished, malleable and ductile with great tensile strength, high thermal and electrical conductivity, softer when rolled, of 2.6 specific gravity and melts at 1252° F (675° C).

Types of Plates

Aluminium plates of 80% aluminium and 20% iron for denting are used in offset plate making. Rolled plate has yield strength of 2 tons per square inch and ultimate tensile strength of 2½ tons per square inch. Offset plates are made in rolling mill, hardened and reduced to required thickness by cold rolling. Crystal structure of aluminium is closer and finer, gives fine grain surface with better hold for water, but shorter in life than zinc. Aluminium takes slightly sharper and deeper grain than zinc and due to relative hardness, is capable of giving longer impressions.

Aluminium plate weighs less than half as zinc and less cumbersome to handle but must be handled carefully to prevent kinking which cannot flatten. Aluminium being whiter and brighter makes the image areas visible. But its surface is quickly covered by oxide film on exposure to air.

While nitric acid has no effect, sulphuric and hydrochloric acids dissolve aluminium, slowly, and rapidly when hot. Aluminium dissolves rapidly in caustic soda and caustic potash solutions with the evolution of hydrogen and formation of alkali-aluminate.

Thickness of zinc and aluminium plates for surface and deep-etch process varies with the press size from 0.009 to 0. 12 inch for demy to 0.25 inch for 46 x 72 inches size machine. Plates should be of required gauge as mentioned in operation manuals of offset machines, tolerance, at least one side free from scale, scratches and dent. If plate is buckled, it will not lie flat on vacuum frame or on press cylinder and registration in colour work will be affected. Gauge tolerance for smaller size plate is + or 0.0005 inch and for larger size plate or 0.001 inch. Plates should have good resistance to abrasive and dimensionally stable.

Zinc		*Aluminium*		
	Annealed sheets	*Lithographic plates*	*Annealed sheets*	*Lithographic plates*
Tensile strength (lbs per sq. in.)	Below 10000	22000	13000	22000
Elongation %	0	12-15	30-33	3-4
Number of 90° bends to break	—	20-30	—	5-7

Composition of litho/offset plates: Zinc 99%, lead cadmium, iron 1%. Aluminium 99%, silicon, manganese and iron 1%.

Mechanical properties of zinc and aluminium are:

> Image areas of offset plates are olephilic or grease attracted and non-image areas hydrophilic or water loving. Metal forming the image area is selected for its ability to accept ink while metal forming non-

image areas is selected for ease in moistening and its ability to be desensitized to ink.

Copper in combination with oxygen and sulphur is found in copper pyrites or chalcopyrite and malachites or cupric carbonate. It is a lustrous metal with pinkish brown colour, malleable and tough and is a good conductor of heat and electricity. It has 8.95 specific gravity, melts at 1976° F (1080° C), slowly tarnished in air acquiring dull reddish colour but due to moisture becomes coated with green deposit called verdigris. Copper is readily dissolved by nitric acid but slowly affected by hydrochloric or sulphuric acids. Ammonia dissolves copper in the presence of air. It is softened by heating to dull red heat.

Multimetal plates when compared to zinc have advantages like saving of graining time, uniform plate quality, lesser stoppages on printing machines, etc. They have smooth surface to obtain better reproduction of tonal values and point sharpness. Compared to zinc, bi-metal foil has enhanced number of tonal values to 16. Damping is 1/4 that of grained zinc plate due to separation of water and ink carrying metals.

With proper care, it is possible to print 10 to 20 lakhs impressions. However, bi-metal plates are not economical for short and medium run but suitable for newspapers in multicolours. Bi-metal plate consists of two metals one having preferential affinity for ink, the other for water.

In bi-metal plates copper is common for image areas. Aluminium, stainless steel and chromium are chosen for non-image areas because these accept water in preference to greasy ink. When copper and chromium are used together they are usually electroplated on zinc and steel plates, called polymetal plates. Bi-metal plates with zinc, iron or aluminium base are electroplated on one side first with copper and then with chromium, layers being thin, copper being 0.0000 1 to 0.00 1 inch thick and chromium being 0.00005 inch thick. Chromium layer has a dull, matte appearance to retain moisture while printing. Electro-chemical voltage series of metals are decisive for their selection. Ink carrying metal acts positive to hydrogen electrode.

In voltage series, it stands to the right of hydrogen whereas water carrying component of plate consists of a metal standing to the left of hydrogen and acting negatively to hydrogen electrode. Ink carrying metal remaining copper, by electroplating, chromium coat acting as water carrying constituent is applied to copper layer. Other water carriers may be aluminium, nickel or steel.

Bi-metal plates may be grained or ungrained. To make grained bi-metal plates, base plates are first grained and electroplated with copper and chromium. Electrolysis is adopted to coat layers of copper and chromium, an oxide layer on aluminium plate surface called anodising and electrolytic graining.

Anodising is a means of electrolytically producing film of aluminium oxide of controlled thickness on surface which is highly water receptive and resistant to chemical action and abrasion on the press. Anodised plates, though used mainly for deep-etch process, are also used on wipe-on and pre-sensitised plates, resisting corrosion and oxidation.

Possible types of bi-metal plates are electroplate, an image metal on a plate of non-image metal forming an acid resistant positive image on the layer of image metal, etch away the image metal from all areas except image areas and remove acid resist from the image area, and electroplate a non-image metal on a plate of an image metal or on a plate which carries surface layer of image metal, forming a stencil or negative image by acid resistant coating on the layer on non-image metal, etch away non-image metal to lay bare the image metal in positive image areas removing protective stencil from non-image areas.

Base	*Non-image metal*	*Image metal*
Stainless steel	Stainless steel	Copper
Aluminium	Aluminium	Copper
Plastic	Aluminium	Copper
Mild steel	Lead	Copper
Mild steel	Chromium	Copper
Aluminium	Chromium	Copper

Bi-metal foil is supplied gummed and packed in cardboard roll, on opening they are checked for creases and ruptures, cut to required sizes, gum washed in water basin before use.

Two metals may be carried on a third to make tri-metal plate. Besides affinity for grease or water other considerations that have a bearing on choice of metals include suitability of metal to form top layer for electro-deposition on lower layer. Top metal should allow suitable processing technique to be used and it should be possible to dissolve top metal without affecting lower one.

Tri-metal or polymetal plates are made from base plate of zinc, iron or aluminium; an electroplated layer of copper on base plate; electroplated layer of chromium, i.e. non-image metal over copper, only layers of copper and chromium being affected by plate making and in printing.

Re-used Machines

It came to pass that many dealers of used graphic arts equipment practised their skills, spreading joy and goodness in the oversized pages of the most widely-read and most well-respected paper for graphic arts readers.

And so many of them spoke of their minds and their hearts to the classified ad manager of this publication, and they told him secrets of their experiences in dealings of the heavy iron; and he listened.

And in the fourth month of the ninth year of the ninth decade of the twentieth century of the modem era, there was produced a very wonderful issue of this most-revered paper, and it was called the "Used Equipment Roundup".

Thus it was that the classified ad manager gathered to himself their notes and records of such secrets as he had collected over time from these wise and seasoned veterans of the trade.

And he shifted through them, and pored over them and digested them, and drank much of the bitter fruits in order to understand them the better, and meditated upon these pearls of wisdom at length.

And when he could stand no more, he distilled them into words, and his head swam with the richness of it, and he began for all who would read of it.

1. No rule on buying used equipment is more important than this one.

   If you haven't had business dealings with the seller personally, ask for references. Any reputable dealer will be happy to supply you with a list of satisfied customers.

If you buy through a private sale, you may think you're getting a really "hot deal". On the other hand, you may just get burned.

Any used equipment dealer will tell you: his reputation is his most important asset. Take advantage of this fact and get the goods on your man before the goods go on your van.

2. The worst thing you can do is to buy equipment that is just sufficient to handle your present needs (unless you have no plans to grow).

If in six months you find your sales have outgrown your machinery, you'll be faced with taking a cash loss on the disposal of your present equipment and a loss in production time when you set up its replacement.

Plan carefully for the short term and the long term. Be sure the equipment you're getting today will be compatible with whatever you intend to add down the road.

3. Be prepared to travel, if necessary, to see equipment in operation. This, of course, goes in spades for major piece.

   Don't take the seller's word for it that the machine runs perfectly" or "just like new".

If you don't feel you have adequate knowledge with regard to the purchase, take along an expert to check the machine's performance. If you have to, pay a qualified independent serviceman or experienced operator-mechanic to go along with you when you make your inspection.

Whatever you do, don't rely on a "friend who used to be in the business" or a brother-in-law who once worked for a printer, or the like.

4. This is a perfectly obvious, straight-forward rule-and one that is overlooked almost every day.

   Before you buy, ask yourself: will this machine fit through my door? Up the stairs? Down the stairs?

If your shop is on the second floor, will you have to hoist it up the side of the building to get it in? Then what?

If you're in the basement, can you get it down there without having to dig a special tunnel for it?

Will the floor hold it safely?

Will you have to completely disassemble it? Who's going to pay for the expense of moving it if it turns out it won't go in?

If you don't manage to get it in, will there be enough room left to run it without continually hitting or falling over something?

Think ahead. It may save you a barrel of aggravation.

5. Make sure your available power source is compatible with the machine you're buying.

Many paper cutters and larger presses require 550 volt or 220 volt three-phase power. If you don't have three-phase hydro in your building, you may have a problem. It may be very expensive to install it; it may even be impossible.

If your building does have three-phase hydro, you will still have to install a small transformer. This however, should not present a major difficulty.

Whatever you do, don't confuse 220 volts one-phase (domestic hydro) with 220 volts three-phase (industrial hydro).

6. Remember that "reconditioned", "refurbished" and "rebuilt" are sometimes used interchangeably.

Find out exactly what has been done to the machine, and by whom. Ask a lot of questions. If the answers aren't forthcoming, or seem vague or noncommittal, pass on the deal. Too often "reconditioned" machines are sold with nothing more elaborate than a fresh paint job.

Inspect your potential purchase inside and out before you make a commitment.

7. Every machine, no matter how well it runs when you first get it, is destined to need service and/or replacement parts sooner or later.

When it does, will you be able to find a reliable technician to work on it? If you do, will he be able to get the parts he needs without waiting weeks or months for them? If it is an obsolete model, parts may not be available at all.

Bargains can sometimes be had on machines with unfamiliar names-but beware if you need service.

If, like most people, you can't afford lengthy down time, stick to equipment made by manufacturers with established networks of service and parts suppliers. When it breaks down in the middle of your busiest time, you'll be glad you did.

8. If delivery and installation is not included in the price, you will have to pay movers, carpenters, electricians, etc., out of your pocket. Have you figured this into your calculations?

In addition, if the equipment you are buying is unfamiliar and/or complicated, is the seller going to provide any kind of training?

If not, you may find the true cost of the equipment is a great deal more than you anticipated after you add the extra time it will take for an operator to learn by himself how to run it properly and the productivity you lose in the process.

9. "The best laid plans of mice and men", as they say, can go awry.

What if, after all your careful consideration, the machine doesn't perform up to your expectations, or your needs change faster than you expected? Will the seller take back the machine? If so, on what terms?

This is an important point to establish. In the case of a private sale, you will have to dispose of the equipment yourself. Some dealers, however, offer "trade up" or "trade-back" programs with varying terms and conditions.

10. Whatever "guarantees" or "warranties" are included by the dealer, make sure you have them in writing.

    There's nothing worse than going back sometime later with "I thought you said..."

At the same time, you should satisfy yourself that the seller is in a position to give up to his promise.

Printing on Screen

It is perhaps seldom realized that the twentieth century is not so much the 'atomic' age as the age of mass communication better, faster, more efficient international communication; an age of which the atomic race is only one aspect.

'Visual communication', a term coined only recently, embraces the graphic and typographic arts.

Since the second world war the output and standard of printing have grown to an extent no one could have possibly anticipated.

This tremendous upsurge has affected even remote and obscure processes of printing and graphic reproduction. Fifteen years ago screen printing was not a major printing process; it has now emerged from comparative absurdity to acceptance as the fourth basic method of printing stencilling. From a handicraft first introduced at the turn of this century, screen process printing has developed into a mechanized industry.

The concept of a crude process used only for short runs is giving way to an appreciation of the special characteristics, effects and advantages of screen printing; new and unexpected applications in contemporary printing and graphic technology are being researched and applied almost daily.

Specialized industrial applications of the process, as for example in textile, ceramics and wallpaper, are being intensively developed in many fields hitherto unfamiliar to the letterpress, lithographic and intaglio printer.

Screen printing is essentially stencilling, through a sieve consisting of a tightly stretched fabric. A stencil is defined by the Concise Oxford Dictionary as a 'thin plate of metal etc. in which pattern (interrupted when necessary by a thin bar of the material left to prevent pieces from falling out); is cut out.' 'Stencilling, the COD goes on to say, is to produce (pattern) on surface; ornament (surface) with patterns; by brushing paint etc. over stencil plate laid on the surface. Hence stenciller .... (etomceler sparkle, cover with stars)'.

This is an excellent summing up of the most obvious and important characteristic of screen printing, with the emphasis on shape, ornament, brightness, sparkle and paint quality. Screen printing can be defined in exact terms as: selectively blocking out a sieve-like screen fabric, silk, metal or synthetic, and forcing a viscous ink through the mesh openings by means of a squeegee rubber on to a flat, curved or irregular surface of paper, metal, glass etc. which has been placed in register on a base board, table or special device.

The term silk screen printing is therefore inadequate and inaccurate; in addition to silk bolting cloth, other materials such as stainless steel, nylon and terylene are in constant use today. In Western Europe the term serigraphy is current, derived from drawing on silk (Latin-sericus, Greek-graphein) on the analogy of lithography.

As it is often difficult to distinguish a screen from a lithographic print, it is important to consider the special characteristics of screen printing. It is essential for the printer, print buyer and designer to know and recognise these particular qualities in order to realise their full potential.

The stencilled character of screen printing is the decisive factor throughout as it results in a relatively thick ink film, with depth of hue, and variable covering power, depending on the type of ink; screen prints have a certain graphic solidity. Screen printed half-tones are usually limited to between 45-65 screen; on examination they reveal a characteristic heaviness in the shadow areas and rather forced highlights, with a narrow range of middle tones. Type-matter down to eight point can be printed satisfactorily even during long runs, provided a letter design suitable for reproduction by screen printing is chosen and that the printer knows his job.

Tools and Equipment : The basic printing equipment consists of a frame carrying a screen and stencil. This gives the printer maximum freedom with flexibility in stencilling without limitations on size, surface, rigidity or section of the material. It allows the regulation of the ink film thickness and the use of a very wide range of inks from mat to glossy, transparent and opaque; colour changes are quickly made, an attribute which, for instance, has helped to establish the process in textile printing.

The printing frame, a relatively simple and cheap item of equipment, can be easily made to a specific size. This simplicity of equipment and the easily acquired basic operation of squeegeeing have led to the mushrooming of many backroom printers; as a fast turnover is essential for their survival, quality, performance and prestige of the process have consequently suffered. But it has also enabled graphic artists to express themselves more freely, and directly than is possible with traditional autographic processes and as a result screen printing design has been greatly enriched. The preparation of stencils is faster and simpler than litho plate or letter press engraving and the materials are cheaper.

Setting up for manual or machine printing is not elaborate; thus giving the screen printed job a fast start. Printing speeds are slow compared with other process, especially slow with manual printing; hand production ranging from 100-400 iph according to the type and size of the job. Nevertheless, runs of 10,000 are not uncommon. The mechanization of screen printing has resulted in a considerable speeding up with top speeds in the region of 3,500 iph while average speeds of 1,000 iph have helped in maintaining consistent quality.

Because of the special formulation and the thickness of the ink layer, screen process prints cannot be stacked immediately after printing. Ink drying therefore is a major factor in slowing down production and causing bottlenecks. Even the most expensive and elaborate drying equipment has not yet succeeded in solving this problem.

Due to the relatively brittle nature of stencil materials they are more likely to break down during long runs than metal blocks or plates; register depends on a number of factors such as humidity, which are difficult to control. These are limitations to be carefully considered. A less important but often mentioned aspect is the 'mess' and smell associated with screen process printing. The former limitation can be avoided by organization and craftsmanship, the latter by improvements in ink formulation and the introduction of proper ventillation and air conditioning.

Printing Method : The earliest examples of these are signs and fabrics. Today there are few aspects of modern living, in home, street or factory, which are not affected by new developments of the process. By its versatility, screen printing has lent itself increasingly to advances in graphic and industrial technology; it has played an important role in the growth of the plastic and electronic industries. Marking processes, i.e. container and bottle printing, transfers, dials, etc., would be inconceivable without screen printing.

Metal, glass and plastic signs in flat, or three-dimensional units, plastic packaging pre-filled or vacuum formed are invariably screen printed. The rapid growth of television advertising has given a great boost to the printing and production of display and point-of-sale materials. The demand for bright, patterned textiles and wallpapers has extended the use of screen printing into these two highly specialized and competitive fields. Thus more conventional uses have been outstripped by specialized industrial applications.

Screen printed half-tones for posters, in size ranging up from increasing quantities. Photo-mechanical techniques, such as posterization, with a quality close to gravure and collotype, have affected design, and are leading to novel new uses.

Monetary Aspects : When is screen printing more economical than any other printing process? This question, asked quite often, is difficult to answer while allowing for any and every eventuality.

As can be seen from the general characteristics of the process, screen printing might often be thought in fact to be the more expensive process. Nevertheless it is still used because of the special graphic effects sought by the designer.

Many different factors decide the use of any printing process; the size and character of the design, the number of workings, the quantity required, the material selected or specified, the competitive cost. But there is no denying that where rich graphic colourful results are sought, screen process has a quality not easily matched by other printing processes.

A further aspect needs some clarification. It is true to say that a screen printing business can be set up with very little capital. It is equally true that, unless the printer has experience, a thorough knowledge of the process and excellent business connections, he will quickly run into trouble in the highly competitive field of printing.

Tools and Machinery : The screen printer's equipment is, by tradition, crude and simple. Even now, the simplest and cheapest equipment can be found side by side with expensive precision machinery in up-to-date establishments. Is such expensive equipment necessary? The flow of new machinery, printing aids, and equipment seems to indicate real and pressing needs. For example, fast machines could not be built without new and efficient drying equipment. The growth of screen printing would be retarded; the expansion into new fields could not take place.

The screen printer's basic equipment consists of a frame, hinged to a base, the squeegee, a piece of flexible rubber mounted in a handle, and some sort of drying rack. Frames are mostly made from timber, even some machines have wooden frames or insert bars to hold the silk. Aluminium frames have been introduced since 1948 on account of their greater rigidity, lightness and freedom from distortion. The screen fabric has to be stretched tightly over wooden frames by means of battens, glue or tacks; some of the latest aluminium frames include stretching devices, which allow quick and even tensioning of the fabric, with easy adjustment of parts.

The screen fabric must be drawn tight for stencil adhesion, register and sharp printing by the use of special stretching devices, ranging from simple floating bar frames to expensive and complex stretching tables. The squeegee consists of a rubber or synthetic blade fitted into a wooden or aluminium handle. Special squeegee sharpeners are used, as blades have to be kept even and ground to a variety of profiles according to the needs of the designer. The printing table must be rigid and of a convenient height for feeding in stock and printing. Hardboard, aluminium or plastic bases are best. Register marks made from card, gummed paper, plastic or metal are placed on the surface.

Vacuum base tables are a great improvement. They consist of a plastic or aluminium base with small perforations connected to a vacuum pump. The air is exhausted as the frame is lowered and the vacuum released when raised. This prevents the stock from adhering to the screen fabric after printing because of the highly viscous screen printing inks. The stock is held firmly, tight to the base, making faster printing possible. The one arm squeegee (a further improvement introduced about ten years ago) travels along a shaft mounted on the table opposite to the printer, enabling him to pull the squeegee along without effort, thus making it possible for one operator to print even 60 in. x 40 in. posters. These tables have micro-register adjustments.

The German SPS tables have an automatically moving hinge bar, which transform them into semi-automatic machines. Stainless steel fabrics stretched by a pneumatic device and squeegees holding a blade on an identical principle are designed for aids to high precision printing. There are a number of specially constructed precision printers on the market; they are essential for the exacting demands of electronic circuitry, dial printing and marking.

It is difficult to find a parallel in the orthodox printing processes for the sieve-like fabrics used in screen printing. It is perhaps nearest, by analogy, to the printing plate, as the sieve carries a negative image of the design to be printed.

Choosing the right screen fabric influences the quality of the screen printing. It is important therefore to understand the structure and behaviour of these fabrics, to correctly assess screen printing technique. Improvements in existing fabrics and the recent introduction of synthetic materials such as nylon and terylene have opened up new fields to the screen printer.

The original fabric used by screen printers was identical with the flour miller's sieve the silk 'bolting' cloth-hence 'silk' screen printing. Silk has a number of advantages, such as relative cheapness and wide range of width and qualities. It is hygroscopic and coarser in weave than metal or synthetic fabrics. Quality and register can be seriously affected by the cloth tightening with heat and slackening with dampness. Silk bolting cloth is produced in two basic weaves; interlock and plain weave.

The interlock type weave consists of full-gauze, where all warp and waft threads are interlocked at their intersections, and of half gauze, in finer weaves, where only every other thread is interlocked, with alternative threads passing over and under each other. Plain weave silk cloth consists entirely of such threads. Therefore though it is less rigid than interlock, the mesh openings are larger and more regular. This results in a thicker ink film and better definition, as the mesh opening is unaffected by knots or twists.

Nylon and Terylene are used increasingly now a days. Synthetic fibres consist of a single smooth filament. Plain weave construction, a greater ratio of mesh opening to thread, fineness, imperviousness to humidity and certain acids, are their main advantages over silk fabrics. Disadvantages are: the price, and difficulties with stencil adhesion unless the fibres are roughened up. An additional drawback is caused by lack of elasticity. When the stretched fabric slackens it is impossible to tighten it any further.

These can be conveniently grouped together. A fine,

monofilament thread with large regular mesh openings, and plain weave structure is characteristic of these fabrics. They are costly; accidental dents render the damaged area useless; the thread needs very thorough degreasing for the adhesion of dischromated gelatine stencil materials. Mainly for these reasons metal fabrics are usually employed by transfer and industrial printers, who require long wear, a fabric unaffected by heat or humidity, and fineness of definition with a heavy ink deposit.

Where special inks are needed for ceramics, plastics, fluorescence and phosphorescence, resists and adhesives, screen printing is the in-ideal process as these inks depend on the thickness of the ink layer for their maximum effect and perfect bonding to the surface. There is no other process capable of printing to vacuum formed plastics; the same applies to the printing of luminescent dials and certain ceramic applications. Fluorescent screen printing inks have been found more lasting and stronger, as the strength of colour depends on the thickness of the ink film. Resists printed on copper-plastic or copper-paper laminates also depend on the same factor. Pinholes in the resist will render the circuit useless.

The latest developments are intended to help printers in individual ways by providing inks which work best under certain drying conditions in relation to certain surfaces; thus tackling the problem of drying at its source-the formulation of the ink. It is claimed for instance that vinyl inks, developed in the United States, dry in ten seconds on twin jet dryers and in twenty seconds on a jet dryer; but drying time is increased to over ten minutes if left to dry on drying racks. This new approach to ink formulation is of the greatest importance for the process. With increasing mechanisation and faster printing speeds the printer has now a wider choice of inks; with new drying and printing equipment, faster drying is now practicable.

In the early days of 'silk' screen printing, about fifty years ago, only a few stencil materials were used; these were prepared by screen printers. The classic book of Hiett and Middletone, written and compiled at that time, carries a wealth of information on how to prepare pigment paper, how to shellac paper, and so on. Today screen printers are in much better position. There are numerous excellent supply houses at their disposal; they can choose from many new and improved materials brought regularly on to the market.

Stencils can be grouped conveniently under three headings; hand drawn, knife cut and photographic. Hand drawn stencils are worked on the screen surface itself with various filters. White lines are obtained by blocking out with glue, shellac or paint; black lines and textures by drawing with lithographic ink or crayon. The latter technique, 'serigraphy' popular in the United States among artists, has led to acceptance of the process for autographic print making. In this country a full appreciation of the potentialities of this technique for prints is unfortunately still lacking.

Knife cut stencil materials are most commonly used by screen printers. The earliest stencil material, paper, is still in use today for large letters, backgrounds and when heavy ink deposits are required. Paper is too fragile for long runs, any detail of small letters must be kept in position by connecting ties, showing typical stencil effects. To overcome this paper was shellacked and then ironed on to the screen after the printing areas were cut out. Further improvements resulted in the well-known profilm and bluefilm, paper laminates; the former coated with shellac, the latter with fish glue. Bluefilm was introduced when it was found that cellulose inks destroy the shellac coating of profilm stencils.

These heat-adhesive materials are being slowly replaced by solvent-adhesive knife-cut stencils. Developed during the last ten years in the United States, adhesion to the screen fabric is affected (as the name implies) with a special solvent. The stencils are made in a more expensive plastic material, but are easier to see through; quite small detail can be cut sharply, and the ink layer can be regulated. Available in a wide range of colours, any coloured original can be worked from without difficulty.

Further research has resulted in a new plastic-base water adhesive cutting film. It can be used with any ink, does not require special solvents for adhesion and is easily removed with water. Other plastic films are removed with cleaners, Profilm is soaked off with methylated spirit, Bluefilm washes off with water.

The introduction and perfection of photographic stencils has been an important factor in the steady advance made by screen printing. These stencils now make it satisfactorily possible to print type down to eight point even during long runs, to keep accurate register, to render fine detail and clear halftone subjects. Duplicate stencils can be produced quickly and accurately from the same original and identical stencils for subsequent reprints. Photographic stencil materials are long lasting, relatively cheap and most are easily removed from the screen. A positive transparency is required for their production, but photography as such is not always required as it is possible to produce these transparencies with hand methods also. The quality of the transparency is of the greatest importance. Transparent parts must be clear and opaque areas impervious to light with sharp, dense edges. Only stable plastic base materials and process plates or films should be used.

Photographic stencil techniques are based on the tanning of colloids by light. A stencil is produced by preventing the rays of light from reaching parts of the gelatine and then washing off those soluble areas. Even illumination from a light source rich in the blue special range is needed. Unless stencils are required continuously no bulky and expensive equipment or dark room is required.

Types of Fabrics Used : All screen fabrics irrespective of material are numbered to denote the fineness of their weave. Silk bolting cloth numbers end at 25, the equivalent of approximately 250 threads per lined inch. Numbers 10-12 are used by most screen printers for the average job, but meshes from 14 onwards are needed for halftone printing. The 'quality' or thickness of the thread is expressed by X. The most commonly used quality is XX. Nylon and metal meshes carry on in fineness where silk leaves off. There is no international coding system for fabrics and their grade can only be ascertained therefore by consulting charts supplied by each manufacturer.

Different Inks : Screen printing inks have specific characteristics, totally different from orthodox printing inks. They must pass through small openings without clogging, and dry fast on the printed stock. There is no ink on the market as yet which can completely satisfy all these requirements.

As we have already noted screen printing started as a branch of sign writing. It is not surprising therefore to find that the first inks were decorators' oil paints suitably altered for the process. These inks are still with us today, but adjusted to drying faster, with thinner ink film. The characteristics of opacity, a heavy ink deposit and slow drying (mainly by oxidation), have remained. There are mat or gloss inks; if a transparent base is added they can be used for transparent over-printing.

Natrocellulose inks adapted from aircraft finishes were introduced after the second world war. A thin film ink was obtained with an egg shell litho-like finish. Faster drying was achieved by evaporation; the thinner film made the printing of halftones and of fine detail possible. These inks are self-dissolving, screens can thus be left without the danger of stencils getting hopelessly clogged; they do not require thinning and do not skin up. The main disadvantages are, translucency, expense, special solvents and a strong unpleasant smell. Some of the cleaners have a low flash-point and therefore these inks come under the regulations of the Cellulose Act. The clear base mixed with metallic powders makes an excellent metallic ink and a range of trichromatic colours is available for halftone printing.

Great efforts have been made by ink manufacturers during the past ten years to perfect screen printing inks, developing an ink with the advantages of both oil base and cellulose. The 'synthetic' inks were the result; these dry by evaporation with a thin film, but are more opaque than cellulose inks. The solvent is white spirit, but they do not skin up and are self-dissolving as cellulose inks. The unpleasant smell has been eliminated. There are now a number of these inks on the market, suitable for a variety of surfaces, drying mat, semi-mat or glossy.

In the modern age of mechanisation and automation, it is comforting to know that craftsmanship still reigns supreme in the field of silk screen printing. Nevertheless, a wise silk screen artist endeavours to make best use of the facilities which photography has extended to this process. In the past, the silk screen artist also used to be endowed with drawing and designing ability but that is not so at present. Thanks to photography, any design can be photographed and most of them can be reproduced by silk screen.

The versatility of the process is unquestionable since one can print on almost any surface-paper, board, fabric, glass, bakelite, wood etc. and it is not even necessary that the substrate receiving the ink should be plane and flat.

Before preparing a photostencil, one must have a sharp positive of the design or original to be reproduced. Most of the silk screen reproduction consists of line work though halftone work has also been attempted successfully.

The conventional method of making a photographic positive is by contacting a negative on a piece of process film. The negative is made on a process camera or any other camera suitable for copying work. The original design is placed on the copyboard of the camera and evenly illuminated by a suitable illuminant which may be carbon arc lamp or white light fluorescent tube or photoflood lamp to name a few. The camera lens must be a good anastigmat. An apochromat lens would be ideal but quite expensive at the same time. Having focussed the original to the desired size, a sheet of orthochromatic line film or ortho lith film is loaded in the camera and exposure is given to the original.

The orthochromatic film is not sensitive to red region of the spectrum (600-700 millimicrons;). Hence the film can be processed in a dark room fitted with red safelight. Development is done in the developer recommended by the film manufacturer. If the recommended developer is not available, any one of the following developers may be used.

Caustic-Hydroquinone Developer

Solution A

Hydroquinone	25 gm
Potassium hydroxide	50 gm
Water to make	1000 c.c.

Solution B

Potassium hydroxide	50 gm
Water to make	1000 c.c.

For use, mix A and B in equal volume just before use. During development, the exposed areas of the film are affected and the silver halides present in these areas are converted into a form of black silver. Thus opacity is produced in the exposed areas. The developed film is then quickly washed in water in the following solution:

Sodium thiosulphate (hypo)	250 gm
Water to make	1000 c.c.

The above solution reacts chemically with the residual silver halides forming a water soluble complex so that when the negative is washed, the soluble complex is removed from the gelatin layer.

Hydroquinone-Carbonate Developer

Sodium Sulphite (anhydrous)	150 gm
Hydroquinone	20 gm
Sodium Carbonate (anhydrous)	50 gm
Potassium Bromide	10 gm
Water to make	2000 c.c.

The above is a single solution developer which must be used undiluted. Development time is five minutes at 20° C.

Whichever developer is used, if the negative is correctly made, the design will be obtained in a transparent form against an opaque background.

A positive is now made from the above negative by contact printing. This operation is performed in a printing cabinet of the vacuum type. If such a cabinet is not available, a photographic contact printing frame may be used. If that too is not available, two thick glass plates may be used. The emulsion side of the film is placed in contact with the emution side of the negative.

The combination is held together between the two glass plates. Exposure is given through the negative using a frosted glass filament lamp. Light will be transmitted through the transparent areas of the negative (which constitute the image of the design) and expose the film. There after the film is processed as in making the negative. The result is an opaque image against a transparent background.

Instead of preparing negative, a positive can be directly prepared by chemical reversal. In this method, the copy is exposed and the film is developed in the recommended developer. The exposure must be somewhat greater than normal and has to be determined by trial and error. After development, the negative is well washed in water. Then the silver formed in the exposed areas is removed by 'bleaching' in the following solution:

Solution A	
Cupsic nitrate	300 gm
Potassium bromide	10 gm
Acetic acid	150 c.c.
Water to make	1000 c.c.

Solution B	
Hydrogen peroxide	2%

The working solution is prepared by mixing A and B in equal volumes. The solution dissolves the gelatin in the exposed areas. When 'bleaching' is complete, white light is switched on and the bleached negative is washed in water. The unexposed silver halides in the image areas are now exposed by the light. The film is then redeveloped, washed and fixed. The result is positive.

The original is a Flag in two colours-red and blue. A negative (ii) is made from the key drawing. The negative is retouched with photo-opaque leaving only the red areas open. A positive (iv) is made from this negative which will be used in making the red printing photostencil. The key negative is now washed and dried. It is again retouched (v) to stop out all areas except blue. Another positive (vi) is made from the negative which will yield the blue photostencil.

Although it is possible to prepare photo stencils for halftone reproduction, the result cannot be of a high quality. The limitations imposed by the process make it mandatory (i) to use a screen not finer than 33 lines per cm (85 lines per inch) and (ii) to avoid fine tonal gradation because it is neither possible to maintain fine isolated gelatin dots in the shadow nor force the ink through very fine openings in the highlight areas of the gelatin stencil. For best results, negatives (halftone) must be made on a process camera using lith films or coarse magenta contact screens. The negative is contact printed on high contrast film to obtain positive with dense and sharp dots.

The positive (line or halftone) so prepared is now used in obtaining a photostencil in gelatin. This can be done either by the direct method or by indirect method commonly known as transfer method.

In the direct process, a layer of gelatin of suitable thickness is deposited over the silk screen. A number of coating solutions have been recommended by different workers. The following is a typical formula which gives fairly good results:

Gelatin	90 gm
Sodium Carbonate	2 gm
Potassium bichromate	20 gm
Glycerine	7.5 c.c.
Water	1000 c.c.

Gelatin is the film forming colloid which is rendered light sensitive by potassium dichromate. Glycerine makes the stencil pliable so that it may not develop cracks. Sodium carbonate raises the pH of the solution by reducing its acidity, a dye such as methyl violet may also be added to impart colour and improve the visibility of the image in the stencil.

In preparing the solution, gelatin is first soaked in about 600 cc of water and then warmed to a temperature of about 45° C to obtain an emulsion. The dichromate and the carbonate are separately dissolved each in 200 cc of water. When the gelatin has dissolved, the carbonate and bichromate solutions are added taking care that the temperature is maintained at 45° C. The glycerine and the dye are added last. The emulsion is thoroughly stirred.

For coating, the emulsion is warmed to 45oC and applied to the screen by a wide camel's hair brush. Both sides of the screen are coated and care is taken to obtain a film of even thickness on the silk screen. Drying is effected by a fan. Both sides of the screen are then given a second coating. The coating and the drying operations must be carried out in yellow light otherwise the coating solution is likely to get fogged.

The sensitized screen is now printed under the positive. Actinic light should be used for exposure. Development is done in water at 45° C. Both sides of the stencil are developed until the unexposed gelatin has been washed away leaving a clear cut design in the stencil. Development is arrested by applying cold water. Linen sheets are then used to absorb as much moisture from the stencil as possible. Further drying of the stencil is done under a fan.

After printing, the gelatin stencil is soaked in twenty per cent solution of sodium or potassium hydroxide and then scrubbed under warm water until all traces of gelatin have been removed.

The transfer process though somewhat expensive is extremely popular these days since it is quick working and gives excellent results if the manufacturer's instructions are followed. A large variety of materials is obtainable based on transfer process of which two are being described below.

The first is a presensitized red pigmented gelatin coated on a transparent polyester base of good dimensional stability. The product is commercially available as 'Five Star' and is manufactured by Autotype International Limited, England. The film can be handled in yellow light. Stencil preparation is extremely. The film is first cut to the desired size.

The positive is placed in contact with the non-gelatin side so that the stencil will be right reading when viewed from the gelatin side of 'Five Star'. While maintaining a firm contact, exposure is given through the positive using a source of actinic light such as a carbon arc lamp or mercury vapour lamp. Sunlight may also be used. The sensitivity of 'Five Star' lies mostly in the ultraviolet and blue region of the spectrum. Exposures vary a great deal since there are many variants. It is therefore best to find correct exposure by first making a trial exposure.

The next step after exposure is hardening of the exposed areas of gelatin. This is done by immersing the film in 1.2%

solution of hydrogen peroxide at 20° C. The commercially available hydrogen peroxide has its strength expressed in 'Volumes'. Thus a 20 volume solution contains about 6% of hydrogen peroxide.

The gelatin film is then developed in a spray of warm water at 40-45° C until all the unexposed gelatin has been removed from the image area. The silk screen which has been previously cleaned is moistened with water and the stencil is applied to the underside of the frame carrying the screen. Moisture is removed by gently dabbing with clean newsprint which is placed inside the frame. Thereafter, the stencil is allowed to dry in gentle breeze of a fan. The base support is then peeled off.

In another indirect process, the film material is supplied unsensitized along with a liquid emulsion and a sensitizer. The emulsion and the sensitizer are first mixed and then coated on the unsensitized film through the silk screen. The coating is allowed to dry after which the backing material of the film is removed. Exposure through the positive is given as before so that the image will be right reading when viewed from the top side of the screen frame. Develaopment is done in plain water. Finally, cool water (20-21° C) spray is directed over the surface until the image areas are washed away. The stencil is then dried as before.

2

Jobs in Production

Every newspaper is designed to meet the needs of its customers. Although more or less all newspapers now-a-days get the same news, yet their presentation differs according to the requirements of their readers. The readers of a quality newspaper require detailed articles. On the other hand, the readers of a popular tabloid require more visual impressions and the spoken word. In a Tabloid newspaper the photographs and the headlines are given more space whereas the text is short. These headlines and the pictures can convey the story of a news at a single glance. Thus, we see that the layout and type faces of a newspaper are very important along with the contents of the information.

Various Types

It is said that there are 5,000 different type faces in the world which are used in the various alphabets of different languages. Of course, a journalist is not concerned much with the typography. But this is the main tool of the sub-editor of a newspaper. A fount of type is a collection of letters, numbers and other devices such as punctuation marks etc., all of the same character and belonging to the same family. In fact, a series of type faces consists of several founts in different sizes. A family of type is a collection of founts and series all of the same basic design, but in different sizes and weights or widths.

The weight of a type face is referred to by its x-height. In each family of type there are certain letters that project upward from the main body of the letter. For example, b, d, and h. Still, there are certain letters that are projected downwards like g, j and p. Similarly, there are other letters that are shaped entirely within the main body like a, e and x. And the height of these letters is known as the x-height.

Type faces are measured in points. A point in the system used in most English speaking countries, is 0.0138 inches or 1/12th of a pica (0.166). There are approximately 72 points to the inch. The point sizes refer to the measurement of the body of the letter. The text sizes most commonly used in newspapers are from 4-3/4 to 12 points. For headlines 14 to 96 points are used. A variety can be given within the body type by using a contrasting type face within the same family—usually either bold or italic. Some papers also begin a story or sections of stories with a larger letter, usually two or three lines, known as a drop letter.

Style and Design

Sometimes, to give importance to the beginning of a news story, the introduction is set across two or three columns in a larger point size than the story that follows it. For this, sometimes a contrasting type can also be used. Generally, if a bold type is used for the first two or three sentences of an introduction, then the story should go into an intermediate point size of the standard body type for the next two sentences which should be set across either two columns or in a single column, depending on the layout of the page.

The type faces which are used in the printing of a newspaper determine its character. Some newspapers even have a specially designed type character. Although most of the newspapers may not have a definite character, yet they also have a planned series of type faces which are available to the sub-editors. Every newcomer must try to know the type faces which are used in his newspaper.

Newspaper Layout

The number of type faces which are used in a newspaper should be small enough so that people are able to handle them in a hurry. Still, the number should be sufficient enough for different effects. Very large and very bold faces are needed only for special occasions, when some really big story is to be published. Generally, modest type faces are needed to headline the usual run of stories.

The layout of a page is very important in the production of a good newspaper. The layout should be such that the greatest amount of information is printed on a page to give variety. But, this may be kept in mind that it should not create any confusion. There is no doubt that every paper has its own style. Some of the newspapers have now-a-days moved from a vertical make-up to a horizontal style. Generally, the horizontal style is only useful, when the number of lengthy articles on a page is small. In such a case, lengthy headlines across four to six columns can be given. But one thing should always be remembered that a page should give the look of being clean and neat from the top to bottom.

Ink for Printing

Printing by the rotary letterpress method from rubber stereos originated in the last years of the nineteenth century and inks for the process consisted of aniline derived dyes dissolved in alcohol or water; hence the adoption of the generic name of aniline inks. Since 1935 development in printing machines and ink formulations has been dramatic and the range of substances printed has increased so that the term "aniline" has been rendered obsolete. The term "flexographic inks" came into use in 1952 and the use of the word "aniline" together with its chemical associations of toxicity and odour largely disappeared. In recent years the quality of print produced by the flexographic process has improved greatly. The process was originally limited to the printing of paper bags and sacks, but with recent progress in the design of printing presses, stereos and substrates, excellent decorative tone work can be produced.

Special Types : A flexographic ink consists of three basic types of ingredient: solvent, resin, binder and colour. The selection of these is dependent on the end use of the print as well, the substrate to be printed and the type and speed of the printing machine. The ink must be low in viscosity in order to be distributed adequately in the simple distribution system, and yet remain on the surface of the stereo, thus producing a clean print. Many flexographic printing presses are capable of production speeds of 300 metres per minute, and print from reel to reel.

The inks have to be formulated to dry at this speed. When the substrate being printed is non-absorbent, it is essential that all the solvent is removed from the print prior to re-reeling if set off is to be avoided. The solvents used must not attack the various types of rubber or plastic used to form the stereo, the resin system selected should ensure adequate adhesion to the substrate during the life of the print, and the final print is usually required to be odourless.

Before considering the basic formulation of flexographic inks it is desirable to consider the types of substrate printed by this method. This will enable a relationship between the ingredients selected and the end usage of the print to be developed.

The types of substrates may be divided into three groups: paper and board, film and foil.

The range of end uses of flexographic printed paper is vast and includes paper bags, waxed bread wrappers, parchment for fat wrappers, coated papers for labels, kraft liners for corrugated cartons. All may be printed on reel to reel presses and the inks may dry partly by absorption as well as evaporation. The range of ink specifications varies widely and may require resistance to light, resistance to wax, fat, etc. In general there is no problem of adhesion to the surface of paper though the rub-resistance of a print may be important.

Board is usually printed on a sheet fed press. Large quantities of corrugated board for subsequent case making are printed flexographically. The major requirement is for rub-resistance during transportation. The surface contour of papers and board influences the quality of the print achieved. Tone printing using fine screen is only possible on smooth surface, and it is more common to print tone designs on film and foil surfaces than on paper when using the flexographic process.

The use of film for flexible packaging has developed rapidly in recent years. Accent is placed on the production of flexible films which have excellent barrier properties and which can be handled by a variety of packaging methods and machines. The two major film types have been based on regenerated cellulose and polyolefin films. Uncoated regenerated cellulose film has poor resistance to moisture. The use of a coating based on cellulose nitrate and wax increases the moisture resistance of the film and enables it to be heat sealed. An improvement in moisture and gas barriers can be achieved if a coating of polyvinylidene chloride (pvdc) is applied.

Polyethylene and polypropylene films have excellent moisture barrier properties, and it is possible to coat polypropylene with pvdc to improve the barrier properties.

Inks cannot be absorbed into the films, so that adhesion to the surface of the substrate must be obtained by the resin system and the solvents must be removed during the printing operation. When certain coated films are being printed, it is possible to improve ink adhesion by heating the web, thereby fusing the ink to the coating, but care should be taken to ensure that no film distortion takes place as a consequence of the heating.

Other films which are printed flexographically include polyester, nylon and polyvinyl chloride.

Aluminium foil used for flexographic printing is usually no thinner than 0.009 mm when unlaminated. Thin gauge foils may be used for confectionery wrappers, thicker gauge for certain lidding operations, and laminated foils for a wide range of package protection.

In certain cases, aluminium foil may be washed with a primer which prevents oxidation and promotes ink adhesion. In view of the non-absorbency of the surface, inks must be based on resin systems having excellent adhesion properties. The inks must be very flexible, have good solvent release and exhibit no tendency to block in the reel.

Flexographic inks are composed principally of colourant (dye or pigment), resin and solvent. The ink types may be classified in general terms by sub-dividing according to the main types of basic ingredient. It is usual for the ink manufacturer to market inks under trade names pertaining to the resin type used, as this selection is closely linked to the properties and end use of the ink. Inks may be considered by colourant as (a) dye type and (b) pigmented inks. In certain cases, blends of dye and pigment may be used in the same ink; for example, a combination of titanium dioxide and dye. Such an ink type is classed as semi-pigmented. Water based inks may be considered as a sub-group of pigmented inks.

The dyes most commonly used in flexographic inks are salts, usually the hydrochloride, of basic dyestuffs. They are soluble in alcohol and many of then) are soluble in water. The dyes are usually "laked" with tannic acid or a similar product. This process increases the solubility of the dye in methylated spirits, develops colour strength and greatly reduces solubility in water.

The tendency to bleed in wax, glycerine and other treatments is also reduced. As a general guide, in amount of tannic acid equal to the weight of dyestuff should be used in the ink formulation. The lightfastness of the dyes is improved by laking, but it is still poor (Blue Wool Scale 1). High acid value resins of a phenolic type may be used in place of, or in combination with tannic acid as a laking agent, thereby reducing the amount of additional binder which may be required in the ink formulation. It should be noted that the use of a particular laking agent may affect the shade of the dye Solution considerably.

Dye based inks are widely used on paper for bread wrappers, bags, etc. where no lightfastness requirement is demanded. Because of their almost Newtonian behaviour, low viscosity inks of high colour strength may be formulated enabling clean printing to be obtained. The migration tendencies of basic dyes do not encourage their use on plastic films or in contact with a wide range of products.

The dyestuffs most commonly used are:

Auramine	Victoria blue
Magenta	Rhodamine G
Malachite green	Methyl violet
Rhodamine	6G

Soluble dyes having considerably greater lightfastness and resistance to fats, etc. are available and may be used for special applications. The dyes vary in solubility and in general are much less soluble and of lower colour strength than the basic dyes. Suppliers' specifications should be consulted before using certain dye/solvent combinations. The main uses for these lightfast dyes are for foil printing, where the transparency of the dye can give striking decorative effects. Many of these dyes are metal complexes of which the following are examples:

Solvent Yellow	19
Solvent Yellow	45
Solvent Red	102

Because of the wide scope of work printed flexographically, the range of pigments used is broad. In general terms the requirement of the pigment is that it shall have low oil absorption, high colour strength, economic price, and stability in the appropriate resin/solvent combination.

The rheological behaviour of the pigment in a flexographic system is influenced by the method of preparation of the pigment, the incorporation of wetting agents, the conditions of precipitation and washing. Pigments of apparently similar chemical constitution may have vastly differing flow and storage characteristics in the same resin system.

The main types of pigments used for general purpose work are :

Organic

hansa, and benzidene yellows

permanent red 2B

PMTA blue, violet, green, pink

phthalocyanine blue, green

lithol reds

permanent red 4B

lake red "C"

Inorganic

lead chromes	molybdate orange
titanium white	carbon black
bronze blues	(iron blues)

For particular specifications, e.g. soap resistance, other pigment types will have to be used and some of the above may not be suitable for all resin systems and substrates. It is important while formulating ink that the stability of the ink during storage be examined in addition to the more obvious requirements of flow, adhesion, product resistance, etc.

Accelerated tests should be conducted to establish the viscosity and shade stability of ink systems.

The function of the resin component of the ink is to act as a dispersing medium, carrier and adhesion promoter for the pigment. In the introduction it was noted that adhesion to the substrate may be entirely physical, as in the case of ink penetration into paper or board; or physical/chemical, adhesion being obtained either by hydrogen bonding to or chemical reaction with the Substrate surface. Resins of various chemical type may therefore be used, but a prerequisite is that they shall be soluble in suitable solvents for the printing process and they will release the solvent rapidly during the drying stage. Resins may also be divided into two broad classifications: non-film forming and film forming. The latter provide a continuous dry film on the surface of the substrate, examples being cellulose nitrate, ethyl cellulose, and polymeric resins.

Formerly, the basic resin used in pigmented flexographic inks was shellac. It has good wetting properties for the pigment, has adhesion to a wide range of substrates, and is soluble in methylated spirits. However, shellac has slow solvent release characteristics, low heat resistance, and has recently become very expensive compared with other resins. Alcohol Soluble maleic resins have largely replaced shellac in systems which require the use of hard resins obtainable at a more economic price.

Of the film forming resins, cellulose nitrate is the most commonly used in solvent based flexographic inks. It has excellent pigment wetting characteristics for almost all pigment types, and has excellent solvent release and heat resistance. The fact that it is compatible with a wide range of synthetic resins allow its use in inks for a variety of substrates. Pigmented dispersions in cellulose nitrate, known as chips, may be prepared which can give excellent gloss and transparency, which may be of advantage when surface printing on non-absorbent films and foil. Cellulose nitrate may be used in conjunction with other resins to produce curing ink systems, giving heat resistant formulations more resistant than conventional inks.

Ethyl cellulose is also used widely in solvent based inks. Though the pigment wetting and flow characteristics are not as good as cellulose nitrate, ethyl cellulose has excellent solvent release, low tack, good film forming properties, and is especially useful in dye inks when no resin-dye interaction takes place.

Polyamide resins have excellent adhesion to a wide range of substrates, including polythene, polypropylene, foil and pvdc coated film. Particular care must be taken to ensure that the solvent system required for a particular grade of polyamide resin is compatible with the stereo material being used.

The use of acrylic resins has increased in two specific areas. The advent of the use of pvdc coated films for good packaging and the consequent requirement for heat resistant inks with good gloss necessitated the use of acrylic resins, which have good compatibility with cellulose nitrate and cellulose esters, and have solubility in suitable flexographic solvents. Disadvantages of acrylic systems are their tendency to "string" at the printing stage, causing dirty working, and the problems of solvent solubility and resin compatibility.

The use of acrylic resins in water based systems has increased, mainly due to the rapid increase in the price of shellac.

Other resins used in flexographic inks include polyvinyl butyral, polyvinyl acetate and polyvinyl chloride, all of which are used for specific purposes. The skill of the ink formulator is in the selection of the appropriate resin combination to meet the printer's and the end user's requirement.

The function of the solvent component of the ink is to dissolve the resin and enable the ink to be handled in the ink duct, transferred to the stereo, thence to the substrate. When non-absorbent substrates are being printed, the solvent must be entirely removed during the drying operation of the printing press. The choice of solvent is dependent on:

(a) the resin system selected, which may be predetermined by the substrate and the end use requirements.

(b) the substrate being printed.

(c) the composition of the stereos.

(d) the flow characteristics of the ink.

(e) the speed and drying capacity of the printing machine.

(f) restrictions which may be imposed by operators' or end users' requirements or legislation.

The most common solvents used are: water, methylated spirits, ethyl isopropyl and normal propyl acetates, isopropanol and normal propanol, and 2-ethoxyethanol ("Cellosolve").

In certain cases aliphatic and aromatic hydrocarbons (SBP solvents and toluene), and ketones may be required to enable the satisfactory solution of particular resins. When these and high concentrations of ester solvents are being used, special precautions in the use of stereos must be taken.

With the advent of the photopolymer plate, restrictions on the use of certain solvents are even more severe.

The following table indicates the suitability, or otherwise of various types of stereo materials when used with solvents. "R" indicates that the material will give satisfactory performance. Those marked "C" maybe used with care, when print quality is less critical, and stereos made from another material would be undesirable. The materials marked "N" should not be used because the stereo may be severely swollen and even disintegrated by the solvent.

This table should only be used as a general guide. Most inks are not based on single solvents, and stereo materials may vary in composition. In case of doubt, further information should be obtained from the stereo manufacturer.

These are used to modify the ink system to meet the final requirements of the print.

Plasticisers are particularly important when printing on plastics films and on foil. Being in effect a non-drying solvent for some resin systems, they impart flexibility. However, the addition of plasticiser lowers the heat resistance of a resin and when added in excess can give rise to blocking. The correct selection of various plasticisers can improve ink adhesion on certain substrates.

Waxes are incorporated to impart resistance to rubbing and scratching. They may be included in the ink either as a pre-dispersed medium or by the use of a micronised form stirred or milled directly into the ink. The most commonly used wax is polyethylene. For certain particular requirements or non-blocking characteristics, silicone fluids or fatty acid amides may be included in the formulation.

Solvent Resistance of Stereo Materials

Solvent	*Natural rubber*	*Nitrile rubber*	*Butyl rubber*	*Photopolymer plate*
Alcohols				
ethyl alcohol	R	R	R	R
iso-propyl alcohol	R	R	R	R
n-propyl alcohol	R	R	R	R
Esters				
ethyl acetate	N	N	R	N
iso-propyl acetate	N	N	R	N
n-propyl acetate	N	N	R	N
Ketones				
acetone	C	N	R	C
methyl ethyl ketone	N	N	R	N
methyl cyclohexanone	N	N	R	N
Glycol ether				
'cellosolve'	R	R	R	R
Aromatic hydrocarbons				
toluene	N	C	N	N

Contd....

Solvent	*Natural rubber*	*Nitrile rubber*	*Butyl rubber*	*Photopolymer plate*
xylene	N	C	N	N
Aliphatic hydrocarbons	N	R	N	N
Water	R	R	R	R

R = Recommended

C = Caution

N = Not recommended

Water based inks require special attention, the two problems associated with inks of this type are foaming in the ink duct and during the manufacturing operation, and the possibility of mould growth. There are various anti-foam products available to the ink maker, many based on silicone derivatives.

The two areas of concern are whether the anti-foam is effective in the resin system being applied, and whether the anti-foam may affect the printing stereos and the print quality. Certain compounds may effectively eliminate bubbles from the surface of ink being agitated in a duct circulating system, but may also cause craters in the ink film which are transferred onto the stereo immediately prior to printing. Anti-foam additives may contain hydrocarbon solvents which severely attack stereo rubbers, causing swelling and Subsequent print distortion. It is recommended that non-harmful fungicides be used to eliminate the likelihood of mould growth in water based inks during storage.

Ink Making : Three distinct groups of ink type will be considered initially:

(a) Dye based inks

(b) Water based inks

(c) Pigmented inks-solvent based.

These have been developed from the original aniline inks. The inks are formulated from solutions of basic dyestuffs which are laked to increase alcohol solubility, colour strength and reduce water solubility.

The main solvent used in dye based inks is denatured ethyl alcohol (methylated spirits). Both 64 overproof (op) and 74 op grades are used, and the former contains approximately 5 per cent of water. This small amount of water helps to stabilise the dye solution, but too much would cause precipitation of the dyestuff.

Dye based inks are usually used for printing on paper, the end product being general purpose bags, wrappings, waxed bread wrappers and sweet wrappers. They are rarely used on plastics films due to the tendency of the dyestuff to migrate into the film.

The inks produced have low viscosity and high colour strength, and can print at very high machine speeds due to the penetration of the ink into the paper stock. Should the drying rate of an ink need to be increased, acetone or ethyl acetate may be added. Retarding of ink drying may be achieved by the use of glycol ethers, though it must be realised that the retention of any solvent in a print may give rise to objectionable odours. The problems of set off caused by retained solvent and other factors will be discussed later.

The adjustment of an ink for drying rate is dependent on the drying potential and printing speed of the machine, the area of type face, etc.

The best results are achieved by correct initial formulation in cooperation with minor modification by the printer at the press side. For instance, some printers may wish to add 5 per cent of retarder to an ink to maintain clean printing from a small type-face, and others would complain that this addition would slow down the drying rate of the ink so that the production speed would have to be reduced. A typical formulation is:

Dye Based Waxed Paper Ink

10.0	victoria blue dye
2.0	methyl violet dye
12.0	tannic acid-or equivalent
6.0	shellac solution (50 per cent in 64 op meths)
5.0	"cellosolve"
65.0	methylated spirits (64 op)

When auramine yellow and rhodamine B dyes are being used, it may be found necessary to increase the amount of laking agent used to minimise the wax bleed of the dyestuffs. Inks intended for use on sweet wrappers which may have to undergo a glycerine treatment to improve flexibility, should be tested for resistance to water and glycerine.

Inks may be formulated on 74 op methylated spirit, provided some additional water is included. The use of resins improves ink transference from the stereo and hardens the ink film, in addition to being considered as possible laking agents. The incorporation of small quantities of ethyl cellulose may reduce the tack of the ink and assist in overcoming ink penetration through very absorbent papers.

Ink based on more lightfast dyes are most often formulated for adhesion to aluminium foil. The dyestuffs require no laking agent to adjust their resistance properties.

A starting formulation for a lacquer for shellac washed foil would be:

45.0 methylated spirits (74 op)

15.0 ethyl acetate

5.0 "cellosolve"

5.0 plasticiser

20.0 cellulose nitrate

10.0 shellac varnish (50 per cent resin)

Dye based inks are manufactured by making solutions of the dye and laking agent in the solvent, either by cold or hot blending on high speed stirring equipment. It may be necessary to allow the solution to stand for a period to allow undissolved particles of dye to be settled or be filtered. The solutions may be prepared in concentrated form for subsequent blending with other varnishes and solvents or, alternatively, by mixing dyestuff, laking agent, varnish and solvent, thereby eliminating the manufacture of the concentrated solution.

Dyestuffs are fully transparent and therefore do not give bright colours when used on coloured papers, e.g. brown kraft. Some opacity may be imparted by including a percentage of a titanium white base to the dye ink. The medium into which the white is dispersed must be suitable for use with the dyes. These semi-pigmented inks may also be used on lightweight papers, which may become very transparent when waxed.

Other pigment/dye mixtures are used either to produce specific colour effects, or to increase the colour strength of a fully pigmented ink with a low viscosity dye concentrate, though the possibility of interaction of the dye with the pigment must be closely investigated.

Fully water based inks must not be confused with water reducible inks. The latter may consist of inks based on organic solvents which may be partially reduced with water. An essential feature of these is that the resin used must also be soluble in the solvent/water system.

Water reducible systems are not widely used, but interest is shown when supplies of solvent are limited or when the use of water as a slow drying solvent may assist in obtaining good print quality. The scope of water based inks will be discussed more fully.

The traditional water based inks consist of resin systems which are dispersed in water. Naturally occurring resins such as casein are readily soluble in water and may be suggested as an ink vehicle. However, it will be observed that the resistance of a print of this type of ink to water will not be satisfactory.

The ideal formulation is that which although water based, will have acceptable resistance to water when the print is dried. Traditionally, shellac is the main resin used, which can be made water soluble in an alkaline solution. Suitable alkalis are caustic soda, ammonia, or triethanolamine. The resulting varnish usually has a pH between 7.5 and 9.0. Because the varnish consists of a soap rather than a true solution, water based inks are very sensitive to water reduction. The use of certain pigments may be precluded because of the effect of the pH of the varnish system.

The advantages of water based inks may be summarised as follows:

Excellent press stability is achieved because of the low evaporation loss from the ink duct. The print quality is not impaired by ink drying on the stereo.

There is no solvent attack on the stereos, and photopolymer plates may be used.

Obvious economies are obtained in using water as reducer and cleaning solvent, both for price and availability reasons.

There is no fire hazard.

Typical water based flexographic inks may be based as follows:

Red Water Based Ink

19.0	calcium lithol red
60.0	alkali solubulised shellac-water varnish
5.0	polyethylene wax compound
15.75	water
0.25	silicone oil

Blue Water Based Ink

12.0	phthalocyanine blue
10.0	barium sulphate
65.0	solubilised acrylic resin-water varnish
5.0	polyethylene wax compound
7.75	water
0.25	silicone oil

The disadvantages are the poor level of gloss and the slow drying rate which, if conventional methods of drying are used, restricts the use of water based inks to highly absorbent substrates. Developments are proceeding to establish the feasibility of using radio frequency drying equipment in conjunction with water based inks on plastics films and foils.

The main uses of water based inks have been in the paper sack and carton field, where highly absorbent papers are used and the non-inflammability property is a major advantage. High press speeds are obtainable and the print becomes satisfactorily water resistant shortly after printing.

Due to the high increase in the cost of shellac, various synthetic resins have been used in waster systems. A wide range of acrylic resins is available from which water/alkaline solutions may be obtained. Solid resins may be soluble at pH 7.5 to 9.0, and certain emulsions may be solubilised at this degree of alkalinity.

Extending pigments are used to reduce the raw material cost of inks. The use of lead chromate pigments in water based inks is frequent in view of the advantages of low cost and high opacity. The use of these toxic pigments may be restricted by local regulations, and the pigments may be affected adversely by the pH of the vehicle or alkaline adhesives used in board manufacture. The wax compound is necessary to provide a rub-resistant print, which is particularly required for the corrugated case and paper sack market. Various materials may be recommended for use as anti-foam additives. In certain cases it may be found necessary to include in-can preservatives.

The temptation to include solvents in water based formulations should be avoided, particularly when problems of fire hazard may arise. High concentrations of pigments in water paste form are available, from which water based inks may be manufactured by a stirring technique rather than the grinding of dry pigment into a suitable vehicle system. This method should show manufacturing cost savings for the ink maker.

In recent years there has been a major development in the use of inks which are suitable for heat transfer from a carrier web (usually paper) to fabric. This is based on the use of disperse dyestuffs which sublime at high temperatures. The requirements for the print are for good print quality, low initiation cost, ability to print wide webs, and a water based flexographic system is often used as the vehicle for these dyestuffs. The main property of the print on the carrier web is that the resin used does not interfere with the subliming properties of the dyestuff. The formulation of ink is a very specialised technology; the selection of the dyestuff is influenced by the composition of the fabric and the resistance properties required from the transferred print. Advances in the technology have produced ink systems which are suitable for heat transfer printing onto most synthetic fabrics, and more recently onto natural fibres.

A typical starting formulation for a heat transfer ink would be:

10-20 per cent	disperse dyestuff
60-70 per cent	solubilised acrylic resin
5 per cent	wax medium
15 per cent	water

This classification includes the widest range of resin and solvent systems. As indicated earlier in the chapter, the choice of resin and solvent is always influenced and often predetermined by the substrate to be printed and the specification to be met by the print. It is therefore appropriate to consider the resin system in parallel with the substrates indicating the basic formulation types and the requirements which may be stipulated when using certain substrates. It is important to realise that certain ink systems may be satisfactory for use on a wide range of materials with only minor modifications. Others may be restricted in use because the formulation is too complex or too expensive to be used for relatively low performance requirements.

Web offset heatset presses are running faster and faster every year. Production speeds will reach 3,500 feet per minute by the end of the 1990's. This will be a significant improvement over the 1,200 to 1,400 feet per minute generally accepted as the standard in the early 1970s. But speed alone is not a valid criterion for measuring efficiency in today's rapidly changing pressroom. Productivity and paper waste reduction are increasingly important factors which must be considered.

One basic question which must be answered is what does productivity really mean? A good working definition for most printers would simply be excellent press and ink runability combined with minimum downtime for web breaks and blanket cleaning. There are, however, several external factors which affect ink performance in the drive to achieve high productivity.

These variables include paper, distribution of the fountain solution, plant water quality, solvents, plates, blankets and rollers. These variables play pivotal roles in how well ink will, or will not, print. But none are more critical than the paper surface, the chemical characteristics of the fountain solution and their combined compatibility with the ink chemistry.

Use of coated paper for web offset heatset publication work has increased substantially during recent years, but has not kept pace with the 33% growth of the printed insert market from 1981 to 1986. In 1986, more than 16 billion flyers and inserts were printed on uncoated stock. They were produced for a wide range of end-use markets but most were related to advertising.

This parallel growth in productivity and printing has increased the burden on the paper substrate. The most important characteristics of paper are absorptivity, roughness, surface strength, brightness, wet strength, caliper, pH, conductivity and sheet formation. It is very important that paper stock be consistent from roll to roll, have good gloss and ink holdout along with a lack of blistering and delamination. It is absolutely essential that the paper does not contribute to blanket contamination. It is obvious that the testing of inks and coated and uncoated stocks is necessary if one is to predict what final properties of the printed surface will be achieved on press.

After paper, the second most important variable is the dampening system and how effectively it controls the fountain solution. The principal function of the dampening system is to transfer a constant thin film of solution to the non-image area of the printing plate and to assist in emulsifying water into the ink to form a proper, stable emulsion. Dampening systems can be divided into low energy types, medium energy systems, and high energy brush and spray equipment. All of these systems depend upon controlling the lithographic dampening or fountain solution whether it is acidic or neutral. The solution contains many ingredients, ranging from buffering salts to use of protective colloids and emulsifying agents.

What does productivity really mean? A good working definition for the printer would be excellent press and ink runability combined with minimum downtime.

The main functions of the fountain solution are to keep the non-image area of the plate clean and to form a micro-emulsion .of water in the ink. This provides the press with a cooling and purging effect. While fountain solutions have other functions they all focus on controlled emulsification between the ink and the fountain solution. This emulsification must be carefully performed to allow the transfer of ink to the form rollers of the press and plate. Without proper emulsification, water can breakout and stripping can occur.

Emulsions are formed through both chemical and mechanical action. It is essential that the proper formulation of ink resins and vehicles be selected for compatibility with wetting agents in the fountain solution. It is also important that the press and the dampening system design be such that the amount of energy exercised does not interfere with the stability of the emulsion. The stability of a water-in-ink emulsion can be of prime importance as opposed to an inverted emulsion.

It has been discovered that the shape of a curve that is obtained when one plots the concentration of fountain solution in an ink vs. time axes study can be helpful when attempting to predict printability. The stability of emulsions and the shape of curves can be drastically altered when substances such as isopropyl alcohol are substituted for the glycol ethers generally found in the solutions. Many of the ethers, such as butyl cellosolve tend to alter paper coatings by solubization and to act as peptizing agents on the gel structure of the inks.

Other important considerations are conductivity and pH. Conductivity, which in its basic definition is the ability to conduct an electrical charge, can vary due to extractions from paper, ink, plant water, on any change in dilution of the fountain solution. pH can cause an interaction between the paper and the fountain solution, which in turn, can affect drying time and ink receptivity. It has been proven that careful monitoring of these two variables can improve print consistency.

Discussions about paper, fountain solutions and emulsification are very useful but they lead to the most important subject of all. That, of course, is ink and how it is affected by these variables.

Lithographic ink has remained basically unchanged since it was first developed hundreds of years ago. The main ingredients have remained constant, except for concentration and chemical nature. It still consists of pigments, resin or solvent vehicles and additives. Most ink chemists would agree that the composition of lithographic ink, whether it is being printed at 1,200 feet per minute or 3, 500 feet per minute, is similar, except for rheological structure, that is its floor characteristics.

The fact is that for many years, resins have been utilised, including modified rosin esters and functional hydrocarbons. So have the long oil linseed alkyds and aluminium gallants. Also, petroleum-based solvents and slip additives are still used. One is prompted to ask, if this is the situation, what has changed to enable us to print at higher speeds on today's variety of substrates? The answer is quite simple. It is not so much that the composition of the building blocks has changed but that the structure has been rebuilt. The corner stone, in this case, is rheology.

There are several factors involved with rheology, but the most important are tack, viscosity and yield value. It has been discovered in recent years that those inks which have excessively large increases in shortness (yield value divided by viscosity) after emulsification are likely to show poor performance on press regardless of the shape of the emulsification curve.

Another conclusion drawn from studies and rheological measurement on fountain solution/ink studies is that thermodynamic stability of such emulsions is necessary for optimum press performance. In particular, the shear and thermal stability of ink/fountain solution emulsions is generally desired for optimum lithographic performance and can overcome some deficiencies of press mechanical condition.

There have been some major advancements in pressroom equipment and raw material design. But there is still no single factor that affects printability more than the rheological characteristics of a printing ink and it is there that ink manufacturers are concentrating their research.

Good press performance of an ink relies largely upon the optimum selection of raw materials, and upon correct fabrication. Once this selection has been carried out, the continuing operational performance of that product will then depend upon the maintenance of standards, both in raw material quality and manufacturing.

The extreme value of testing and controlling raw materials and finished inks is thus apparent, and it is proposed to examine this area in the detail that is necessitated by its importance.

Methods of testing belong essentially to two distinct types:

(1) Numerical determinations-those that can be expressed in identifiable quantities such as tack values, acid values etc.

(2) Comparative tests based on simple non-quantifiable tests of factors such as shortness, degree of flow etc.

As many of the properties of printing inks are either ill-defined, or not well understood, it is not surprising that many tests fall under the second category.

In some cases, it is necessary to check the product in the form of a laboratory print. This invariably involves visual assessment, and highlights the still dominant reliance upon the human observer, who is more efficient in many ways.

As long as the ink maker is not less critical than the printer, printer's customers or other assessors, it is likely that his decisions will be acceptable, particularly as his method of assessment will be the same as the others.

Any planned testing programme should first involve an estimate of the testing required. In estimating, certain questions need answering, such as:

(1) Is the test realistic?

(2) Can the length of time required for the test be justified?

(3) Is the test necessary?

(4) Is the testing adequate?

(5) What are the limits of any test?

If these points are covered in the planned programme, then problems arising as a result of fluctuations in raw materials, which can be a major source of problems if left uncontrolled, will be minimised.

It is thus the primary objective of any new product development to include a testing program that adequately covers both a quality performance test on that product and more fundamentally includes an assessment of raw material quality.

Different Used Techniques : In order for raw material testing to have any meaning, the sample taken from a delivery of material must be representative of the bulk in all respects. This is a simple and perhaps obvious statement, but if the sampling is not carried out efficiently, then a batch may be incorrectly assessed and this could possibly result in costly repercussions at some future date.

A single delivery of material may contain several drums with the same batch reference number as well as others with a different reference. Ideally, samples should be taken from all containers and each tested accordingly. But where this is not considered practicable, one may take a calculated risk and examine samples taken at random from containers of nominally the same batch.

The following is intended as a guide to sampling different kinds of material:

> Resins which are delivered in lump form, may well also contain some smaller pieces and fine powder. A composite sample should then be taken which is representative of the proportions of each grade present. It must also be remembered that there is a specific reason for resins being delivered in lump form (usually to prevent oxidation) and so they should only be crushed, where necessary, immediately prior to the actual raw material testing.

The vibration in transit of a cask of pigment may well have caused some segregation of particles of different size. Hence, the cask should either be tumbled before opening or several samples taken at varying levels in the cask with a special auger-like tool.

Liquids should be thoroughly stirred or the barrels tumbled before opening to ensure that no separation into distinct phases has occurred.

Quality control sections, whether concerned with raw materials, intermediates or finished inks, carry a great responsibility for the efficient working of a company. Decisions must be made in all testing departments on the tolerance limits required: if these limits are too narrow, then ink production can be impeded and late deliveries could ensue, whereas too wide limits can, of course, have a detrimental effect on both quality and reproducibility. For commercial purposes, a working compromise must be reached: some testing will be regarded as essential, and further testing, while desirable, may be uneconomic. The ink formulator must bear a great responsibility in setting these limits as he alone is fully aware of both the final ink specification and of the raw materials which are essential to the success of his particular formulation.

Comprehensive testing of raw materials has the advantage of reducing the range of tests needed at the finished product stage, and hence a faster service to the consumer. However, this advantage is partially offset by the necessity to test deliveries of some of the more versatile raw materials in a wider range of formulations than those in which the batch may eventually be used. The individual ink companies must, therefore, balance their testing resources to give the most advantageous results.

In the remainder of this chapter, a relatively comprehensive guide to the testing of both raw materials and finished inks has been attempted but it is impossible in the scope of such a section to include all the highly specific tests which could be carried out. Where standard test methods are included, only the salient points have been given and the reader should refer to the published test procedure for the practical details. References are also quoted throughout the chapter for the reader to further his background knowledge in specific areas of testing procedure.

Quality control of pigments is particularly difficult as a single pigment can be used in a wide variety of vehicle systems to give inks for many different end uses. Hence, the testing procedure must be selective and it can logically be divided into three sections. Firstly, limited testing can be carried out on the dry pigment itself to ensure the batch meets the specification for shade, strength, particle size, oil absorption, moisture and volatile content. The second and possibly most important consideration is to compare the ink making characteristics of the batch against the master standard in the ink maker's own vehicle systems. Finally, provided the batch meets the specification to date, prints from the sample and standard inks are checked for their resistance properties.

Since the pigment particle size will affect such fundamental properties as strength, hue, rheology and stability of the finished ink it would seem desirable to check particle size or at least the average size distribution as part of the quality control procedure. However, in the size range of most pigments (less than 1mm) the majority of the standard techniques for sizing (e.g., gravitational sedimentation, optical microscopy) are slow and inaccurate. Only two methods are suitable for particle size measurement in this range: electron microscopy and centrifugal sedimentation. Electron microscopy is an expensive method and requires an experienced operator but is capable of producing very accurate readings.

The disc centrifuge is now the preferred technique and results compare favourably with those obtained using electron microscopy. However, neither of these two methods is simple and quick enough to be used as standard quality control procedure on each batch of pigment and the ink maker therefore places greater emphasis on the dispersion of the pigment particles in the finished ink.

The oil absorption of a pigment will depend on:

(1) The type of pigment (i.e. whether it is a lead chrome or barium lithol).
(2) Particle size and size distribution.
(3) Particle shape.
(4) Surface characteristics of the sample, such as those obtained by treatment to improve wetability or even simply due to absorbed moisture.

If the oil absorption of the pigment varies from batch to batch then formulation changes will have to be made to the inks and clearly this is undesirable. Since the factors affecting oil absorption cannot easily be measured, the test is reduced to a purely empirical comparison between the batch and master standard. The actual test method is given in BS 3483, Part 137; 1974, the result being quoted as the mass (or volume) of oil required to wet 100 g of pigment. Alternatively, the sample and standard can be dispersed in a measured amount of oil and the relative consistencies of the two samples can then be compared.

Absorbed moisture may affect the ease of dispersion of some pigments and this should be determined on each batch of pigment according to the method in BS 3483, Part 6; 1974.

A temperature of 105° C is chosen for this test as at higher temperatures volatile matter may be lost which is an essential part of the pigment: this is especially true of carbon black and pigments on an aluminium hydrate base.

All pigments should be checked wherever possible in the vehicle systems in which they will be used in production, but in certain cases where the pigment is used in several different types of inks this will result in a lengthy testing procedure and a selective range of formulations must then be chosen. This should include oil and liquid ink formulations (where appropriate), a vehicle system which is used in bulk with the test pigment and one which is a more difficult medium for ease of dispersion. The method of dispersion in the laboratory should:

(1) Simulate production milling methods.

(2) Be rapid and comparative.

(3) Utilise small quantities of pigment so as to retain a single master standard for testing as many batches as possible.

For example, bead mill dispersions with liquid and oil inks can be simulated in the laboratory by a high speed stirring technique using a standard weight of beads or steel balls in a known amount of ink. Small triple roll mills can of course be used to represent their larger production counterparts, but care must be taken to avoid any alteration to the roller settings in between milling the standard and batch pigments.

The first test must be to ensure that the batch of pigment disperses at least as readily as the standard and to an equivalent degree so that costly production milling time will not be lost. Dispersion is measured on a fineness of grind gauge. This is a hardened steel block containing a shallow groove which is graduated in depth from zero to, for example, 25 or 50 microns. A sample of ink is placed at the deep end, drawn down with a steel blade towards the shallower part, and the dispersion is taken as the point at which the continuous ink film breaks down across the groove. However, care must be taken in interpreting the result if discontinuity in the ink film occurs higher up on the gauge due to the odd oversize particle. It is then important to determine whether these scratches are caused by undispersed pigment particles, or by, for example, wax or dried ink, and this can be confirmed by examination of a smear of the ink under a microscope.

Once the correct dispersion level has been attained, the trial ink can be compared with the standard for strength, hue, gloss and flow (or consistency). Firstly, the flow is checked as it is impossible to obtain meaningful comparative prints unless the batch and standard have very similar consistency. Liquid inks having near Newtonian flow properties can be compared by viscosity measurements using any of the standard techniques (e.g., Ford and Zahn cups). Oil inks, however, are more difficult to assess by instrumental measurement and for the present purpose are probably best compared by checking their consistency with the aid of a palette knife, and by a comparison of their relative flow properties on a vertical glass plate.

The strength of the trial pigment is then assessed on a drawdown at full strength and at reduced strength as a 'bleach'. The drawdown is carried out by placing small quantities of the standard and test inks about one inch apart on the top sheet of a securely held pad of paper and firmly scraping them towards the operator with, for example, a 3 inch wide blade. Initially, the blade should be held nearly vertical to reproduce a film thickness comparable to a printed film weight and then finally the blade should be brought almost parallel to the pad to give a thick film weight-the mass tone of the ink.

The drawdown should be carried out on a semi-absorbent paper on which a broad black band (19 mm wide) has been previously printed so the opacity (or transparency) of the batch and standard pigments can also be compared.

The bleach technique involves dilution by mixing (not

grinding) a coloured ink with a much larger quantity of opaque white so as to eliminate any minor differences of gloss and hue. In the case of yellow inks, the eye cannot differentiate small strength differences and so sufficient blue is added to the bleach to bring the hue into the blue-green region.

Hue and gloss can be measured by instrumental techniques but normally a visual comparison of a drawdown and print is sufficiently accurate. The undertone and top tone of the inks can be assessed using the thin film of the drawdown and the thicker mass-tone respectively. Gloss can also be checked on the drawdown but, more accurately, by examination of a print of the batch versus standard on an appropriate stock.

Provided the pigment matches the standard on the tests conducted to date, the appropriate resistance checks are carried out. Many of the characteristic properties of a pigment are a function of its chemical nature and hence are unlikely to vary from batch to batch unless an impurity is present. Pigments are, however, coated to provide easier dispersion in different vehicle systems and this can give rise to batch variation especially when the pigment is obtained from an alternative supplier.

All the resistance tests are carried out on prints of the batch and standard inks rather than on the dry pigments themselves, but it is important that an appropriate vehicle system be chosen, e.g., it is pointless to try and check the heat resistance of a pigment when a low softening point resin is present.

As the lightfastness of a pigment is a function of its chemical nature, it is only necessary to carry out random spot checks but attention should be paid hereto pigments used in inks where lightfastness is an important criterion, e.g. wallpaper inks

Pigments will show higher lightfastness at full strength and therefore it is important that a realistic strength print be submitted for test. For example, a PMTA pigment should rarely be tested at full strength, since its main application will be as a toner pigment. As pigments for use on wallpapers could often be used in tints, it is advisable to test these at both full and tint strengths. Prints should be prepared on a good quality paper which does not yellow on exposure to light or contain artificial brightening aids which are destroyed by ultra-violet radiation.

The exposure of prints to daylight is too lengthy a procedure to be suitable and the use of an artificial source is therefore adopted. The only light source to have an emission spectrum close to that of daylight is the xenon arc and provided a filter is used to reduce the amount of ultra-violet radiation a result comparable to the daylight exposure is obtained in a much shorter time. Other light sources such as the carbon arc and mercury vapour lamp are not recommended as the results bear little comparison to those obtained under daylight conditions.

Another factor which greatly affects the lightfastness figure is the effective humidity which is dependent on the relative humidity and temperature of the surrounding air and the surface temperature of the pattern. The average effective humidity value for daylight exposure in Britain is 45 per cent and therefore the test apparatus should be capable of approximating to this figure.

In order to numerically classify the lightfastness results obtained the prints are compared with a set of eight pieces of wool, each dyed with a different blue dye which has been carefully graded to fade after a set of exposure to light. This is known as the Blue Wool Scale and the scale ranges from one (poor lightfastness) to eight (excellent) according to the number of the wool dyes which have test method. The procedure for mounting and assessing samples is given in as 4321:1969. But it is worthy to note that the term 'fading' includes not only a reduction in strength but also changes in hue, brightness, darkening or any combination of these factors.

Heat resistance of pigments is a critical factor in the areas of tin printing inks (and other metal coatings) and wallpaper inks which will be subjected to hot embossing. The pigments are simply tested by placing prints in a suitably heated oven for a set period of time, the actual conditions depending on the end usage of the print. The prints are then compared with an unheated sample for changes in strength, hue and brightness.

Pigments to be used in soap and detergent wraps should be checked to ensure no impurities are present which are liable to cause bleed problems. Although test methods for both soap and detergent resistance are given (BS, 4321 Test methods 6 and 7 respectively) the manufacturers of these products have their own test methods which are generally more severe than the British Standard tests.

A typical soap resistance test as provided by a leading manufacturer, is as follows:

> A 25 per cent soap gel is made up and allowed to set. The gel is moistened and the print to be tested is first soaked in water to prevent curling (one minute for paper and five minutes for board). The print is then placed face down in the gel and left for 15 minutes, after which time it is examined There should be no sign of bleeding at this stage. The print is then replaced and left for three hours before being further examined. After this period there should be preferably no bleed, although a slight bleed could be considered acceptable.

Testing for detergent resistance is becoming more complex with the advent of the enzyme powders and more recently "solvent" powders. Provided a pigment passes the above test, it is unlikely to fail with the standard soap powders and therefore detergent resistance should be assessed with an enzymic powder. (Note: To date no standard test has been published for resistance to the "solvent detergents").

A typical detergent test resistance is as follows:

> A five per cent solution is made up using the appropriate enzymic detergent in water. Two filter papers are soaked in the solution, one is placed on a glass slab and the print to be tested is placed face down on filter paper. The second filter paper is then laid on top and a further glass slab provides a sandwiched effect. The print is then examined after three hours and there should be no bleed although a slight bleed could be considered as acceptable.

This test can be conducted either by streaking dilute sodium hydroxide solutions on to a print (e.g. 2,3 and 5 per cent) and examining the dried streaks for discolouration or as in the British Standard test (BS 4321 Test method 5) by sandwiching the print between filter papers previously soaked in a dilute alkaline solution. In this case, the filter papers are dried after a set contact period and then the degree of staining is assessed with the aid of a grey scale.

Acid resistance can be carried out in a manner similar to BS4321 Test method 5 above but replacing the alkaline solution with either dilute hydrochloric acid or dilute acetic acid. The latter reagent is normally used where the print could come into contact with vinegar or pickles.

Wax resistance is essential for inks on waxed paper bread wraps, ice cream cartons, certain vending machine cups and similar applications where the substrate is made more water resistant by immersion in molten wax (usually paraffin wax). The standard test (BS4321 Test method 10) involves immersion of the print in the molten wax for five minutes after which the wax is allowed to run over the margin surrounding the print. The margin and the wax in the basin are then examined for discolouration.

This test is becoming increasingly important as more and more products are being stored under deep freeze conditions.

On carton board, the vehicle system (or overprint varnish) will normally provide adequate deep freeze resistance and testing of the pigment is not necessary.

However, for polythene printing the deep freeze resistance of the finished pack is a function not only of the vehicle (usually straight or modified polyamide) but also of the pigment as well. The deep freeze resistance of the pigment in these cases is not so much a function of its chemical nature but of the pigment coating and therefore quality control of each batch of pigment is essential for this application.

The severest conditions met by the print is not when the pack is actually under the deep freeze conditions, but during the stage of thawing on removal from the refrigerator, and hence the test normally conducted is one of water immersion.

A typical test is as follows:

> The print is immersed in water for a period of at least one hour and a maximum of five hours. The print is then flexed between the knuckles ten times and should show no more than five per cent removal. A second portion of the print is then blotted dry and should show no more than five per cent removal when checked by the Scotch tape test.

Binding of Books

The binding (finishing) operation has been grossly dependent upon the skill and efficiency of the manual work-force. The skill normally acquired through years of experience gained under the expert guidance of senior members of the family as the binding has been a family oriented craft\trade.

Binding or Post-Press Operation being one of the most important functions in presenting and preserving the printed material, can be described as follows:

(1) Pre-Press Binding or warehousing

(2) Post-Press Binding/Finishing

Warehousing/Pre-press Binding

White-paper warehouse

Printed-paper Warehouse

Binding/Finishing Warehouse

Paper is stored and cut before being issued for Printing. Equipment required-Guillotine/Cutting Machines.

Printed sheets are stored awaiting instructions for Finishing. Book printing invariably involves binding in parts thereby saving additional expenditures of binding.

Simple forms of finishing (cutting & trimming) e.g. pamphlet and magazine binding including packing and despatch functions are performed.

Equipment required-Guillotine/Cutting Machine, Wire stitching and Dab-Press etc.

Extensive range of Cutting Machines (Guillotine) are available as follows:

(a) Hand Clamp and hand-levered Cutting action with 4-5" opening; Size: 26", 32", 36" & 42".

(b) Semi-automatic heavy duty with Foot-clamp and motorised Cutting action with manual or motorised back-gauge movement with upto 5" opening; Size: 26, 32, 36, 42 & 48".

(c) Automatic with self-clamping, motorised back-gauge, safety device, 5" opening etc. Size: 33" & 42". Optional Magnetic Clutch and electronic Photocell safety device.

(d) Automatic with Hydraulic clamping and Cutting action, Safety device, digital display, Air cushion table etc. Programmable. Size: 33", 42" & 48".

The modern machines should incorporate the following features for accurate cutting efficiency and reliable trouble-free performance:

(i) The knife fall is so engineered that the cut is made at 90 degrees with the table and provision for adjustment to take up wear etc.

(ii) Clamping should be adequate and adjustable to various levels to suit different types of stock. The clamp action should be complete before the knife strikes the paper.

(iii) The back gauge must be easily moved by hand or be powered. It should be easily locked in position and when locked immovable. The back gauge should be parallel to the cutting line and adjustable both vertically and horizontally.

(iv) Knives should be of good quality and of good depth to allow many regrinds: easy and swift knife change facilities with fine setting adjustments.

(v) Cutting sticks should be easily adjusted, changed or turned.

(vi) Side plates should allow the cutting of small areas accurately.

(vii) There should be accurate gauging and presentation of the cutting distance in a position which is easily read.

(viii) Suitable safety guards in, accordance with the rules & regulations of Factories Act.

(ix) Other facilities e.g. micrometer settings, air-cushion tables, illuminated tables, power-operated back-gauge, photo-cell operated guards and Programmable for multiple Cuts.

Post-Press Binding/Finishing

Folding

Scoring & Creasing

Gathering

Insetting

Collating

Wire Stitching/Stabbing

Thread Sewing and Stitching

Binding Terminology

Styles of Binding

Perfect/Adhesive Binding

Spiral wire and Plastic-comb binding

Embossing, Die-cutting, Round-cornering, Varnishing & Laminating.

Folding

One of the most common and important operations. Folding may be done by:

(i) Hand

(ii) Machine-Semi Auto/Auto.

A sheet of paper has to be folded in accordance with the agreed imposition so that the printed pages will appear in correct sequence. A sheet of paper may be folded in various ways and the folds may be at right-angles, parallel or a combination of both right-angle and parallel folds. (See Illustration 'A').

Folding is an important operation because the final appearance of a job may be spoilt by inaccurate folds causing uneven margins which cannot be rectified in subsequent operations.

(i) Hand folding-Sheets are folded by hand with a bone of folding stick, when the number of sheets required to be folded does not justify setting up a Folding Machine or when the scheme of imposition is unsuitable for machine folding.

(ii) Folding machines of various patterns and capacities exist, and these are capable of folding sheets at speeds greatly in excess of those possible by hand-folding. The method of folding is by either knife-blade or buckle-fold principle or combination of both.

The capacity of a Folding machine is determined by the size of sheet to be folded and the number of folding units. Folding machines are either hand-fed or fitted with automatic feeder (Simple Pile feeder or Continuous Paper feeder). Different thicknesses of paper stock and any alteration in the size of sheet entail adjustment to both the folding mechanisms.

The following characteristics of the printed sheet will effect the folding quality:

(a) The forme should be centered on the sheet, unless there is a good reason for it not to be so.

(b) Back-up should be accurate, the back mark in correct position and signatures properly located.

(c) Sheet size constant with clean edges.

When thick material, such as board, thick cover paper, manilla etc., is folded, its surface becomes damaged and ragged at the fold unless it is scored or creased before being folded. This is done on a rotary scoring machine or a bander scorer by making a blind impression into the material to compress and stretch the fibres so as to produce a score or crease which will permit the material to bend without its surface being broken and the fold becoming ragged.

When a job consists of more than one section, the sections, which have been folded separately, have to be collected together in complete set ready for binding. This operation is known as gathering. In order to distinguish one section from another signatures are used.

Signatures are generally capital letters or figures printed at the foot of the printed matter on the front page of each section in alphabetical or numerical order so that the sections can be gathered in correct sequence and later checked. A gathered job consists of separate sections collected together in correct order as complete sets of signatures.

The placing of one section within another is known as Insetting. For example, if an 8pp. section is inset in the middle of another 4pp. section, a 12pp. section results. The smaller section being wrapped round the larger section. The pages have to be imposed accordingly otherwise the folios will not be in correct sequence.

Insetting is an operation which has to be carried out with more than average, care as insetted sections cannot subsequently be easily checked. An insetted job is one in which the centre section forms the middle round which all the other sections are wrapped. Inset should not be confused with an insert which is a loose piece of paper or board inserted between the leaves of a book/pamphlet and not secured in any way. After folded sections have been gathered, they are collated, which means that they are examined to ensure that they are complete and that the signatures are in correct sequence. On machine-gathered or cheap work, this examination is often dispensed with. Collating marks or 'back marks' are sometimes printed on the back folds of gathered jobs and in this way the operation of collating is simplified because any displacement of sections or other errors in gathering can be seen at a glance.

The cheapest and fastest method of binding single section or insetted work and the method most widely used for magazines and pamphlets is wire stitching. In this operation one copy of the insetted sections, opened at its centre, is placed on the saddle of the machine. Wire, fed from a reel is automatically cut to the correct length for the stitch and driven by the stitching head through the back fold, being clenched beneath at the centre to form a staple which holds the sections firmly together.

Gatherer stitchers are more elaborate machines having an endless chain feed device on which the separate sections are placed, either by hand or by automatic hopper feeders, before being carried under one or more stitching heads. This type of machine permits the insetting of sections to be carried out at the same time as stitching and greatly increases output as the operation of the stitching heads is automatic.

Gathered work, consisting of separate sections, is stitched through the side at the binding edge from front to back. This method is known as stabbing, side wire stitching or flat wire stitching Round wire is generally used for saddle stitching and flat wire for side stitching. The wire is usually galvanised steel, but brass or copper is used when non-rusting wire is considered desirable. The gauge of the wire varies according to the thickness being stitched and the hardness of the paper. Stitching machines are available in India as single-head or double-head power-operated for a capacity ranging from 5" to 1.25". Paddle-operated machines are capable of handling stock upto 9/16".

Preparations of Book : Gathered sections are sewn and insetted work is stitched through the back fold, just as wired jobs are stabbed or stitched, but linen thread is used instead of wire.

Sewing is used in better quality magazine work and in bookbinding, and may be done either by hand or on a sewing machine. Machine sewing is quicker than hand sewing and has the advantage that stitches are independent of each other so that every stitch must be broken before a section can be removed, whereas a single break in the thread of hand sewn work is sufficient for removal of a section because each stitch is made with the same piece of thread.

Modern machines using straight needles may be grouped into hand-fed, semi-automatic and automatic versions.

Certain terms are used in connection with bindery and warehouse work, some of the same are quoted as follows:

(a) Head or top is the edge of a page or book parallel to and above the printed matter or used to indicate the upper positions on any form of binding.

(b) Tail is the edge parallel to and below the printed matter or the lower positions on any form of binding.

(c) Back, spine or binding edge is that portion of a book or pamphlet where the sheets are secured together by thread, wire or other means or corresponding external portion of a book/pamphlet.

(d) Foredge is the edge of a book or pamphlet opposite the back, spine or binding edge.

(e) Cover is any material cut to size for the binding of a book or pamphlet.

Styles of Binding

(a) Edition Case Binding

(b) Letterpress Binding

(c) Stationery Binding

Today the majority of books having stiff cloth covers are bound in this style. This method of binding is known as casing because the cover is prepared separately from the sections making. Cutting Printed Sheets and Folding; pasting End Paper; Gathering and collating sections; sewing collated sections; smashing; trimming edges; gluing of back; rounding and backing; back lining; Case making & Blocking.

This is the name given to those styles of binding used for reading books as distinct from books used for written records such as accounts books. Edition Case binding is a branch of Letter-press binding. The work of letterpress binding may be divided into sewing, forwarding, covering and finishing. This includes the binding of account books, manifold and duplicate books, receipt books, cheque books, and memoranda books, loose-leaf books, punching and creasing sheets for loose-leaf binders.

The style of binding books which are to be used for written records of either a temporary or permanent nature needs to be different from that for books printed for the purpose of reading.

A type of Binding which has become very popular due to its economy and flexibility. What can be easier than gathering loose sections to form book blocks, jogging these, preparing the spines, gluing them and applying a cover.

Perfect Binding or Adhesive Binding can be defined as a method of binding books with adhesive as the only binding medium not involving thread for sewing or steel-wire for saddle stitching. The development of a fully Automatic Adhesive Binding Machine began in the latter part of the nineteenth century, but it was not until after World War II, with the development of suitable adhesive that the process became popular.

Perfect Binding holds a challenge to book binder and machine manufacturer alike. There really are considerable differences between producing large quantities of thin paperbacks as economically as possible, binding bulky telephone directories or mail-order catalogues in such a way that they will stand-up to frequent use over long period.

For achieving best results with adhesive binding, it is essential to study the size of the book, type of paper, grain of paper and the cover, these variable factors are required to be balanced for selecting the most suitable glue and parameters of machine setting accordingly.

Adhesive binding, also known as 'Perfect', 'Patent' or 'Threadless' binding is being used extensively in binding industry because:

1. It produces flat-opening books of any thickness.
2. The books can be either paper covered or cased-in.
3. Adhesive-binding can be done in an un-interrupted work flow.

The Perfect bound book passes through the following stages:

Loose sections or sheets are gathered (manually or mechanically) to form book-blocks and transferred for feeding manually for slower machine and mechanically in-line for faster machines. Built-in vibrating mechanism helps the book blocks to have even spine.

Spine Making : The back-bone (spine) of the book is prepared by mailing-out a section of the spine leaving about 3/4" of the head and tail uncut thus providing a paperhinge. The cutters make a serrated pattern on the surface of the back-bone and roughening cutters prepare an ideal spine for a strong adhesive bond. The paper dust is removed with the help of a vacuum pump to avoid any dust particles transferring to Glue-Tank.

The characteristics of adhesive used in perfect binding are fast drying, flexible and strength to with-stand constant use. The three basic glues used are: (i) Cold Glues, (ii) Animal Glues & (iii) Hot-Melt Glues.

(i) Most Cold-Glues are polyvinyl acetate with plasticizers which form a tough flexible film that dries slowly therefore require additional drying energy.

(ii) Animal Glue is a fairly fast setting gelatine that becomes brittle within a short period of time once the liquids of which the glue is formulated have evaporated.

(iii) Hot-Melt glues have no wetting agent but rather are melted by applying high temperatures. Once applied to a book and cover, the hot-melt adhesive cools rapidly to a solid flexible state that lasts indefinitely.

Paper covers can be scored (creased), aligned and applied to the back-bone immediately after Gluing.

The back-bone with the cover pasted is nipped from the bottom and the two sides.

The bound-books are delivered on their spine with help of sticker arrangement. Belt delivery can be attached for faster transfer.

3

Different Phases

Making the many diverse and independent functions inside the newspaper plant fit together like the intricate parts of facing executives. But there is no substitute for a harmonious blending of these production factors into a unified effort, and nothing else contributes more to the profitable and satisfying rewards to be found in newspaper publishing.

In the same way that a fine automobile spins along on four well-balanced wheels, newspaper production depends on four carefully aligned factors: flow of work, saving of time, capacity standards and expense regulation.

Significent Tasks

Publishing a newspaper requires a ready flow of ingenuity, work, copy, films, and metal. To keep that flow evenly paced and uninterrupted requires clear organization, constant supervision and direction, and the most careful and earnest cooperation.

From the start of the publication period until press time, the news department must keep newsworthy information flowing into the office and the composing room. As any good reporter knows, there is nothing so stale as old news. At times a reporter may think the editors or publishers are hard taskmasters, but actually they are compelled by tradition and by the practical copy flowing steadily. That's newsgathering.

Covering, writing, and editing stories; picture taking; and other newsgathering responsibilities are no different on a weekly than on a daily. They are merely done by fewer persons; and even though the production interval is a full week, a steady flow of copy must be maintained once work on the weeks issue is begun. An alert and efficient editor will do the following

1. Plan ahead. Once an issue is out. Work must begin on the next. In fact, much of the work must be planned days before the date of issue.
2. Keep a date or futures book to reveal what subject matter is to be covered immediately and what news stories are in prospect. This serves a twofold purpose; the paper is not so likely to missimportant stories and assignments can be made according to an organized plan.
3. Use judgement in making assignment. The editor knows which reporters are best equipped by temperament, knowledge, and experience to handle specific types of stories.
4. Plan for early completion of stories to go on inside pages. Which are made up first. Interesting copy must be available at all times for quick makeup.
5. See that department editors plan and complete features and stories well in advance. Some publishers measure the worth of department editors as much by how well they plan ahead as by the quality of the copy produced by their staffs.
6. Clear the news wire machines regularly, sort copy in an orderly fashion, and edit it rapidly. For the daily

newspaper the wire machines roll out endless sheets of news from all parts of the world. The problem lies in what stories to select and when to send them to the copydesk or into the computer. Only experience will develop the kind of foresighted judgement needed for the job.

7. Keep a backlog of time copy handy-features and other material that may be used to fill in on days when general news is light.
8. Edit copy carefully to avoid revisions in proofs, which may cause delays near press time.
9. Write headlines plainly and transmit them with copy to the composing room. Late headlines cause delay and often are placed incorrectly in makeup.
10. Read proofs promptly. A dilatory and inefficient proofreader may wipe out all the speed put into copy preparation by the news staff.

"We made a general outline of the type of material to be used in the Small explains. Then we proceeded to assign specific stories to reporters, and the fact that we told them that they should have one in every three or four days seemed to increase their interest. Naturally we had to have close cooperation and a great many staff meetings."

For a fiftieth-anniversary edition, the publisher of a small daily began formulating plans a year ahead and began actual work on the edition six months before it was to be distributed. The publisher first drew up a general plan, deciding that edition should have ten sections, each dealing with a particular phase of the community's development in which the newspaper had an important part. Next, each section was planned, with a list of the local advertisers who should be represented and the phases of community development to be covered in news and feature stories. Each prospective story was carefully outlined so that the reporter, upon receiving the assignment, had a clear understanding of what facts should be included. A deadline was set for each section. Pictures were taken, copy was prepared and printing of the section took place within a month after work was begun on the edition.

Work then started on the next section, which was to be written, edited and printed within two weeks. That two-week schedule continued until the ten section were completed. Each section was stuffed inside those previously printed, and the constantly developing edition was stored in a protected corner of the pressroom.

The work on the anniversary edition extended over a long period, but by careful planning it was done by the regular staff during some welcomed overtime ours without interfering with work on daily issues.

Work should proceed steadily and evenly in every section of the business department. Records in the office must be as up to the minute as the news that appears in the day's issue if the newspaper is to meet the standards of a going concern. This can be realized only by :

1. Giving definite instructions to office help.
2. Having proper forms for tabulating required information.
3. Issuing statements and making collections promptly.
4. Avoiding delay in answering correspondence.
5. Acknowledging all advertising and subscription orders immediately.
6. Paying bills promptly and taking advantage of discounts.
7. Maintaining adequate personnel and equipment.

A publisher encourages efficiency, accuracy, and promptness in the business office by requiring up-to-date facts about the business. Forward-looking business managers are making dramatic use of computers for keeping an almost instantaneous check on minute details of the business operation.

Keeping ahead in preparing and selling advertising and feeding copy to the composing room in a way that will keep the machines busy is the advertising department's job. To accomplish this, most newspapers have deadlines for advertising copy.

The Bloomington, III., Pantagraph has an advertisements of such perishables as fruit and meat. On those the deadline is 5 P.M. the day before publication.

Advertising Headline Requirements

Size of ad	*Days Preceding publication*
Double page	5 days
Single page	4 days
Half page	3 days
Quarter page	2 days
Smaller ads	1 days

The composing room refuses copy that does not conform to this deadline schedule. Such a schedule puts the advertising department on its toes and counteracts excuses from the composing room.

When putting out a special edition, the steady flow of advertising copy to the composing room for many weeks prior to publication is a important as a steady flow of editorial copy. The Atlantic city, N.J press stimulated its advertising force in a unique way for a special edition. To provide competition and thus create a steady copy flow, members of the staff were selected by team captains of the "Write Sox" and "Purple Hose". A "nine-inning game" started with last week in December and continued until mid-February. Each page of advertising counted as a run. Each week counted as an inning. The keenness of the competition reflected in the final score; Purple Hose, 51; White Sox, 50.

Other techniques used to maintain a more even volume of advertising are:

1. A special rate to merchants who carry a minimum amount of daily or weekly advertising.
2. Bonuses and commissions for extra volume produced by salespeople during slack periods.
3. Definite linage goals established with suitable rewards for the staff when the goals are reached.
4. Last year's linage figures kept constantly before the staff.
5. Special pages of cooperative advertising produced for otherwise dull periods.

Some newspaper have found it advantageous, as far as stimulating the flow of advertising copy is concerned, to offer discounts to merchants who deliver their copy "camera-ready" to the newspaper. This practice obviously eliminates the work of the advertising representative in obtaining the copy from merchants, and relieves the newspaper of typesetting, composition, proofing, and delivering finished ad proofs for approval by the client.

No department of a newspaper runs more risk of getting off balance in its work flow the circulation department Papers. Papers must be delivered to homes at regular hours each day or week, and they must be in good order or subscribers are dissatisfied. Circulation totals must rise continually at least remain stabilized at a profitable level.

A carefully planned adaptation of a semi-automatic book keeping machine-the National Cash Register book keeping machine, Model 3100, with a 26-inch carriage has eliminated much paperwork by district personnel in the circulation department of the Santa Rosa, Calif, Press Democrat. Formerly, the district staff posted their "stops" and "starts", then totaled their new draw for each route or dealer and turned in the completed figures to the book keeper. Under the new draw for each route or dealer and turned in the completed figures to the bookkeeper . Under the new system, the stops and start for each route or dealer go at once to the book keeper who posts them on the daily draw sheets, arriving at the days draw as well as at the cumulative total for the month. When the total draws at the last day of the month are compiled, figures are immediately available for posting the monthly billings, without the necessity of balancing the month's work.

Rapid circulation growth led the Toronto, Ont., star to modernize its mailing room to speed the movement of papers from the presses to trucks and other carriers. To supplement the equipment it already had in the mailing room, the star publishers had their research-engineering department design a machine to feed bundles directly from a Cutler-Hammer paper conveyor, end on the roller-slat conveyor, and then directly through a company-designed automatic self-feeling, wire-tying machine. This specially designed bundle feeder is know as the Star starter.

To the casual spectator, the mailrooms of modern metropolitan dailies are marvels of mechanical ingenuity, where the pace of activity can become quite feverish as the pressroom hits full production. Conveyor systems are customized to speed freshly printed sections of the newspaper in sometimes bewildering configuration-horizontally, vertically, around curves, and through machines that automatically insert stack count tie in bundles, address, or perform other specialized duties.

The Memphis publishing Company has added a computer-directed system that determines automatically the distribution of bundles through chutes to waiting trucks four floors below. Some of the specially designed equipment for faster and more efficient mailroom operations can give this part of the newspaper plant an exciting appearance.

A perennial problem facing circulation managers is that of carrier turnover. Some newspaper deposit to a carrier's credit half the value of a U.S. Savings Bond when he has been on the route three months. To collect the bond, the carrier must stay on his route nine more consecutive months and do good work.

Management once looked upon the composing room more as a necessary evil than as a profitable operating department, but this attitude has been changed by time studies, cost systems, and analyses.

An unusually detailed presentation of desirable trends in newspaper makeup was provided in comments by the judges of the 1979 Typoraphy and Design Contest of the Inland Daily press Association, as reported in Editor & Publisher magazine. The judges were Hayward Blake, Evanston.IIL, graphic designer; and two educators from the Medill School of Journalism at North-western University: Assistant Dean Dave Nelson and Professor Jack Sissors.

Here are some of their observations:

1. The better newspaper use functional rather than formula makeup. Traditional newspaper have a sameness that makes them look designed by formula, whereas the best tend to use makeup that fits the news.
2. Wider columns appear most functional and attractive.
3. Newspapers do not waste white space but are careful to distribute it throughout any given page.
4. Column rules are disappearing.
5. Newspapers tent to use type family throughout the paper.
6. Varying the graphic treatment of special sections tends to create interest.

Here were some of their criticisms:

1. Too many nameplates are too large too ugly.
2. Bad standing heads suggest that many newspaper managements should buy the service of a graphic designer.
3. Too many newspapers use italics too much instead of saving it for use as a contrast face.
4. The use of the same kind of rule borders for boxed stories and advertisement should be avoided.

5. Too few subheads are use to break up body type.

Subheads should be boldface and of a typeface that represents a change.

Firm policies on typographical usage and makeup variations will contribute much to the flow of work in the mechanical department.

Time-saving Techniques

Newspapers today buy time as well as talent. The rate of pay to most newspaper employes is as much on the basis of time as ability. The tendency among labour leaders is to have work measured by the time spent rather than by its productive power. Employes work a specified number of hours each week, and a half. When manufacturers are buying time of his sort, they want as little of it as possible.

Time clocks used in some newspaper plants not only calculate the hours put in by employes but also make them conscious of their responsibility to make time count and to give full measure. There is some question, however, about the advisability of time clocks since they may have an undesirable psychological effect on employes. This some publishers have learned, is true for the editorial, news, and clerical department. However, there usually is some from of checking in and checking out where a large number are employed.

Non-productive work time includes such time-consuming operations as repairing machinery, plate removal and storage, cleaning up the composing room, and losses due to machinery breakdown. Daily coffee breaks and vacation periods represent many non-productive hours for which the newspaper willingly pays the same as for productive hours.

In some plants there has been a tendency to abuse the privilege of coffee breaks by staying out longer than the time agree upon between employer and employes. To avoid this, a number of newspaper serve coffee in the plant.

Vacation policies are established mainly on the length of time a person a person has been on the company payroll. On some newspapers the employe works for the company for year before a paid vacation is earned. In addition to the prescribed vacations, six holidays are generally granted during the year: New Year's Day. Memorial Day, Fourth of July, Labour Day, Thanksgiving, and Christmas. Many newspaper make a birthday. With smaller newspapers, vacations and holidays may be on a less formal schedule.

Speed in making assignments, preparing copy, and editing is important in the newsroom. To accelerate work there.

1. Help the reporter off to a quick start by clearly outlining the assignment and explaining its importance.
2. Have sufficient telephones in the newsroom to avoid any bottleneck in phone calls.
3. Organise routine telephone calling, such as that for the society page.
4. Have plenty of copy paper on hand, conveniently placed.
5. Have enough typewriters or editing terminals so that reporters need not wait to write their stories.
6. Keep average sentence length reasonably short.
7. Hold copy reading marks to a minimum.
8. See that reporters as well as copy processors understand copy editing standards and proofreading symbols.
9. Devise simple deadline schedules.
10. Provide chutes, elevators, pneumatic tubes, or other types of carrier systems to convey copy quickly to composing room.

For covering special events and correcting situations within the editorial-news office, special timesaving arrangements sometimes are necessary.

To achieve quick coverage of the home football games of the University Miami, the Miami, Fla., Herald has a wire machine installed in the press box, and the operator punches out the story on a direct wire to a phototypesetting machine in the composing room. Thus the type is set direct.

Visitors to the editorial-news office to report happenings, to discuss editorial policies, or to complain about how certain items were handled often consume much of the editor's time. To cut down this wasted time, the Winston-Salem, N.C. Journal and Sentinel carried in its columns a series of "Talks with Readers". One carried an informal photograph of the publishers sitting on his desk, glasses in hand, explaining that newspaper publishers have the tremendously difficult job of managing an operation that is both a business and a public service.

Other pictures explained the duties and trials of the editorial director and staff; and copy indicate why certain stories appear in the paper even though the staff, if it could have its way, would prefer not to use them and explained the impossibility of "suppressing" any news story. Discussing one newspaper towns, the publisher side: "The Journal and Sentinel are only of moderate size, yet last year it cost something like three million dollars to publish these papers. Publishing costs explain why nine out ten towns are served by only one publisher".

Functioning of an Office

In a fast-moving newspaper organization it is imperative that accounting methods keep pace with other operations. Modern accounting equipment saves many expensive hours of manual labour.

As part of a general modernization programme in the accounting department, the Cleveland, Ohio, press installed a Remington Rand accounting machine. Which handled the accounts payable record work in less than half the time required under the newspaper's previous of the work, the daily time ran to an average of seven and one-half hours. Using the new accounting machine, a single operator handled the same work in an average of slightly less than three hours a day.

Leslie Moeller, former director of the School of Journalism of the University of Iowa, cites other ways to save time and reduce costs in the newspaper business office.

Writing letters cost money and a printed memorandum sheet take the place of a letter. It is less expensive to print and quicker to type, and you do not have any extended addressing of salutation. The fact that the space is smaller helps to cut sown on the long-windedness which often seems to go automatically with the full-size letterhead.

Another step cost cutting is to shift to a postcard. You can carry your letterhead on the reverse side, and if you wish you can make a satisfactory carbon from such a postcard. If you use ten of these cards a day in place of standard letters your overall saving will be at least $150 a year if you take into account postage, printing, cost stock, secretarial time and of the other factors.

Modern dictating equipment will save you much time and money. Many publishers who type their own letters can save real money with this equipment. If your plant is small and you do not use a full-time secretary, you will find it easy to hire a stenographer who would like to work a few hours a day. The equipment is not complicated; you will be able to use it in a few minutes, and any competent typist can learn to transcribe in a little while.

Saving time in the advertising department is a matter of carefully planning copyrighting and sales work, giving special consideration to the wants and needs of readers and prospective advertisers and providing proper training for personnel. Some tested time-savers are:

1. Printed layout sheets, for preparing any size ad up to a full page, save many minutes that otherwise would be spent measuring space and ruling borders.
2. Flat-topped filling cabinets permit advertising services to be arranged in order for quick reference and to be opened immediately without going to a table or a desk.

3. A file where advertising ideas for special days each month, anniversaries, special weeks, and the like are compiled.
4. Standard forms for writing classified advertisements and for soliciting want ads by mail enable the ad taker to prepare the ad as it is received and help the mail advertiser to arrange facts systematically and estimate the cost easily.
5. Tilt-top, broad-surfaced copyrighting tables raise moral of the advertising department, encourage neat layouts, and speed production.
6. A timetable should be provided for sales personnel to make regular calls on prospects without duplication of effort. Each salesperson should be given a specific list of prospects or a definite territory to over.
7. A sticker on proof to be delivered to the advertiser indicates when proof was delivered and the time proof must be returned to the office to have corrections or changes made.

In many newspaper plants much time is lost in handling general advertising copy in the composing room, due to careless preparation of order and instructions by the advertising department. To improve this situation in its plant, the Green Bay, Wis., press-Gazette instituted a system whereby ad material was field by date rather than by product. After that there were few missed insertions, repeat ads were handle almost automatically, and old printing material was eliminated.

Careless handling of layouts is expensive. The copy should be clear, readable, and understandable for the compositor. Much copy prepared by merchants and submitted to newspapers should be redesigned and retyped before it goes to the printers.

Advertising sales personnel for the Chicago, III,. Tribune are trained to sell more than an advertisement- they sell a campaign. The idea is use by telephone solicitors in the classified department. They are trained to tell a caller "I'll start your ad today for seven days," which often converts a potential one-time ad into a multiple insertion order. It takes no longer to sell a seven-time ad than it does to sell a one-time ad, or to sell a series of 13 display ads than to sell a single ad.

All advertisers are billed at the open rate by the Carroll, Iowa, Times-Herald and if the account is paid by the tenth of the following month, contract advertisers receive discounts ranging from 16 percent to 28 percent depending on the space used. If a customer uses less space than previously and thus reduces the allowed discount, a call is made to suggest ways of qualifying for a larger one.

Discount are listed on the rate card, but the contract states that they are given "for a consistent and adequate advertising programme." Since the discount also is based on prompt payment, it serves to keep collections in good order and to eliminate otherwise necessary work by collectors, according to James W. Wilson, publisher.

With the impending conversion to the metric system facing it, the Iowa City, Iowa, press-citizen was one of the first newspaper in the nation to begin computing all its advertising measurements and contracts in centimeters rather than in column inches. Adjusting early to the new system has already begun to produce savings in time required to educate advertisers and readers to the change. Other pioneers in the transition to metrics include the Bangor, Maine, Daily News, the Columbia, Mo., Missourian, and the Ypsllanti, Mich., press.

Questions to consider in the circulation department are:

1. How may we lessen time consumed in stuffing when the newspaper is printed in several sections?
2. How may we speed transit of the paper from the press to delivery trucks?
3. Could we reach outlying points of our circulation area by some better delivery methods?

4. Are any of our carriers to begin and complete deliveries more promptly?

Stuffing papers by hand is a long and troublesome task. Tying bundles and getting them ready for delivery may also be time consuming. The Des Moines, Iowa, Register and Tribune has made a number of changes in its system of transporting papers from the press to the delivery trucks.

"The overhead conveyor system, once used for moving papers around our mailroom, has been removed," says J. R. Hudson, circulation manager, and stockers have been installed on the press conveyors. Tying machines now in operation use a plastic tape fastened with a metal clip. The old Pollard Ailing machine has been replaced by new Magnacraft equipment and the mail list has been transferred to the computer. We no longer use the Wallastar tying machine. The bottom wrapper on out bundles is now put on automatically with equipment built by our own machine shop people."

In a major redesigning of its mailroom, the Grand Rapids, Mich., press installed high-speed feeder tables and roller conveyors to link inserters, tyers, and loading dock in a timesaving operation.

The importance of getting papers to readers rapidly is never overlooked by an alert circulation manager. At one time, the Salina, Kans,. Journal served 16 town in 3 counties with daily delivery by airplane. A licensed pilot flew 180 air miles and delivered 1,000 papers per day, 5 days a week.

Another pilot flew 275 air miles to deliver 2,000 paper per day. The papers were wrapped in round bundles and each was dropped from 20 to 50 feet into field at the edge of the town where papers were to be delivered by car; but bad weather prevented airplane delivery only a few days in the year. For four week one winter, skis were used on the plane for safe landings at Salina on return trips forced landing was made in two years, and that was caused by the collapse of an oil strainer.

Circulation in the area doubled in the two years of airplane delivery.

Circulation distribution is a continuing problem for all newspapers. They can improve distribution by applying these timesaving methods:

1. By going to press at regular times. Late runs upset the entire delivery system.
2. By providing mailers with good equipment and teaching them now to use it. A mailing machine that operates poorly in stamping addresses on newspapers or wrappers can easily cause late mailings. The same is true regarding a mailer who does not understand the machine operation.
3. By tracking papers to carriers who deliver in outlying districts, thereby enabling them to start promptly.
4. By using motorcycles for delivery in suburban and rural areas, where homes are far apart and routes are long.
5. By rewarding carriers who complete their delivery routes within reasonable time and with no complaints.

The composing room is one of the most expensive departments of the newspaper organization, and there is consequently a tremendous loss involved in any careless management or waste of time. If materials are scattered, it is hard to concentrate employes operations. Loss also occurs when employes do not have enough material when needed or when they must wait to use a piece of equipment.

To reduce production bottlenecks, the Cleveland Ohio, press installed a Haploid FotoFlo photocopying camera in its composing room. This equipment produced an advertiser's layout full-page size in seven or eight minutes per photocopy so that everybody concerned could start work simultaneously. In addition, time was saved in the engraving department by furnishing photocopy type proofs in reverse, such as black on white and type with screened backgrounds, for the general run of advertisements.

With an week Positive Printmaker, the Lexington, Mass., Minuteman a weekly newspaper with a circulation of 9,5000, reports a saving in time of 48 hours per week in production, plus many hours formerly required for editorial layout work. The Itek 1113, made by the Itek Graphic Products company, requires one minute to make positive prints from original photographs and eliminates tedious "stripping". An additional benefit is that errors are almost totally eliminated.

Time reduction in the mailroom was achieved by the San Antonio, Tex., Express and News when it installed a new Sheridan on-line inserter. A twin-delivery arrangement per minutes a top speed of 36,000 fully inserted copies per hour.

At the New York N.Y. Wall Street Journal satellite plant in Orlando. Fla., fantastic strides have been made in remote control economy of operation.

The six unit Gross Metro offset press is run by a computer console that provides instant, response in the supply of ink, water, or registration adjustments. The management has reported what may be record times for edition start-ups and also believes that losses from newsprint waste have been reduced to the lowest experienced by any newspaper.

The highly automated Gannett newspaper have found that productivity per person has improved by 9 percent since converting to modern electronic production in the mechanical department. Also the Spilled newspapers have noted that fewer people are turning out greater results with improved equipment so that the average of hours worked of hours worked has declined 3 percent despite an increase in number of pages and volume of advertising produced.

The Raleigh, N.C., News and Observer and Times has trimmed its composing room force from 101 to 57 since conversion from letterpress to often, with electronic data processing equipment added.

Another remarkable achievement in timesaving is that of the Minneapolis, Minn., Star and Tribune. According to Paul Brainerd, assistant to the operations director, the newspaper is showing up to 30 percent in overall timesaving; 85 percent in markup; 50 percent in pasteup; and lesser reductions in proofreading, keyboarding, making corrections, and the like.

Detailed as some of these time whittling steps may seem to be, they to be they all add up to increased efficiency and higher profits.

Elementary Factors

Another basic factor of production is department-by-department capacity. The desire to increase production always exists, and it is the responsibility of management changes wherever practicable and advisable.

Adequate lighting, ventilation, and safety condition must prevail in all departments before production can reach a satisfactory peak. The reporter becomes drowsy and sluggish if forced to prepare copy under a dim light. Advertising personnel who have difficulty pulling mats from cabinets in shadowy corners lose time that should be spent in copy preparation and selling. Compositors need the benefit of good lighting. Accidents in the pressroom are less likely when there is proper illumination.

Newspaper publishing in many instances is an around-the-clock operation. Consequently, the lighting system must be adequate and independent of natural light is effective only within a few feet of the windows and varies greatly depending' on the weather. Illumination must be adequate not only in quantity but also in quality. The correct combination provides high visibility of detail and overall seeing comfort.

According to William H. Kahler, lighting engineer for the westinghouse Electric Corporation, Cleveland, Ohio, the composing room should have general illumination of 20 to 30 foot-candles provided by low brightness luminaires such as semi-indirect fluorescent equipment, and each machine should be equipped with a supplementary luminaire to furnish at least 50 foot-candle on the copy.

Lighting plays an important role in the pressroom where operators must maintain precise control of modern high- speed machinery. Fluorescent luminaires of the enclosed, vapour-tight type are recommended. Each luminaire contains two 40-watt fluorescent lamps and consists of a steel housing, inner white-enameled reflector, and a hinged dust-tight cover. Illumination along the sides of the press is about 40 foot-candles. The light inside the press is considerable less, but here again quality is more important than quality. The direction and diffusion of light from the continuous rows of fluorescent luminaires provides excellent visibility on the press cylinders and permits quick plate changes.

Every newspaper plant presents an individual lighting problem. A combination of careful planning, reliable lighting equipment, and regular maintenance will contribute to high production standards, efficient plant operation, and better morale among the workers.

The physical comfort of employe's has a strong bearing on their capacity to produce. Maintaining an even temperature within the newspaper plant the year around eliminates many problems that otherwise would arise. Air- conditioning is expensive, but it contributes greatly to the speed and composure of those responsible for producing a newspaper efficiently and promptly. Temperature has its effect on machinery as well as personnel. An every temperature and humidity should be kept in the pressroom for the proper operation of the presses—state electricity develops easily under adverse conditions of frost and moisture. Some provision must be made for removing surplus heat or fumes that might be produced by a piece of equipment. Efficient ventilation is the obvious answer for all departments where stuffy or odor-laden conditions of air prevail.

Publishers, as well as other manufacturers, are bound by their own responsibility and to a certain extent by law to provide safe working conditions for employes. But machinery around a printing plant presents hazards even under the most extensive protective provisions.

Lack of uniform safety measures for printing plants is the cause of many accidents. A worker transferring from one plant to another usually finds different machinery and different safeguards. A great variety of signaling methods is used in printing plants throughout the country to indicate staring of a machine—bells, horns, whistles, flashing lights. Another cause of server and sometimes fatal accidents is the location of the power control button, which is in almost as many different positions as there are machine. This makes it extremely difficult for workers to shut off the power in an emergency if they are not familiar with the machine or if they are on one side and the button is on the other. However, several devices have been created to shut off power automatically when anything happens to prevent smooth operation, and these should be considered in developing plant safety.

Preliminary steps have taken by the American Standards Association to develop a safety code for signaling devices and control for graphic arts equipment. In addition, strict regulation codified and enforced by federal and state and governments under the general supervision of the Occupational Safety and Health Administration keep the publisher informed of detailed requirements for the elimination of plant hazards.

Fire hazards develop easily in a newspaper plant if the situation is not watched carefully. An analysis made by the National Fire Protection Association of 1,053 fires in the printing industry reveals these general cause; common hazards, 52 percent; Special hazards, 27 percent; unknown causes, 21 percent. These special hazards are further broken down into the following types; paper ignited by gas dryer or static neutralizer flame, 35 percent; type-metal melting, 17 percent;

ignition of paper shreds by friction sparks from processing units, 21 percent; ignition of gasoline, naphtha, alcohol, and kerosene used in cleaning, 11 percent; ignition of benzol and other ink thinners, 9 percent; overheating of the glue pot, 2.5 percent; ignition of collodion deposits, 2.2 percent; ignition of varnish vapours, 2.5 percent; overheating of wax, 1.8 percent; miscellaneous, 4 percent.

In the news department it is difficult to say how much copy a good reporter should produce in a day. That depends to a great extent upon the type of beat to be covered or the kind of copy requested. Some reporters will turn in enough in a day to fill five columns. On some of the large city newspapers the management will be satisfied if its best reporter will turn in one good news story each day or fill one good assignment. The requirement standards on some newspapers are higher than on other, depending on how exacting the editorial-news department is regarding the style and accuracy of copy.

The reporter, as well as the executive, can easily estimate the cost per story or per column of the copy submitted. Employers sometimes remark that a beginner "writes the perfect story, but has yet to learn the tempo of the newspaper. The stories cost too much".

News department production standards may be raised by an alert editor who keeps in close touch with readers and knows how to explain their attitudes to staff members.

The publisher of the Washington, Iowa, Journal, in a unique survey questionnaire, asked readers: "If you were the Journal editor, how would you change the paper?" The questionnaire was a full newspaper-page size. The questions touched every department, feature, advertising idea, comic, panel, occasionally, regular column, editorial, and so forth that appeared in the Journal. Readers were asked to check readership as "always," "occasionally", "seldom", or "never" and to comment on whether the feature or department was liked "very much" "just so-so", or "not at all". The reverse side of the page had space for additional comments and the name and address of the newspaper, with postage prepaid so that the form could be folded and returned by this means the publisher used reader reaction to point out to staff members the standard of interest created by their work in the news and advertising department.

The state editor and the public officials of the South Bend. Ind., Tribune made personal visits to public officials of small communities in the circulation area. In each community they called upon the mayor or president of the city council and the superintendent of schools, asking their cooperation in obtaining news events in their communities. Reception of the idea was excellent. Officials were gratified by this evidence of the Tribune's interest and became good community reporters.

The interest of staff members in better reporting may be stimulated also by:

1. Providing regular and conscientious criticism of stories and methods.
2. Posting samples of excellent reporting and feature writing from other papers.
3. Holding staff meeting to discuss methods that should be used in following important leads and covering outstanding events.
4. Offering rewards to staff members for good story tips.

Valuable suggestions for improving methods in the business office may be obtained from employes. A suggestion box prominently placed and labeled with an appeal for entries and an announcement their own performance and cooperate in improvements.

Bert Stolpe, while director of promotion and public relations for the Des Moines Register and Tribune, concluded, on the basis of a survey, that American and Canadian newspapers are not getting maximum value from the tens of thousands of minds assembled in their plants. In the great mass employe mind lies the future of newspaper industry, he contends, for things don't just happen-somebody makes them happen. In this tight era of mounting costs, revenue-producing and cost-cutting ideas are of paramount importance. Other industries are making hay with suggestion programmes. Why not newspapers?"

Other helps toward maintaining a high degree of efficiency in the business office are:

1. Give employes the best equipment the business can afford. A machine that can increase the productive capacity of an employe builds enthusiasm and morale.
2. Recognize accuracy as well as speed. In the accounting department it is better to have statements issued correctly a day late than to have them rushed into the mails without a careful final checking.
3. Pay more for efficiency and less for overtime. In other words, employ efficient help to do a full day's work well rather than low-pay help that will carry you into many hours of overtime.
4. Urge your book-keepers and clerks to complete the work laid out for the day and carry none over for the next day. Each day then has a fresh beginning.
5. Create a congenial but business like atmosphere in the office.

In normal good times the advertising department is expected to produce to the limit. There may be a time, however, when it is necessary to curtail production because of newsprint shortages or mechanical restriction within the plant. Ordinarily it is more difficult for an advertising manager to curtail production than it is to increase it. No advertising manager likes to draw the disfavour of an advertiser by announcing that only so much space is available and no more. The merchant is bound to feel that the newspaper is favouring another advertiser, probably a competitor.

Many types of accounts are handled in the advertising department. There are users of much space; those who run small but consistent day-by-day ads; and those who use an extremely small but amount of copy, probably an inch a week in a business directory, under a special heading, or on the classified page. The salesperson who handles copy for the large-space user naturally produce more revenue than the one who works on very small ads, but at the same time both are important to the newspaper. Small advertisers, if properly handled, may someday be the newspaper's greatest buyers of advertising space.

Incentive plans will raise the capacity standards of any advertising department. To keep its sales force constantly trying to increase the volume of advertising of advertising linage over the preceding year, the Mexico, Mo., Ledger paid each person, every month of the preceding year.

The Wooster Ohio, Record increased its sales of classified display advertising auctioneers and farmers through suggested copy mailed to the "colonels" of that area. "Public sale season will soon be here; have you contacted an auctioneer?" read one of the suggested ads. "If you are planning a spring sale, book it now for a choice of date." Another provided space for the auctioneer's picture under the heading, "More Dollars, No Worries! Auction sales Are My Business." This not only brought advertising from the auctioneers but it also recalled the Record to farmers when it came time for them to advertise their auction sales.

Production standards in the advertising department may be raised by:

1. Establishing goals to be reached within a limited time.
2. Planning special advertising campaigns for single firms on a community wide basis.
3. Encouraging repeat selling.
4. Requiring sales personnel to submit reports showing

the number of firms served, the number of calls made, and the volume of advertising obtained.

5. Checking other newspapers for ideas.
6. Helping sales personnel to become better acquainted with their community and the possibilities for developing new accounts.
7. Stepping up newspaper promotion.

The circulation department has different classes of clientele to deal with which require varied approaches in presenting the newspaper's merits. More time per prospect is necessary for selling subscriptions in rural areas than for those in densely populated urban sections. Soliciting is more successful in the fall than in the spring. People di more reading in the winter, when they are indoors, than in the summer, when they are busy with outdoor work and pleasure. The amount of promotion behind a salesperson also helps to determine the number of subscribers added.

The number of new subscriptions that can be obtained on a route does not depend altogether on the personality and sales ability of the carrier. It is also determined by the time available to devote to selling and by the inducements offered by the circulation department. If obtaining a certain number of subscriptions will qualify for a college scholarship, the carrier may give greater thought to that than to the extra revenue the additional subscription will bring.

The accomplishments of the circulation department depend greatly upon the energy, farsightedness, and ingenuity of the manager. Ed Roberts, former circulation manager of the Denver, Colo., post, decided that circulation could be increased by efficient carrier service and route management as well as by direct solicitation by carriers and special salespeople. To test the theory, he evolved the following simple plan:

1. A monthly point contest within each district based on the success with which a carrier handled the route and produced orders.

2. A suitably engraved award to the carrier in the entire city who was outstanding for each quarter, presented with the pomp and ceremony appropriate to the importance of such recognition.
3. Insignia indicative of outstanding records established over several months or years.
4. Some form of scholarship to reward outstanding carriers on a annual basis.

Circulation sales personnel will do twice as well in obtaining new subscribers in a given area if they are sent there as part of a well-organized campaign with special incentives and rewards for honest effort and with plenty of promotion behind them.

In a summer campaign to increase rural circulation, one newspaper sent a reporter into the country with a member of the sales staff. Before the salesperson began to talk about the merits of the newspaper, the reporter drew news from practically every family visited about the children, poultry, livestock, or crops. On some weekly newspapers, a man and his wife make up the reporter-sales combination.

The superintendent of the mechanical department knows how much copy a composing machine operator should handle in a day. The way the work is laid out, the encouragement given by the supervisor, and the condition of the plant are important, too. The business manager should have a clear understanding of production possibilities and should confer with the superintendent about conditions in the mechanical department and their effect on production. The abilities of the compositors, press operators, and other employes should be discussed freely with the superintendent; and the poor performers should be worked with to improve their capacities, or they should be weeded out.

The speed with which an advertisement is set depends to a great extent upon its nature and the condition of the copy. If the copy is poorly laid out and instructions are not well outlined of the copy. If the layout calls for unusual arrangement of cuts and type, or if it contains much solid matter and few display lines, more time will required than for a conventional arrangement of type and cuts with much white space. Any simplifications in setting ads will raise capacity standards. Accuracy as well as speed must be sought in composition because careless work means excessive corrections, and that cuts production capacity.

Proper care of presses and paper stock will step up pressroom efficiency. For example:

1. Cleaning the press regularly and oiling it at proper intervals will help to prevent costly stops.
2. Care in adjusting forms on the press increases capacity by permitting top running speed. Even more important, such care prevents accident.
3. A sufficient supply of newsprint for the run, placed conveniently before starting, will prevent capacity-cutting interruptions.
4. Careful handling of newspaper will prevent web breaks on presses using rolls and will prevent stoppages and waste on presses using flat sheets.
5. Good-quality inks will permit capacity speeds and produce clean impressions.

Control of Budget

The necessity for watching expenses and regulating them so that they comply with income has a definite effect on production. When expenses are rising, it is not always possible to keep income within the same range of increase. Management then is compelled to guard expenses with an austere eye and to handle operations with a firm hand.

In the light of these mounting costs, it is important that the newspaper manager analyze the amount and character of all phases of work in the newspaper office and plant. By so doing, standards can be set that will aid in determining hourly pay rates, size of staff needed for operation of a given plant unit, kind of employes wanted, and standard time required for each operation.

Expenses mount easily in the editorial-news department, where the best efforts should go into producing copy that will give readers what they want and make the newspaper a credit to its community. Publishers have been interested more in improving personnel than in increasing it. Less help of greater efficiency is better than more help of low caliber.

Reporters and others in the news department should understand the publisher's desire to produce a good newspaper as well as the problem of doing so when expenses are bouncing against the ceiling. Persons in other departments of the newspaper organization and even residents of the community, with the proper approach, may be induced to give assistance that will help to hold down production expenses.

Employes in the advertising and circulation departments should be encouraged to be alert for news tips as they go about their regular duties. Residents of the community who really have a "nose for news" often become helpful part-time reporters and are willing to serve at little expense. The agricultural committee of the National Association once suggested that newspaper that could not afford to pay the wages offered college-trained reporters could develop good farm reporters in their home communities, and such home-trained reporters could write successfully for farmers who were looking for better ways to increase their farm incomes-incomes that were to be spent at hometown retail stores.

Other ways of curtailing expenses in the news department are:

1. Challenge each member of the reporting staff to produce a feature story a week. Most reporters are busy, yet they will gladly tackle a special assignment. One summer when a member of the staff was absent most of the time, the managing editor of a small newspaper

asked each of those remaining on the job to turn in an additional feature story each week. This proved to be a sort of contest to see which could produce the best feature story, with the result that plenty of local material was produced without employing extra help.

2. Have reporters carry cameras. Many newspaper publishers when hiring journalism school graduates as reporters ask for those who know how to use cameras. A combination reporter- photographer is a valuable staff member because the pictures enliven the stories and this saves the publisher the expense of employing a photographer. Almost any reporter, if supplied a camera, can be trained to use it. There is always the possibility, however, that for a time at least interest in picture taking will be so great that more photos will be taken than the newspaper can use. Photographers and photographer-reporters should learn to select their pictorial matter with care because the camera is valuable when used for pictures of unusual interest but expensive when used for routine shots.
3. Engage district reporters on a pay-per-item basis. Select a news-conscious person in each of the four or five main sections of your city and agree to pay so much for each item written that is termed newsworthy by the city editor. This brings in news at minimum cost from sources not usually touched by regular reporters.
4. Invite persons interested in community history to write articles. Facts of extraordinary community interest never before revealed may find their way into the columns of your newspaper by this means.
5. Have some member of the staff devote a certain period each day to other newspapers in search of local interest articles. Newspapers from which such articles are taken are complemented when you consider their copy worthy of your columns and they readily grant permission.

The care and attention given to cost studies, receipts, and general expenses by those in the business office help greatly to regulate expenses in other departments. A good way to control costs is to set up a budget. Also, use these economy measures for buying materials, supplies, and services:

1. Centralize the buying authority in one person.
2. Wherever practical get prices from two or more suppliers.
3. Be sure you have "minimums" for each item so that repurchases automatically come up well in advance of the "out-of-supply" date. This avoids rush shipments and permits ample time for proper cost-saving buying.
4. Watch your costs for office forms. Many can be produced on a duplicating machine at nominal cost. The copying machine may cost less than 41,000.
5. Keep purchasing records showing names of suppliers furnishing services or supplies, date and cost of the last order, and annual requirements.

The business office must watch expenses and effect economies in other departments as well as in its own. It knows that contemplated expenditures must be consistent with the newspaper's financial ability. Administrative department conferences may result in a change in the newspaper's page width and column sizes, in elimination of the optical scanner step in computerized composition, or in the sale of company-owned trucks to be replaced rented delivery cars.

Not many advertising departments give serious, consideration to production costs; their main goal is volume, and often it is volume at any cost Expense regulation, however, should be applied in this department as in all other. Consideration might well be given to the cost of producing every ad, from the two-line local to full-page display.

Some small advertising accounts require so much time and attention that they cost more than they bring in. Some of that cost is unnecessary. Salespeople who have been handling accounts on a personal basis may be do just as well by telephone.

The classified advertising department's success at selling by telephone should represent a challenge to those who sell display advertising. The manager of a small daily newspaper selected one of the best phone saleswomen in the classified advertising department to use the telephone a few weeks before Christmas to see how many small display Christmas greetings ads she could sell. She made a list of prospects, then clipped from the ad service all the Christmas greetings material she could find. She laid out hundreds of small ads, mostly 2 columns by 3 inches, using her own judgment as to what each prospect might be willing to buy.

With the copy before her she called each prospect, read the copy planned, gave the cost, and in nine cases out of ten landed the order. She was paid a commission of 10 percent above her regular salary. For two weeks she more than doubled her income and at the same time sold more display advertising at less cost than many of the regular sales staff.

Other means of reducing expenses in the advertising department:

1. Eliminate some of the free service given to general advertisers in promoting advertised products. This is a service feature of the advertising department that, in connection with most accounts, may be abridged or expanded without seriously affecting results.
2. Insist on customers having their copy ready when the advertising representative calls. Many valuable moments, for which the publisher pays well, are lost when the representative is required to cool his heels while the merchant makes up his mind about copy to be used.
3. Insofar as possible have merchants prepare their own advertising copy. Many newspaper advertising

departments have increased department expenses and spoiled advertisers by preparing all copy for them.

4. Urge advertising copywriters to avoid use of fancy composition that requires extra time in setting.
5. Set monthly linage goals for advertising sales staff and pay bonuses to those who exceed. This speeds up selling and increases volume.

Newspaper delivery operations sometime may be combined to provide more satisfactory service and at the same time reduce delivery costs. The Janesville, Wis., Gazette delivers papers to farmer subscribers from trucks that take papers to carriers in country towns. It delivers 2,000 papers to rural residents, while covering 900 miles a day at a cost of 15 cents a mile. Considering the fact that so many farmers receive delivery from a truck used to convey bundles to dealers and distant carriers, a fair portion of the cost is chargeable to delivering to farmers.

At one time the Independence, to Examiner had an arrangement with carriers of the Kansas City, Star whereby they delivered the Examiner while delivering the Star. This was done at far less expense for the Examiner than if the paper maintained its own trucks, and it provided additional revenue for Star carriers.

The efficiency of a circulation department may be increased and expenses may be reduced also:

1. By inducing rural correspondents to sell subscriptions. Many weekly and small daily papers pay a commission to correspondents for subscription collections in their area. One newspaper puts on an annual subscription contest with its correspondents, offering prizes or boriqaes to those obtaining the greatest number of subscriptions. This is in addition to the regular commission paid on subscription collections. Newspapers have found this to be an effective and economical way of building circulation at a reasonable cost.

2. By employing a man and wife as a manager team for the circulation department. With the man as manager and his wife a assistant manager, a unified salary more than takes care of family expenses. Furthermore, the manager is free for house-to-house solicitation, knowing that his wife will take care of details in the office. This arrangement work out well for the Columbia, Mo., Missourian, where Mr. and Mrs. Jack Carr were in charge of the circulation department, and at the Willows, Calif, Daily Journal where Mr. and Mrs. Oscar F. DeSoto directed circulation.
3. By using a simplified from of bookkeeping for the circulation department. The more details to be watched the more opportunities there are for errors.
4. By watching all accounts and seeing that payments are made promptly overdue accounts are hard to collect and often are never collected.
5. By closely watching the pressrun each day and the number of paper sold and delivered. Newsprint is costly and may be wasted by overruns.

The mechanical department superintendent often has opportunities to reduce expenses by more careful distribution of work and by observing the way employes perform at the machines, at the makeup tables, or in the pressroom. Attention to minor details sometimes results in savings.

The production manager of the Gannet newspapers says that considerable extra cost in a great many pressroom is due to the fact that papers changing in size so rapidly. The trouble begins in the advertising department. Too often the people there do not seem to realize that by adding two pages they increase the number of employes needs in the pressroom by two or three, who a great many times are working at over times rates. Sometimes it even increases the number in the mailroom.

For many years the Ottawa, Ont., Citizen relied on outside

help for all its electrical work, care of machinery, and minor repairs; and costs ran high. Finally when a new building was erected and a new press installed, a full-time position was given to the electrician who installed wiring for the new building. Since the electrician also had some knowledge of welding and machine shop practice, the publishing company set up a modest machine shop with a drill press, are welding set, grinder, and other small power tools. The savings on minor repair jobs more than covered the expenses of this full-time operation.

General Expenditures

Overhead expenses in the mechanical departments of newspapers may be cut down in other ways:

1. By having a superintendent who knows enough about the machinery to make minor repairs.
2. By making negatives or plates for other newspapers and business firms. The rental cost of an offset camera of a platemaker is sometimes divided between several newspapers receiving material from the same machine.
3. By hiring a helper in the composing room to do the office janitor work, thereby combining two jobs in one.
4. By having compositors double as press operators. This is a satisfactory arrangement in the plants of small dailies but could not be worked out in large unionized shops.
5. By arranging working hours in 35-hour or 40-hour shifts to avoid overtime hours.

Many other factors-postage; width of newsprint roll; cost and availability of paper, ink, film, and other materials; general economic conditions; unpredictable personnel problem-will have a bearing on production. Among the constant factors today, it may be said that the degree of modernization of technology will probably have a more direct effect on flow of work, saving of valuable time, capacity potentials, and regulation of expenses than any other single influence over which management may have control.

Processing Skill

The photographs can be almost as important as news releases. A good picture is worth any number of words for it can communicate a point quickly and succinctly, and in any language. Editors like pictures and many a mediocre press release has found a place because it was accompanied by an eye-catching or interesting picture.

However, adding photographs just for the sake of it is not a good idea. Photography is extremely expensive and should only be undertaken if it is necessary-which is not the same as being marginally useful or pleasant. There are, of course, occasions when photographs are taken to please the chief executive or for company records. This is all very well in its way, but do not make the mistake of thinking that the media will also be interested; unless the picture tells a real story they will not be.

The true value of a picture lies in its ability to illustrate a point or to act as an eye-catcher both to the editor and subsequently to the reader. If the same picture can achieve both purposes then so much the better. A PR executive faced with the task of showing the strength of steel-capped safety footwear hired a double-decker bus and had it photographed as it drove over the foot of a man wearing the boots. He certainly made his point. Another successful bus picture was taken by the sponsor of a fleet of painted buses from London, Birmingham and Manchester.

The buses were offered to a leading charity to take deprived children on a trip to Woburn Safari Park. The buses were photographed with a few surprised giraffes looking in the windows. All the parties concerned gained publicity which they would probably not have achieved otherwise.

Sometimes, of course, the subject is either so technical or

so complicated that a photograph of the laboratories or of a piece of machinery would not make the point and the use of drawings should be considered instead. Nevertheless there are few editors who do not like to use at least one or two photographs and the relevant drawings might be backed up with shots of the inventor or the experimental staff at work. It is sensible, however, to check with editors of really specialist publications whether or not they can use a good picture.

What you should photograph, depends entirely on editors' requirements. Study the publications on your specialist media lists and get to know what sort of pictures are likely to be used.

A very effective way to achieve publicity for a new factory opening, an exhibition, a fashion show, a lunch or a conference is to issue a photocall or general invitation to photographic agencies and to the picture editors of the daily press. Such an invitation should give an indication of what pictures could be taken or which parts of the event lend themselves to photographs. There may be innovative processes at the factory, new products on display at the exhibition and new designs at the fashion show. A lunch or conference may feature well-known personalities and speeches may be made which will be of interest to the media.

Once you have issued the invitation it is important to make sure that the photographers will be able to do their job. Space must be left so that they get an uninterrupted view, extra lighting may need to be laid on and someone must be on hand to make sure the photograph has an accurate caption. Some free-lances have been known to leave without getting a full caption. You may also need to lay on a messenger service to deliver the film to the newspaper building while the photographer goes on to his or her next assignment.

You should also arrange to take your own photographs of this type of event, for they give you an opportunity to show off the newsworthy aspects of your organisation. You should arrange for both black and white and colour shots, but do make sure that you check the requirements of the specific publications before sending them out.

News of the day-to-day happenings within the organization can be communicated with much more interest by photography. Examples include the installation of new plant, moving an unusual load or shipping fridges to Iceland, the chief executive leaving on a trip to China, long-service presentations and involvement in local community activities.

Technique of Production : This can be one of the trickiest areas of photography, for very often the product is not very different from many others on the market and what differences there are may be difficult to illustrate photographically. So before going ahead with photography of products stand back and assess whether editors will be able to use the picture you are planning.

If you do decide to go ahead, there are a number of ways in which the product might be photographed. It can be photographed on its own or in a likely setting. It can be photographed in its packaging if it has any, it can be photographed in use or it can be photographed in an unusual setting.

Depending on which publications you believe will be interested, you may need to photograph the product in two or three of these ways. The consumer press, for example, will not be interested in any kind of pack shot and brand and company names should be removed or kept very small indeed. There are some publications which simply will not use a picture if it has any brand identification whatsoever.

Shots of the product in use or in an unusual setting are the type to aim for in this area. But do not get too carried away with the idea of a gimmicky photograph. It may just make one of the down-market dailies and thus please the marketing director, but it is probably not going to sell very much of the product. Such a photograph is more likely to help sell the newspapers. On the other hand there may be publications on your media list which will be interested in showing the packaging, particularly if it has any unusual features or uses new techniques. Retail publications, too, are more likely to be interested in close-ups of the product itself or in the promotional and publicity material which will help them to sell it.

For certain types of consumer product it can be very useful to have a selection of photographs to be placed with supporting feature material. Food products are an excellent example. Very often the packaging is too heavily branded to be able to use a straight pack shot and a picture of a plate of soup or a bowl of cornflakes is not going to stun the readership. However, if these items are made up into attractive dishes they can be photographed and used to good effect with features on 'Supper Dishes with Soup' or 'Crunchy Toppings'. Some of this work should be in black and white for use in some regional media, but the majority will need to be in colour.

For economic reasons many consumer magazines are increasing their use of outside photographs. Sometimes these are commissioned for specific features following an approach from the PRO. Others have been taken 'on spec' and placed with suitable magazines at a later date.

Beauty features highlight another problem which can arise if the parent company is based abroad. The parent company, perhaps in France or in the USA, will probably have taken a portfolio of beauty pictures when the products were initially launched in their home country. Very often they expect UK PROs to use the same photographs in their own press campaigns. This rarely works. The models look indefinably 'foreign' and unless the feature is on French or US fashion the pictures will not be accepted by the UK press. A new set of pictures will have to be shot.

Checklist for Photographs

1. Decide if a photograph is needed. Will it be able to tell the story better than the release?

2. Make a list of those media to which the picture will be relevant, showing black and white or colour requirements.
3. On the basis of this list decide what exactly should be photographed and how it should be presented.

Photography is a highly specialized business and apart from the odd record shot it is not usually a good idea for the PRO to take his or her own photographs. For one thing there are usually very many other things at an event which need to be organized and directed by the PRO and a well-briefed photographer can take at least one burden off the PRO'S shoulders.

For product and feature work it is even more important to have a professional. Photographers are trained to get the best out of models and to arrange the lighting to the most dramatic effect, and they are usually very creative as well. Photographers' fees are, of course, quite high and there can also be a problem choosing photographers for events outside the area in which you normally operate. In these circumstances a PRO who has a good camera and who knows what he or she is doing may decide to take publicity shots of local events and newsworthy items such as new employees, new sports facilities or retirement presentations. Remember, though, that this is not the end of the story. The pictures have to be developed and printed to a suitable quality for the media and you will need enlargements, possibly in some quantity.

Some large companies employ their own photographers but often these people are expected to handle a lot of clerical work as well as take and process all the photography. Some of them are very good indeed but it is unlikely that they will have had the opportunity to develop skills in such highly specialized areas as industrial photography, beauty photography or still life.

Most PR executives will need to build up a repertoire of photographers skilled in the areas covered by the media relations programme. A good industrial photographer will not be particularly good at portrait work and a fashion photographer will probably not know how to handle food, so if all these areas are represented by the activities of your company or client organization you will need to find photographers in each field.

The number of photographers you work with in each field will depend upon the volume of work that you have and your personal relationships with the photographers concerned. It is sensible, however, to work with at least two and possibly three different photographers in any one field. This cuts down the risk of a photographer becoming stale and running out of ideas about how to present the material. It also means that if one photographer you know and like is booked up the other one may be free to work with you.

The Sources

***Contact*:** This is a purely visual directory of photographers.

Smaller volumes on photographers specializing in fashion, cars and computers are also available.

Elfand Ltd, Unit 39, Bookham Industrial Park, Church Road,

Bookham, Surrey KT3 3EU.Tel: 01372 459559 Fax: 01372 459699

The directory lists a wide range of creative services including photographers and picture libraries.

Reed Information Services, Windsor Court, East Grinstead, West Sussex RH19 1XA. Tel: 01342 326972 Fax: 01342 335612

This lists a limited number of firms, some of which have branches in different parts of the country. Hollis Annual, Contact House, Lower Hampden Road, Sunbury-on-Thames TW16 5NG. Tel: 01932 784781 Fax: 01932 787844

Two Dock Offices, Surrey Quays Road, London SE16 2XU. Tel: 0171 252 1187 Fax: 01 71 232 2302

National Union of Journalists, 314 Gray's Inn Road, London WC1X8DP. Tel:0171 278 7916 Fax: 0171 837 8143

Other sources include the Yellow Rages and Thomson Directories or services such as Pirns Townlink Network and Two-Ten Photo Assignment. The problem with using these directories is that you have no way of knowing whether a particular photographer has the experience to carry out your work or even if he or she is competent. The agency photographers should be adequate but these facilities can be expensive and tied in to other services.

Perhaps a better idea is to try the news or picture desk of the local or regional newspaper. Most of these publications use free-lance photographers as well as in-house staff and these people have the advantage of knowing what kind of picture their local paper will use.

Choosing the Matter : Always arrange to see some sample work when choosing photographers for specialist work, and if possible have a talk with the photographers in person. You may also want to see the studio and check on any special facilities which might be needed, such as access for large items, a working kitchen or space to build room sets.

This kind of assessment may be difficult if you are looking for a photographer at the other end of the country. Here a telephone conversation will usually have to suffice. But do keep records. It may be very useful to know that there is a first-class industrial photographer in Tyne side or that such and such a photographer near the Exeter depot should not be used again. If the job is very important it may be worth the cost of sending someone whose work you know well to cover the assignment. This may cost more at the time but could save a lot of money in the long run.

The quality of the photographer's work is not the only factor which you may need to check on. It could be that one first-class photographer takes much longer on studio work than another or that another industrial photographer cannot work without bringing in extensive lighting systems. There will be occasions when a slight loss of quality, provided that it is not too great, will be offset by budget gains or less disruption on the production line. The only way to find out this sort of information, short of using the photographer once, is to talk to other people who have used him or her. If you see samples of the photographer's work you will be able to contact the clients who commissioned the work.

If you want to place a picture in the national press it is common practice to work with an experienced newspaper photographer who will advise you on the composition of the photograph. For example, one paper might like unusual angles to a shot whereas another will like to include people in the picture. The photographer will take the pictures with particular nationals in mind and then sell them in for you through his contacts on the picture desk. A fee will be charged for the photographic session with a further fee for selling the picture in.

Checklist for Choosing a Photographer

1. Does the photographer specialize in the area in which you need to commission photography?
2. Have you seen examples of his or her work?
3. Are you sure that the chosen photographer's working methods will be suitable for the job in hand?
4. Do you need to find an experienced photographer who can also sell-in the photograph?

It is rarely sufficient to put the product on the table and expect the photographer to get on with photographing it. The photographer may have sensible suggestions for backdrops and for simple accessories, but very often rather more is required. It may be that the product would be shown off to best advantage in use. This means a decision must be taken on whether the in-use setting can be re-created in the studio or whether the photography should be done on location. It also involves the use of models.

With highly specialized products the models will probably be people who are already working with the product. Professional models do not always look very convincing in a factory or a highly technical laboratory.

If you are using 'real' people, make sure that they will be reasonably comfortable in front of the camera. Some people freeze up and look completely false. The only way to check is actually to point a camera at the people chosen before the main session. Try to keep the pictures looking as real as possible. Too many beautifully clean and pressed white coats, for example, can look staged, and best clothes are quite unbelievable at work.

More often the photographic session will be in the studio and it will be virtually impossible to work with people who are not professional models in these very artificial circumstances. Professional models are trained to look at ease and to be able to produce spontaneous-looking smiles and expressions to order.

Not all models are the curvaceous female variety and studio shots can be set up with less glamorous professional models where this is required. Models, like photographers, specialize in certain types of work and they usually have portfolios to show off how they look in a variety of poses. This specialization can be quite important; there are good reasons why a model specializes in hair fashion photography rather than hands or feet. Indeed pretty hands can be one of the most difficult things for a PRO working in beauty to find.

Most models work through photographic model agencies. Some of these also specialize in male models, children and so-called 'uglies', or the less glamorous type of model. There are also agencies for animal models. Check the telephone directory or *Hollis Annual* Yellow Pages or ask the photographer with whom you plan to work to recommend some agencies. The agency will send you either their complete portfolio or a suitable selection of models to fit your brief.

If at all possible interview all models with whom you have not previously worked. Some models can be a very disruptive influence in the studio, particularly if there is more than one model on the session. It also helps to brief the model in advance so that he or she is aware of what is involved and will bring the right selection of clothes or accessories. If you are using models frequently keep a model book with notes on how each one has been used before, what they look particularly well in and any other relevant notes.

One final point: always make sure that all models sign a release form or contract to ensure that they cannot suddenly demand repeat fees on a photograph which is widely used.

For some types of shot models will do their own hair and make-up, but if you are acting for a manufacturer of hair preparations or beauty products you will probably need to use a hair stylist and a make-up artist. Remember that leading professionals in these fields must be credited in the captions. Do not try to save money by using unknown or inexperienced people in these areas-the results can be disastrous.

For certain types of photograph, particularly those for feature use, you will need to think about the accessories you will use in the photograph. This may simply mean adding a flower, an attractively draped scarf or a glass of wine to the products to be photographed, but it may also mean creating a complete atmosphere.

One product may be used in a feature on Italian cookery while another may be the dominant part of the decor for an elegant drawing-room set and yet another may appear in a greenhouse. For all of these photographs a large number of accessories or props will be needed to create the desired effect.

Photographers who specialize in food or in room set photography will probably have a good selection of props. In addition manufacturers of household goods are willing to lend their products for use in photographs for non-competing items in return for suitable credits. Large shops and department stores will be equally helpful.

However, if you are trying to create a period shot or a specifically national look you may have to hire props. Sometimes the photographers will organize this for you, but if there are a large number of photographs to be taken then you should consider using a specialist photographic stylist whose job it is to provide a good selection of suitable props from which you and the photographer can choose on the spot.

This type of photography also calls for other specialists such as home economists to prepare and present the food in front of the camera, room set designers and model makers. All of these specialists must be chosen with care and with an eye to the particular skills required. Some home economists are excellent at cake decorations, for example, while others are better at all-round cookery or pastry work. If you have not worked in these fields before ask the advice of the photographers. They will have specialists with whom they like to work.

To take really good pictures photographers need to be properly briefed. They are not mind-readers and unless you explain, in some detail, what you are trying to achieve with a particular photograph they will not be able to do their best work. You might, for example, be photographing a tractor. A picture intended to show the pulling strength of the tractor will need to be quite different in composition from one designed to show the gradients which it is able to climb or the revolutionary design of a new gearbox.

Photographers also need to be informed of the printing process involved in the publications for which the picture is intended. Some processes do not reproduce pictures very well and the subject needs to be in bold relief without too much fussiness, whereas other processes are able to reproduce every detail. They also need to know the type of publication for which the picture is intended. The composition of a photograph for the *Truck Drivers Weekly* would be quite different from that for *Science Today* or for *Vogue Magazine.*

For location work it is very helpful to the photographer to visit the site beforehand. A good photographer should, if necessary, be able to produce good pictures without a previous visit, but he or she will certainly produce better results if there has been sufficient time to look round and plan the most effective camera angles. Such a visit should involve talking to personnel to try and understand something of their jobs and to work out how best to tell the story in visual form. Any technical points should be discussed with the relevant experts to avoid any arguments about the pictures afterwards.

Obviously the plant or area manager should be alerted both to any pre-shooting visit and to the photographic session itself. He or she, too, needs to be briefed on the need for and the purpose of the photographs, for it is important to ensure cooperation. Disruption of normal activities should be kept to a minimum. This is important not only in the interests of keeping production flowing but also in obtaining the most natural pictures of the operatives and staff involved.

However thorough the briefing, the PRO still needs to go on the shoot. Once briefed, the photographer should be left to compose the pictures and if he or she says something will not make a good picture this judgement should be accepted. But as the PRO you can smooth the way. You can also check the final picture before it is taken.

Not all location photography is centered on plant, machinery or buildings. Quite a number of 'mug shots' or portraits will be needed as people join the company or move their positions within it. This can be a very tricky area as most people are self-conscious in front of the camera. It is the PRO's job to help relax the subject. You can also brief the photographer on any idiosyncrasies, on interests and on which parts of the person's job might lend themselves to photography. In this way it should be possible to obtain a more interesting picture.

Show the transport manager with one of the lorries in the fleet or talking to a driver, the canteen manageress in the kitchen or the sales director at a briefing session.

In the studio the conditions are, of course, rather different. There is usually less urgency, though the time factor cannot be ignored since studio time costs money. The photographer will be in charge here but he or she will still need a detailed briefing. If other specialists are involved, a general briefing meeting will ensure everyone knows exactly what is required of them.

The PRO should then let everyone get on with their jobs. A point to watch is the delivery of a product or material to the studio. Very often this will be coming from a different department, which should be alerted in good time. Check with the photographer that the material has been delivered a day or so before the appointed date. This gives you time to chase it up if there have been any hiccups.

On location or in the studio some subjects are just not very interesting, and anything which can be used to add interest will be helpful. Human or animal interests almost always improve a picture, but the subjects should be used in a way that is relevant and which helps to explain the subject. Children playing with toys, men putting up prefabricated house units, a family in a holiday resort or a woman using a knitting machine are all likely to enhance the original subject. People in the picture should be concentrating on what they are doing. They should not merely look decorative. A blonde in a bikini does not enhance a jeep nor a cuddly dog a power drill.

Sometimes people are used to give an idea of scale. A man standing beside a combine harvester or an earring photographed with a close-up of the head will help to convey the size of the object.

Always check the final composition before the photograph is taken and ask yourself the following questions:

1. Is the picture relevant to the story?
2. Is it self-evident what the subject is or does?
3. Does the picture tell the story without the need for a long caption?

The next step is to check the detail, and this will need more experience. If the shot is to be sent out in black and white the colour must be ignored and the shot viewed in terms of tones of grey. This means that the sharply contrasting colours green and black will look just the same in the black and white print. It also means that the choice of background colour is vital. An experienced photographer should have pointed out these things but it is sensible to acquaint yourself with some basic knowledge. A black and white polaroid will also help.

Composition can also present many potential pitfalls. One highly experienced PRO tells the story of her first photographic foray. The product was discreetly set out towards the back with the label half turned away. The picture looked attractive and showed a new use for the product. The only trouble was that the photograph was so arranged that it would be very easy for a picture editor to crop the product out of the picture altogether.

Checklist for Setting up the Picture

1. Brief appropriate managers that the session is to take place and arrange for any special facilities or sample product.
2. Brief the photographer in detail on the purpose of the photograph and its destination. Visit the site if possible.
3. Brief any supporting specialists in a similar manner.
4. Look for relevant human interest angles and action in the photograph.
5. Take the photographer's advice on what will and what will not make a good picture.
6. Check any technical points in advance and if mistakes could be made make sure an expert is present

7. Keep disruption to a minimum and try to keep any live models as relaxed as possible.
8. Make a final check on the photograph before it is taken to ensure that it will do its job. Does the picture show the subject off to best advantage?

If you are satisfied with the answers to these questions then go ahead and authorize the picture.

The first point to consider is the number of shots which need to be taken. This will depend partly on the requirements of the interested publications and partly on technical considerations such as variations in lighting and the medium being used. If the subject of the photography is a new type of ballpoint pen, for example, at least two shots will be required, one for the retail trade press and one for the consumer press. The former could include attractive packaging or promotional material, but this would be quite unsuitable for the consumer press. Here a shot showing someone using the pen would be much more appropriate. If the PRO felt that a number of different editors were interested in such a picture he might decide to take two or three different shots: one perhaps with a child drawing or learning to write, another in an office setting and another in the home with a woman writing a shopping list.

If the photography is in black and white the photographer may be working with reels of film rather than with plates, in which case he or she will be able to take many more shots without inflating the price too much. But for some forms of still life, for example, and for colour work the photographer will be working with plates, which are expensive in themselves. These technical aspects of the shoot should be discussed with the photographer in advance and the decision may be made, in the light of the budget as well as of the PR requirements, to put a specific limit on the number of shots.

Quite apart from wanting pictures to enhance the pages of their magazine and which will interest their readers, editors need pictures of the right size and printed on the right sort of paper.

Editors want sharp, well-focused prints which are glossy but not glazed. They should usually be whole-plate size but half-plate pictures, if they are well cropped before being sent out, are equally acceptable. Pictures for television should be 10"x 8" matt, preferably in colour. Transparencies can usually be accepted from 33 mm upwards, but it may help the magazine if plate sizes are agreed before the pictures are taken.

Topicality can be important here. Nothing irritates a daily newspaper picture editor more than an allegedly topical photograph sent through the post. Pictures must be delivered to these newspapers on the day they are taken. If you think there is a good chance of a daily newspaper using one of your pictures but don't feel they are likely to send their own staff photographers, a phone call to the picture editor could arrange the delivery of exposed film immediately after the event.

Take care with the choice of prints. If the photographer has used a reel of film ask for a set of contact prints with the photographer's own choice of two or three of the pictures enlarged. Check all the pictures and crop if necessary. Do not allow the photographer to stamp the back of the photograph. You are sending the picture out and are the contact for further information. Remember too that in times of industrial strife it is possible that the photograph could be blacked if the photographer is not a union member.

All too often 50 or more prints are ordered from black and white photography and sent out indiscriminately to complete sections of the media list. Some PROs have even been known to send pictures out to radio stations. This is extremely wasteful and reinforces the inefficient image of PR executives.

However, there are some occasions when sending a photograph to a radio station is not such a bad idea. It could make it much easier for the presenter to describe an unusual item, and here perhaps a sample of the article itself might make life even simpler. Photographs can also be used to arouse interest in an event which would not otherwise bestir the news editor to cover it.

A good example comes from the PR agency for a hair preparation manufacturer. This company holds a national hair colouring competition every year with regional heats, and radio had shown little interest either in covering the event or in interviewing the winners. However, when shown pictures of the amazing results achieved by the winning entrants, most of the local radio stations near to the regional heats interviewed the regional winners.

Photographs should only be sent if you are absolutely sure that the recipients will be able to use them-even to the press. If only a small number of publications are involved and you are not sure about photographs, ring up and ask.

Some organizations print a sheet of miniature photographs so that editors may choose which, if any, they would like to have. This can be expensive and if a large mailing is going to regional newspapers, for example, it may be more sensible to reproduce one or two pictures on the release and invite editors to request prints, or simply state that photographs are available on demand.

Make sure that all pictures leaving the Press Office are properly captioned and that they are well protected. Pack with cardboard or with hard-backed envelopes and make sure that there are no paper-clips to pierce the prints and that the address is not written on top of them in ballpoint pen.

Checklist for Sending out Photographs

1. Decide the number of shots on the basis of the budget and the interested media.
2. Choose prints carefully and crop where necessary.
3. Have the photographs processed to the right size and on the right paper.

4. Take particular care to get the topical pictures to the daily media the same day.
5. Only send photographs to publications you are reasonably sure will want to print them. Offer photographs to other publications by phone or by stating on the release that photographs are available on request.
6. Take care to protect pictures in transit.

The copyright in a photograph rests with the photographer, not with the person, who commissioned the picture, nor with anyone who is shown in it. If you need to have the copyright for some reason this must be negotiated separately for an extra fee or royalty.

On an important assignment it makes sense to draw up a contract with a photographer so that you are both quite clear about how the photographs are to be used, Consult the *ABC Guide to Copyright*, a publication every PR office should have. It was drawn up by the British Photographers Liaison Committee and is available from the Association of Photographers, 9-10 Domingo Street, London E1Y OTA. Tel: 0171 608 1441 Fax:0171 253 3007.

There exist, chiefly in London, a number of photographic libraries which will supply prints and transparencies on topical or historical subjects where exclusivity is not a requirement. They charge a fee for the use of their material. You are unlikely to be using their services for material to send out to the media, though they could be a useful source of illustrations for internal publications, but you may be able to place some of your material with them for use by other organizations. The Central Office of Information is another organization which may be able to use your photographs.

However, you are more likely to have your own photographic library with reference shots of all plant and personnel and a collection of possible feature material. Too often this library' is a mound of photographs, some without captions, in a single folder or drawer. A secretary or executive has to plough through them all to fulfil every media request.

To be really useful the photographic library should be carefully organized by subject and the system should indicate the following:

1. The date the photograph was taken.
2. The photographer who holds the negative.
3. Availability in colour as well as black and white.
4. The copyright holder if different from the photographer.
5. Brief caption details.
6. The current whereabouts of the picture if you are expecting it to be returned, and a regular reminder procedure.
7. Any restrictions governing publication, such as the correct acknowledgement. It is useful to hold at least two prints of all black and white negatives and to re-order as these are sent out, and to keep black and white and colour libraries separate. A photographic library needs constant updating. Pictures of the chairman ten years ago or the old plant before the renovations are only of interest for the company history and are definitely not for current use. So check from time to time whether pictures should be retaken rather than re-ordered.

Colour transparencies are expensive and, extra care needs to be taken to ensure they are not lost through carelessness or neglect. Every loan should be followed up after a certain period of time. Some companies insist that journalists or other borrowers sign a form to say they will be responsible for any photographs borrowed and they will pay for it in the event that a photograph is lost or not returned before a certain date. This seems to be carrying things a little too far. A number of circumstances in which a transparency could be lost or damaged would be quite beyond the control of the borrower.

You will soon get to know those publications which are regular users of your transparencies, and provided the pictures usually return safe and sound there is no need for such formal contracts. After all, your organization is benefiting from the continuous exposure of its products.

Right Transparency

1. Select a transparency with the right colour balance. Its colours should be a correct combination of hue-the property of a colour that distinguishes it from other colours, of saturation-the relative purity, vividness or intensity of colour, and of value the property of a colour that makes it seem light or dark. Its tonal separations should be rich and distinct so as to result in quality reproduction in multicolour.
2. Select a transparency which is sharp and crisp, containing minute details and nuances. Even separations made on a scanner cannot reverse m inherent lack of sharpness in the picture although it can correct colour casts and improve upon desaturation and poor tonal separations.
3. Select the right format size of transparency for your job. In a 35 mm picture that is enlarged for instance, the grains are enormously magnified in the final reproduction and are almost 3000% bigger in size. Magnification also often results in a loss of detail and clarity in the final picture.
4. Select a transparency that has been correctly exposed. The leeway for altering colour balance during processing cannot alter the quality of a transparency that has been under-exposed or over-exposed during photography or developing.
5. Always use the original transparency for the best printed results. A duplicate generally has more contrast than the original, which has to be reduced by flashing, masking and the use of special film for duplicating.

Make sure that the identical size of the duplicate is used.

Wrong Transparencies

1. Reject a transparency with colour casts. The sensitivities of the emulsions in each film are balanced to reproduce colour as human vision is prepared by experience to see them. Any mismatch of this with the light source leads to an unnatural colour cast. If for instance film balanced for professional studio lighting is used in daylight, the transparency will have a blue cast, daylight film used under artificial lighting causes an orange cast. The final result, an unnatural rendition of colour in print.
2. Reject a transparency in which the grains are evident these particles form a developed photographic image on the film and become even more visible upon enlargement and subsequent reproduction.
3. Reject a transparency with shadows cast by the objects photographed. Human vision interprets such shadows as black and dark grey, while colour film records shadows as blue.
4. Reject a transparency in which glare or polarised light produced by smooth light reflecting surface such as water or glass has dulled the colours and reduced the detail recorded by the film.
5. Reject a transparency with spots. These would stand out upon enlargement in the final reproduction.
6. Reject a transparency with finger prints and scratches.
7. Reject a transparency that is badly mounted. Crude hand mounting results in a transparency acquiring jagged edge fibres.

The process camera plays a very important part in offset lithography. With the advancements in science and technology, the process camera has also undergone a great degree of change. A survey of the Indian Printing Industry would reveal that cameras of all sorts and kinds are being used. Thus we have the old, wooden, manually operated gallery type with a bulky dark slide and the modern, sophisticated, steel frame version fitted with interchangeable lenses, integrator and densiprobe. The old model is still capable of giving a fine performance if handled scientifically so far as black and white reproduction is concerned. For colour reproduction, the scanner seems to have dug its feet in.

Colour separation by electronic means is quick, sure and reliable and in this field cameras are making way for the scanners. Costwise, scanners are very expensive and every lithographic plant cannot afford them. Such plants may borrow scanning services from elsewhere for colour separations and use their own cameras for black and white line and screen reproduction.

Photography Techniques : The function of the camera is to form a sharp, well defined image of the copy in desired size. This is possible provided the camera is fitted with a lens free from major aberrations and having a high resolving power. For practical considerations, the camera lens is built up of several elements instead of a single piece. The composite lens is a convex or convergent lens as only such a lens is capable of forming a real image. (A real image is that which can be brought upon a screen. Your image in a mirror is not real but virtual).

The camera operator is given necessary instructions regarding the size of reproduction, the ruling of the screen etc. It is interesting to note that it is possible to obtain a sharp image at the back of the camera without looking at the ground glass and without any built-in focussing device. This needs some elaboration and explanation. The distance between the plane of the copyboard and the lens is called 'copy distance' and is represented by the symbol u. The distance between the lens and the plane of the ground glass is called 'camera extension' and is denoted by v.

If the focal length of the camera lens is f, the following relationship is found to exist:

$$1/v + 1/u = 1/f \quad (1)$$

(All the distance-u, v and f have been taken as positive)

The ratio v/u is called magnificent and it is denoted by the letter 'm'. If the value of m is one, the image has the same size as the object. However, if m is greater than 1, the image is enlarged and if less than 1, the image is reduced.

If we multiply the equation (1) by u and v separately, we get two more equations as below.

$$1 + u/v = u/f$$

or $$f\,(1 + 1/m) = u \quad (2)$$

and $$1 + v/u = v/f$$

or $$f\,(1 + m) = v \quad (3)$$

Now suppose the focal length of the process lens is 48 cm (You will find it printed on the lens mount). The camera is required to be set in such a way that the image has 50% linear reduction i. e. m = 112,

From equations (2) and (3).

$$u = 48\,(1 + 2) = 144 \text{ cm}$$

$$v = 48\,(1 + 1/2) = 72 \text{ cm}$$

Hence, if you set the copy distance u equal to 144 cm, and camera extension v equal to 72 cm, you will find the image in sharp focus upon the ground glass screen and in fifty per cent linear reduction.

If you want to employ this technique in practice, you have to scale the camera first. This is done as given below.

1. Put any line copy on the copy-board preferably a printed scale.

2. Focus the image manually and visually to same size. Lock the camera.
3. Take a long measuring tape. One end of the tape should touch the Surface of the copy-board. (One of the assistants may be asked to hold the tape like that). Measure a distance equal to 4f from the copyboard surface and make a mark in the back panel of the camera coinciding with this distance as shown in the figure. Let this mark be 'c'.

Find the middle Point of the distance AC and let it be 'B'. Mark the positions of 'B' and 'C' on the lens panel and back panel respectively. The camera has now been scaled. Here is how it operates. Suppose the linear reduction desired is 75% i.e. m = 3/4.

Now, according to camera optics,

$$u = f\ (\ 1 + 1/m) \text{ and } v = f\ (1 = m).$$

Hence putting f 48 cm and m = 3/4, we find that u = 112cm, and v = 84 cm. The distance AB is therefore set equal to 112 cm and BC equal to 84 cm. You may now switch on the illuminants and check the definition and the size of the image. To your surprise, you find that it is in sharp focus and fairly accurate in its degree of reduction.

Having already compromised with the inevitable that colour separations would be prepared on the scanner and that black and white work would be taken up on the camera, the necessity of using carbon arc lamps or an expensive substitute can be dispensed with. Mercury vapour lamps may be used, you can even use day-light fluorescent tubes-four on each side and get fairly satisfactory results. For accuracy in exposure, you have to ensure that the intensity of light emitted by the illuminants is more or less uniform. A voltage stabilizer will be found very useful. A light integrator will almost make the exposures one hundred per cent correct since the exposures would be correlated to units of height and not to units of time.

Normally, the densitometer is not a part of the process camera. However, modern cameras are often fitted with a small 'densiprobe' for evaluating the tones of the copy and determining its density range. The densi-probe can be used for setting the illuminants in such a manner that there is no tonal variation in the plane of the ground glass if a white sheet of paper is put on the copyboard. Illuminants so set will illuminate the copy very evenly. Determination of the end-densities and density range of the copy will enable you to decide the correct detail and highlight exposures and, of course, the flash.

If you are not using an automatic processor and doing development in a dish or tray, here are some useful tips to keep in mind.

1. For best results, the development must be done at a temperature between 20 degrees to 25 degrees C. If the darkroom can be maintained at a temperature within this range, you will also need a development chart as given below.

Measure the temp. of the developer and develop in accordance to the chart.

Development temp. (in C)	20'	21' 22'	23'	24'	25'
Development time (in mts.)	31/2	31/4 3	23/4	21/2	21/4

This chart should be prepared by you by trial and error:

2. The developing solution should be agitated by tilting the dish both in the long and short directions.
3. The amount of developers in the dish must be sufficient to keep the film covered with the developer during agitation.
4. Do not use exhausted developer for development. Formation of yellow colour in the developer is a warning that exhaustion is setting in.

And finally-do not prepare solutions in the darkroom. The dust from the chemicals may become a part of the environment of the darkroom and hence affect the film while you are loading it in the camera. You may later find intense black spots after development which may seem inexplicable to you.

Many printing plants now have automatic film-processing machines to perform the developing, fixing, washing, and drying functions for film and for some specialized papers. Information on processing times and temperatures, and on methods for handling photographic chemicals in processing machines, is available on request from kodak graphic arts technical sales representatives. Mixing instructions for machine processing chemicals are packages with the chemicals themselves. However, even if you do own an automatic film processor, knowledge of the principles of tray processing is invaluable for setting up a quality-control programme for proper processor function.

Process the exposed film in a developer, a stop bath, and a fixer; then wash it in running water. You control each step by time and temperature,.

The developing time and the recommended developer are stated in the instruction sheet packaged with the film.

You can adjust the temperature of the developer to the recommended 68F 20°C by floating the tray of solution in a larger tray of either cold or warm water for several seconds. Don't put water into the developer itself to adjust temperature. The handy Kodak Tank and Tray Thermometer may be placed right in the tray of solution.

You must handle the film exposed or unexposed, in a darkroom illuminated only by the safelight recommended in the instruction sheet packaged with that particular film (most films with the same basic colour sensitivity-orthochromatic or blue-sensitive for example-require the same safelight). The safelight provides light of a colour and intensity that will not affect the film if darkroom work is carried out with reasonable care.

Proper safelight illumination includes lamp-to-film distance and bulb wattage, as well as the safelight filter itself. To check your safelights for safety with orthochromatic emulsions (red safelights), view the safelights through Filter, a dark green gelatin filter. If you can see white light transmitted through the filter, then the safety of the safelight should be questioned. A more accurate safelight test Would be this:

— Make a simple halftone exposure of any piece of copy on Ortho Film.

— Place the exposed but unprocessed film facing up on your work bench. Cover one-half of the image with an opaque card or masking material.

— Place the exposed but unprocessed film facing up on your workbench. Cover one-half of the image with an opaque for 3 minutes. Then process the film.

— Examine the processed halftone image. If you notice a change between the masked and unmasked areas, then your safelights are unsafe and may be contributing to apparent changes in film speed.

The above controls require the following equipment:

Timer	Safelight filters
Thermometer	4 Trays
Safelight lamp	Tray siphon

Preparing the Solutions

Developer	Into one tray pour about a 1/2-inch to 1-inch depth of Developer, mixed carefully according to directions.
Stop Bath	Into a second tray pour about 1/2-inch to 1-inch depth of an acid stop bath, such as Stop Bath
Fixer	Into a third tray pour an inch or so of Fixer. The latter permits shorter fixing times and as a liquid, is easier to mix.

Wash	Fill a larger tray with water and keep the water running. Circulation and replenishment of water by advice such as the preferable.

Place the exposed film in the developer. Do this by dragging the film face-down through the developer and then quickly flipping it over, face-up. Agitate the developer continuously as follows: Raise the left side of the tray about ½ to 3/4 inch; lower it smoothly, and then immediately raise and lower the far side similarly; next, raise and lower the right side, and then the near side, These four operations constitute an "agitation cycle," which requires a total time of about 8 seconds, most operators form a habit of uniform agitation, so that they can more nearly repeat their results on successive negatives. Continue agitation until the recommended time has elapsed.

When a developer solution is used for a large number of negatives, it gradually becomes exhausted. A gallon of developer can develop a film area equal to about 30.8 x 10-inch sheets of film. You should increase gradually the developing time during the useful life of the solution. Discard the solution when you have reached a 50 percent increase in development time, necessary to produce a good negative, when exposure is normal.

Handle the wet film by a corner or edge to avoid damaging the image. Lift it up and let it drain for a few seconds; then quickly transfer it to an acid stop bath. This stops development more quickly than does a water bath and helps keep image uniform. It also prolongs the life of fixing both. After several seconds of vigorous agitation, transfer the film to the fixer.

Important Prints : When your hands have been in solutions, always rinse them in clean water before wiping them on the darkroom towel or before touching anything. This will prevent spots on films caused by contamination from solutions and dry chemicals.

Agitate the film vigorously in the fixer until the film appears to be clear in the unexposed, light areas-usually after about minute in a fresh fixer. Then leave the film in the fixer for the recommended time, to remove the last traces of unexposed light-sensitive material. You can turn the room lights on at this time.

To preserve the image, the film must be washed as recommended in the instruction sheet. After washing wipe it gently with a soft rubber squeegee and hang it upto dry. The film dries more quickly if both of its sides are squeegeed onto a rigid surface such as glass or plastic.

Line negatives are often developed by inspection. When development is nearly complete, you lift the negative briefly from the sink. A magnifier will help you inspect fine detail. By observing the density of the black background, you can learn to judge when development should be stopped.

Assuming proper development, density is largely determined by exposure. You should, of course, estimate the camera exposure as accurately as possible. However developing by inspection does permit you to compensate for some exposure error by stopping short of the recommended developing time or by developing a little longer, whichever is indicated by inspection.

Density scales are used to check many factors which influence photographic behaviour, such as light sources, safelight fog, developers, developer exhaustion and the fundamental properties of the sensitized material. There are, of course, many more applications for density scales in photography.

The need for quick visual reference for checking exposure/ development changes (intentional or unintentional) can be met by using the opposed gray scale. This guide is made by first cutting a gray scale in two, lengthwise; the sections are then joined again, but in opposing directions.

To make the opposed gray scale, cut about 5/8 inch from the edge of the Separation Guide gray scale. Next, cut the 5/8-inch piece into two 5/16-inch strips. Then, join the two strips together in the opposed position so that the 0.30 step is opposite the 0.50 step. Place transparent tape on the back of the strips to hold them together. To square the guide, trim away the high densities on the ends. If convenient, the steps can be numbered or otherwise identified for easier reference.

By including the guide with all camera line copy, you should be better able to match line width rendition from similar copy, confirm normal exposure and development for certain copy, and control development compensation when processing in a tray.

After you have made the test exposure from the line copy target and have determined which exposure work best with each type of copy, make full-sized exposures of each type of copy and place an opposed gray scale next to the copy. These exposures establish the density value at which certain exposure and development conditions will produce the most significant density change in the scales.

The term "break" is commonly used to describe the point at which a line negative of a gray scale appears to have lost most, if not all, of the tonal separation between the steps and shows a major shift in density. This is especially true with very high contrast materials, in which density values in the copy are essentially reproduced as either black or white. Consequently, the guide will look different at the "break" as exposure is adjusted to suit the different types of copy. If the copy has coloured filter is sometimes used to get improved black-and-white separation. The use of a coloured filter may cause slight changes in the "break point" that has been established as being ideal for good line copy without such a filter.

Lithography is a comparatively young process; it being well under 200 years since those famous Senefelder discoveries occurred. As a result lithography has developed alongside established printing processes. Let us look at the way in which a job travels through the lithographic department:

(1) Planning, (2) Reproduction, (3) Camera, (4) Camera Enlarger and Colour Scanners, (5) Processors, (6) Retouching, (7) Layout Assembly, (8) Step and Repeat Machines, (9) Colour Proofing System, Cromolin, etc., (10) Graphic Arts Input Materials.

Planning has always been an important stage in the lithographic process. With the increasing range of platemaking machines, high material and labour costs, the planning stage has become an important contribution to the production programme.

Many planners may be restricted to the simple planning techniques which are related to the class of work or type of equipment available. The importance of establishing high standards in planning is seen in the speed of the later stages of production.

The class of work may vary tremendously from simple book work assembly to multi-colour work. Planning therefore not only demands considerable skills of hand and eye, but perceptual skills in knowing how the job should be approached. This will require decisions concerning the correct techniques to be employed and the selection of materials. Planning also demands an attitude of conscientious responsibility and high standards of cleanliness and accuracy. An appreciation of typographic design and page layout should be a necessary attribute of the planner.

The basic requirement of any original is that it should be an accurate representation of that which it portrays. No amount of skilful retouching or correction can compensate for bad copy. All artwork should be carefully checked to ensure that the proportions are correct and if reduction or enlargement is required, sizes and proportions must be clearly marked. Copy for reproduction normally falls into one of the three categories. These are either Reflex (Flat) or Transparency:

(a) Line, (b) Continuous Tone, (c) Colour Work

Preferably the line copy should be prepared in Black regardless of the colour of ink to be ultimately used in printing and it is essential that it is clean, dense and sharp. Other line copies are Chinese Black ink drawings; pen & ink sketches, art pulls of type matter, scraper board, quarter tone; tints, stipples and bleach out drawings, etc.

Continuous one copy, usually in the form of bromide prints, should have good tonal separation from shadows to highlights throughout the range of the original. No amount of correction or retouching can put this right at a later stage. Other originals are wash crayon from and are normally made of glossy paper.

Flat copy in colour can be easily reproduced. Colour transparencies in size 35mm and 120mm must be absolutely sharp and of normal contrast, i.e., density range of not more than 2.0.

Copies are often presented in the form of dummies and layouts to indicate the nature and position of separate illustrations for an advertisement or composite printing surface. The term "copy" includes all subject matter. Thus a layout of the required complete work is essential either as a visual rough or something more detailed and comprehensive.

Having produced a suitable original, the next step is to photograph it on a large process camera which does not differ fundamentally from the hand cameras used by general photographers. Modern cameras are precision instruments with critical tolerances, sleek styling, anti-vibration precautions, short focus wide angle lenses to save floor space, electromagnetic shutter, integrating light meters, spot on registration devices and reset location controls using dial micrometer gauges with measure to within 1/1000 inch. The cameras are primarily of two types:

(a) Gallery Camera,

(b) Darkroom Camera

These are of the horizontal type and are still in use. These are not attached to a darkroom and stand in a special studio system requiring the dark room to the camera and vice versa after exposure.

These are both horizontal and vertical. Vertical cameras are also of two types. Film loading end of the camera is built into the wall in the case of horizontal cameras, and vertical cameras are positioned in the darkroom itself. The following points are considered whilst selecting process cameras to suit your needs.

Camera Size is determined by the maximum size of negative or image area that can be exposed. The most common sizes are 12" x 15", 16" x 20", 20" x 24" and 30" x 30".

Normal range of process cameras is upto X2 enlargements and X4 reductions. Vertical cameras have a range from 20% to 500%, it comes in size: 16" x 20" and 20" x 24".

The copyboards are suitably provided to cover the entire range and hold different types of copies. Copyboard is supplied as standard, holder and transparency holders on gallery cameras are optional.

Optics used on these cameras and other process cameras correspond to the size of the camera. Apochromatic lenses (suitable for colour reproduction), prism is mounted in the lens (or in modern camera optical reversal unit incorporating front coated mirrors replaces prism, etc.) as and when reverse negatives are required for block-making and despatch plate-making.

Light source for copy used to be provided by set of four arc lamps, suspended in pairs on either side of copy, distance from the copy and angle of the light source is adjustable according to the size of the original being reproduced. The arc lamps have been replaced with Halogen lamps and Xenon lamps in most of the cameras being produced these days.

Provision for inserting gelatine filters in the lens are also available in all makes of cameras. The modern cameras have filter current electric-operated for selection of filters etc.

Darkroom camera are also equipped with a flashing device, switching device, switching on-off through electronic timer.

- Magnetic shutter for precision.
- Exposer timings, the same works in conjunction with the Electronic Timer.
- Modern cameras offer programming facilities computerised auto-focus, auto-size, density correction, on-line densitometer, etc.
- Focussing screen (ground glass) is provided for checking of focus manually.
- There are Roll Film cameras, Plate Maker cameras for small printers.

The environments and working conditions must be strictly adhered to and maintenance procedure should be followed as:

(a) Optics must be protected from chemical fumes and humidity, a bag of celicagell must be placed near the optics.

(b) Dusting of the camera should be done with the help of a vacuum cleaner.

(c) Mechanical adjustment of the camera, i.e., squaring and parallelism between Copyholder, Lens Column and Vacuum Back, must be checked, corrected for error, collometer or a sizing stick provided by some manufacturer should be used for squaring.

(d) Anti-vibration mounting and levelling should be periodically checked.

(e) In case of Arc Lamps, these must be cleaned daily and serviced fortnightly. Whilst using Xenon or Halogen lamps, a log-book should be maintained to record burning hours for having replacements arranged within working life of the lamps.

(f) All moving parts and Vacuum/Suction Pumps to be lubricated weekly.

Camera Enlarger as a photographic reproduction instrument stems from the increasing use of colour transparencies for reproduction including the miniature 35mm and 57 X 57mm, (2 1/2" x 2 1/2") which provide a deciding factor in its development.

It occupies less floor space and is simple to operate. It incorporates latest in technology, i.e., Lens Turret, Xenon Lamps, Vacuum Base Board, Filter Holder, Punch Register System on Base Board and three point location in the transparency Image plane. Cold Cathode lighting, Electronic Flash and Computerised Controls makes it a completely self-contained Camera Reproduction Unit.

Colour Scanning is an alternative to photographic masking methods for the correction of colour originals. The manufacture of photographic masks, to adapt the colour separation to the characteristics of the process colour inks, is replaced by electronic calculation of the requirements involved and the immediate production of separations suitable for screening and platemaking.

Automatic film paper processors are required by units using phototypesetter, colour scanners and for high speed and high volume work in the graphic reproduction departments.

With dish or tray development, consistency is difficult on account of the problem of controlling the solution and standardising agitation. The chemicals are discarded after use, hence the process is uneconomic.

Machine processing using film processors whilst involving initially a large outlay of capital, are money savers, in that one machine can process work of Camera, Scanner and Contact

Printers, eliminating darkroom bottlenecks and cutting chemical cost by 50%. Valuable to space, previously occupied by sinks, drying cabinets, etc. is saved. The machine functions efficiently after 30-45 days or more, after that the chemistry is normally changed and the machine emptied for complete cleaning and servicing.

Hand corrections for monochrome or colour work consists of adding or removing density from the photographic image. The most important method is the dot-etching of screen positives made from continuous tone negatives and in some instances, depending upon the quality of the original and the continuous tone negative, retouching is carried out at this intermediate stage.

Special Retouching Desks can be installed which consist essentially of a adjustable light box with opal perplex sheet or ground glass. A pair of tungsten lamps provide the necessary even light without straining artist's eyes.

For preparing multiple, same size positives from one master negative exposing half-tone positives from continuous tone negatives and contact screens. Composite positives are very often required to be made from two separate negatives for exposing positives for deep-etch platemaking.

All the above operations are carried out on the contact Printing cabinet. The Contact printer should consist of face-down vacuum frame mounted on a cabinet. The vacuum of the frame is adjustable to suit different thicknesses of Films.

The height of which is sufficient to provide even illumination from point light Source. Provision should also exist for adjusting the brightness of the lamp with a dial as a guide for repeat exposures. Timer should be incorporated for accurate exposure. Safe light should also be incorporated for positioning the negative and film etc. The cabinet should be lighttight so that when exposure cycle commences the operator could open unexposed film without fear of fogging material.

The layout is the working basis of all subsequent planning operations. It is a full size technical drawing which indicates the various image positions as they will finally appear upon the printed sheet. It will also include "aids" such as register, collating, fold and trim marks, star targets, signal strips and colour control blocks. These will assist the specialists engaged in subsequent operations such as the printing, folding, collating, trimming and punching operations.

The aims of an accurately produced layout will be to facilitate the positioning of various images, the register of multi-colouring work, ease of production in the later stages, economy in the use of materials and machinery at all stages. In order to fulfill these aims the necessary information must be readily accessible. Good liaison should therefore exist between the planning, production, camera, pressroom and finishing departments

The planner must consider factors, e.g., sheet size; sheet grain direction; type and size of plate used; plate clamp allowance; Paper-grip allowance; arrangement of individual images of varying sizes; areas of critical register; ink distribution over the sheet.

When selecting a table for planning and ruling up no expense should be spared to obtain the best equipment. Layout accuracy in lithographic planning is essential at this point for the production cycle since little can be done at later stages to put bad planning right.

The planner should select a table which is:

- Versatile in use and of solid construction for accuracy for drawing of impositions and layouts.
- for checking of press sheets and assembled flap.
- provision for scribing of negative film or cutting of masking materials.
- adjustable tables allow for varying working postures.
- suitable Glass top to accommodate largest layout sheet.

— stainless Steel Straight Edges with finely engraved scales with facility for locking arrangement.

— layout grippers for holding the Astrafoil.

— table illumination-Fluorescent light tubes for even distribution of light.

The tables should be placed at level to avoid distortion. Each of the two chain driven straight edges can be aligned to move the straight edges parallel across the table and at right angle with Vertical Straight Edge. It is necessary to check this adjustment periodically.

4

Book Printing

When we hold a book in our hands we seldom think of the process, or processes, it has been through before coining into our hands. Whether it is a text book, novel, a legal book, a newspaper or magazine, a letterhead or business card, product literature or a circular, or any of a thousand different kinds of printed matter, they all go through some or the entire process of printing. As recently as the last century, the making of a book was a laborious process which could last several months.

With the advances in technology in this century as well as the increase in literacy, the number of publications has increased phenomenally. In India alone there are more than 25,000 different publications and which figure puts India in fifth place. India also has more than 100,000 printing presses.

Evolution and Growth

We do not know when man first began to write. One can imagine that messages were scratched into the soil or blazes were made on rocks or trees, tens of thousands of years ago. In the beginning of recorded history, the Phoenicians and the

Sumerians, used a sharp instrument to make impressions in a soft clay tablet, which was then baked hard. The Egyptians and, later the Romans and the Greeks, chiseled characters into stone tablets. The oldest papyrus rolls date from about 3500 B.C. and are the first form of paper as we know it today. Writing on papyrus was done using reed pens. Red ink was derived from iron oxide and the black from lamp black. Paper was actually invented in China in the second century AD. It took almost a thousand years to migrate to Europe and the paper mill was built in Italy in 1270 AD.

Books began to take the place of parchment rolls around the fourth century AD. They had to be laboriously written out by hand. The centers of learning were concentrated in the various monasteries and with the Royal houses in Europe and the monks had to write or copy out the books manually with pen and ink. Copies of a book were few and far between.

The first reproductions made by man were from images carved on flat stone. These were intaglio, i.e. indented, representations. An inky substance was deposited in the indentations and then transferred onto paper.

Around the ninth century AD, raised impressions on wooden blocks was used in China. In this period metal plates were engraved and used for reproduction as well. The engravers at this time were goldsmiths. As the demand for books grew, it became obvious that a better method of printing was required.

It was the invention of movable type which made such printing possible. In the middle of the fifteenth century, Johann Gutenberg invented individual type which was used for many centuries after and is still used today for the hand setting of composed material. Gutenberg cast individual characters in a brass or copper mould, in which a character of the alphabet had been punched. The punch was created manually by drawing a character in reverse on the face of a hard steel block and carving out the area around the character. The resulting cast of an individual alphabet came to be known as type. These castings were made for the entire alphabet and in different sizes as well. He then placed the characters together to form words and a complete line of text, clamped the type together in a metal frame, applied ink to the raised surface of the characters and fixed the frame to a wooden wine press. A wine press consists of a wooden screw with a handle on top and a flat plate at the bottom, within a frame fixed over a flat bed. When it was pressed down onto a sheet of paper, the ink left an impression much like a common office rubber stamp.

In this way, he could set an entire page at a time and make several copies in less time than it would take to write out one page. This process came to be known as the setting of type or, in other words, typesetting. Over the next four centuries, the role of the publisher switched from churches, governments, royal families and universities to the Printer. The printer did his own type casting, his own typesetting and printed and bound his own books. The Press, as it was usually called, acted as the publisher and distributor. Minor improvements were made to this basic process the press was mechanized using the steam engine and later electric motors. This kind of press was known as the Letterpress.

The typesetting and printing functions remained with the publisher, and under his control, as is still the case today with certain newspapers, for example. However, there developed a separation between the writer and the printer, the type designer and foundry and the typesetter.

Sometime in the eighteenth century, a machine was invented which provided a method of writing more legible than the pen-the typewriter. Soon thereafter, the use of carbon paper as well as stencils and duplicating machines made it possible for small offices to take over their own internal publishing requirements. Mark Twain was among the first to purchase a typewriter. The keyboard was arranged as logically as possible, not based on the efficiency from the standpoint of the operator, but from the viewpoint of the mechanics of the machine, which kept jamming frequently due to collision of the keys. The most commonly used "QWERTY" keyboard is, in fact, very inefficient from the operator's standpoint.

From the time of Gutenberg till Mergenthaler's Linotype or Lanston's Monotype linecasting machines, there was no practical way to set type by machine. The Linotype (line of Type), introduced in 1880, had a keyboard and the operator typed the text on the keyboard which put together a series of moulds of the characters typed, called matrices, and a molten alloy of lead was poured into the mould forming a complete line of text. This single unit was delivered to the galley all ready to go into the form. The complete line as a single unit was less likely to get jumbled up.

At about the same time another invention was getting developed photography, which was to have a big impact on type-setting. The printing presses were also being improved with automatic sheet feeding of the paper. Drawings and photographs could now be printed by making a block.

By the mid twentieth century, a shift had already occurred from Letterpress to Offset printing, at least in Europe and North America. Letterpress requires printing to be done on a flat bed causing it to be much slower than offset, which uses a rotary drum. While Letterpress requires printing from raised type, the offset process requires exposure of the plate from a photographic negative or positive, and therefore, the use of raised type for typesetting became a liability.

To make an offset plate, the process was, and is, to place a photo negative on a sheet of metal which had been sensitized with a light sensitive chemical and exposed to light. The metal sheet was then washed with a mild acid and the unexposed area got etched, leaving the dark areas of the photograph slightly raised. When ink was applied with a roller, only the raised portions received the ink, which could then be transferred onto the paper.

The need for a photocomposition device became readily apparent. In the 40's, another process was developed to expose type directly onto a roll of film. The First Generation Phototypesetters used the same mechanical principles as was used in the Hot metal linecasting machines. Instead of the moulds for the hot metal, the phototypesetter used a negative film of the characters. Using a lens, a beam of light was passed through the negative and onto Silver Bromide-photographic paper.

The Second Generation Phototypesetters switched from a film negative matrix to a disk, which was essentially a photographic negative of the characters of the alphabet arranged in a circular form. The film was then moved laterally by the space of one character and the disk was spun to align the next character and the light was beamed through to the paper. This was repeated until the entire page or column was exposed. The exposed film was then processed in a dark room and resulted in the positive, which could then be used to make a plate for printing.

The First Generation Photo typesetters were adapted from hot metal models and worked as nearly as possible on the basis of the same principles. A Second Generation machine was one which was especially conceived and designed to set type by photo-mechanical means. Both machines were Typesetters, i.e., both generation machines set type and were not capable of graphics. A Third Generation Typesetter is one which does not expose type directly from photographic masters but reproduces them electronically on the face of a CRT, a Cathode Ray Tube.

The images thus created are in turn photographed (either the same size or enlarged or reduced by using lenses) directly from the screen. Each page was reduced to a number of pixels (picture elements) and the resultant resolution was indicated as Dots Per Inch (DPI). The resolution of these first of the Third Generation Typesetters ranged from 300 to 900 DPI and the prices were upwards of US$ 200,000. However, there were some significant advantages of these digital typesetters-(a) the image on the screen can be manipulated electronically in a number of interesting ways; (b) the setting speed was much faster; (c) there were fewer mechanical parts which present maintenance and reliability problems and (d) one was not restricted to setting images of alphabets only; the CRT was capable of setting graphics.

The Laser was invented in the sixties and has also been applied to Typesetting technology. The laser is capable of generating a very fine and intense beam of light. It is possible to interrupt this source so that the light emissions can be pulsed; it is also possible to deflect this beam of light from a mirror surface. These Fourth Generation Photo typesetters used laser technology to expose film or paper and worked in a raster scan mode.

In Raster Image Processing, instead of individual characters being laid down, a horizontal slice of an entire page is exposed at a time. Using a process similar to photocopiers, laser printers, which could print directly on plain paper, were built but at a very high cost of over US$ 150,000.

The principle of the Laser printer is explained here. The laser printer consists of a photosensitive drum which is sensitive to light. The drum is given a positive charge at one point. As the drum rotates, the laser beam "writes" the black portions onto the drum at another point negating the positive charge. As the drum rotates further, it passes positively charged toner particles which are attracted to the negatively charged parts of the drum at a third point.

The plain paper/film is given a negative charge, which attracts the toner off the drum, and adheres to the paper at still another point. The paper and toner are processed finally by passing through a fusor, which applies heat (at 200° C) and pressure to the toner and fuses it to the paper.

Computers had made an impact on the world soon after

the Second World War, but it was not until the seventies that computer technology was brought within the grasp of the common man. Several companies had started manufacturing Personal Computers in the mid seventies including Commodore, Tandy and Apple. Even IBM, the mainframe manufacturer, launched its PC in 1981. As prices dropped over the years, the use of PC's grew till, today, there are an estimated 80 million installed worldwide. With the advent of the PC, software companies began to write composition software on PC's.

The video terminal represents the single most important development in the field of computerized page composition. Earlier, the process of composition was "blind" the operator of a hot metal typesetter could not immediately see what he had typeset.

The video terminal gave us our first window into this process. More importantly, we now have the opportunity to review and change and also to see the effect of that change. Most terminals have been designed for text processing but since 1984, with the launch of the Macintosh, the graphic arts industry had a terminal which could be used not only for text processing but for all kinds of art as well. WYSIWYG, What You See Is What You Get, was the next step. One could see on the screen the exact layout including graphics, before giving the command to get a hard copy. Video terminals came to be 'Known as front end terminals.

Composition Software : The main categories of composition software have to do with the following:

Justification : which is a broad term for arranging text horizontally across a page.

Hyphenation : which is a sub-set of justification, concerned exclusively with how words should be divided (split), when necessary, in order to achieve better justification.

Pagination : a method of composing text both horizontally and vertically, so that text is properly spaced out to fill a page and appropriately divided into pages.

Editing and Corrections : directed to the elimination of input errors or to resolve problems created during the pagination/layout process or to introduce changes by the author.

Graphics : a very broad term for the input, creation and subsequent editing of non-textual matter, like drawings, photographs, charts, etc.

Networking & Communications : required especially where more than one terminal is used or where terminals of different types are used or when the terminals are installed at different geographical locations.

Operating and File Management Systems : Vital supporting programs

The above categories may or may not be incorporated into one software program. As video terminal systems become more common and more useful and because the editing and correction work may take place at various stages of the composition process, it makes sense to segregate the applications into separate modules rather than to have one large unmanageable program.

Update Techniques

With Terminals becoming more and more common, there had to be a way of communicating between a number of terminals connected to the same typesetter. Different users, the author, editor, artist or illustrator and the composer, needed to exchange files without having to take a hard copy or exchange floppy disks. The solution was to "network" the terminals so that files could be transferred over wires electronically, a Local Area Network (LAN). Also, with Wide Area Network, the author need not be in the same location nor in the same city, even. Files of text or graphics could be communicated over ordinary telephone lines to remote locations for editing, proofing or composing. Different kinds of terminals also had to communicate with each other. Files formatted under one system had to be "understood" by another system.

New Technologies

The publishing industry is coming of age. With electronics progress in the last decade, publishing has come a long way from what it was a century ago. It has, however come full circle in the sense that during Gutenberg's time, the functions of the typesetter, printer and publisher were all under one roof. Later, these functions separated and today are coming together again. By 1983, Tom Hagan, president of CAMEX reported: "In the 1950's and 60's the thrust of development in pre-press systems was to 'get the Lead out'. In the 80's it will be to 'get the Silver out'. We are now striving to eliminate the mechanicals and paste-ups as part of the printing and publishing process... I cannot imagine a more exciting time to be involved in this industry." Publishing systems, today, could be summarized as requiring some or all of the following components:

Front End Terminal

A compact personal computer

Standard keyboard layout

Built-in mouse or other entry system

Output Device

Plain paper output

Fast output of both text & graphics

Storage Media

Large capacity

Scanner

To input graphics or text

Black & white or colour

Suitable Software

"A document printed on a laser printer is acceptable as camera-ready-copy, a printing term meaning that printing plates can be made from photographs of laser printed pages ... using a laser printer to produce camera-ready copy eliminates the long and laborious steps of typing and formatting your document on a photo typesetting machine, proofing it and making corrections, composing it into pages, and proofing it again before printing plates are made. Using the copy produced on the laser printer, the printer need only create printing plates of the copy, and print as many copies of the publication as needed."

In a traditional setter, the image is set on a sensitized medium, such as paper or film. After which the exposed film is passed through a film paper processor. "Film processing machines are designed to carry the exposed film through a series of baths in which the film is developed, stopped, fixed, washed and dried in controlled conditions."

Typesetter Comparison

Photo-Mech	*CRT*	*Lasersetters*	*Apple Photo*	*Laser Type setters*
Font Setting	On film	Floppy Resident	Floppy/ Resident	Floppy
Style Type	Mechanical	Electronic	Electronic	Electronic
Optical System	Flash Tube/ Lens/Mirror	CRT/Lens/ Optic Fibre	Laser/Mirror	Laser/Mirror
Exposure by	Light Non-coherent	Light Non-coherent	Light coherent	Light coherent
On	Permanent Sensitised coating	Permanent Sensitised coating	Permanent Sensitised coating	Renewable Photo Sensitised coating
Imaging	Internal	Internal	Internal	Internal
Fixing	External Wet	External Wet	External Wet	Integral Dry

Contd...

Photo-Mech	***CRT***	***Lasersetters***	***Apple Photo***	***Laser Type setters***
	Chemical Process Removal of Resin	Chemical Process Removal of Resin	Chemical Process Removal of Resin	Thermo Process Deposition of Resin
Output	Positives on Paper/ Film	Positives on Paper/ Film	Positives on Paper/ Film	Positives on Paper/ Film
Master	Film Negative	Film Negative	Positive	Positive
Photo ready			Negative	Negative

In plain paper laser setters, the film paper processor is built in. Since these setters use a dry process of depositing toner on plain paper, the processing consists of the application of pressure and heat to fuse the toner to the paper. The result is a fast output of the finished master without requiring the exposed film to go through the time consuming process described above.

5

Printing of a Newspaper

Communication is a process involving sorting, selecting and sending of symbols in such a way as to help a listener perceive and recreate in his own mind the meaning contained in the mind of the communicator. Communication involves the creation of meaning in the listener, the transfer of information and thousands of potential stimuli-communication enables us to do important things, to grow, to learn, to be aware of ourselves and to adjust to our environment.

Mass media together comprise a new social institution, concerned with the production and distribution of knowledge in the widest sense of the word, and having a number of salient characteristics, including the use of relatively advanced technology for mass production and dissemination of message; the systematic organization and social regulation of this work; and the direction of the message at potentially large audiences who are unknown to the sender and free to attend or not.

Global Industry

The mass media institution is open, operates in the public sphere to provide regular channels of communication for messages of a kind determined by what is culturally and technically possible, socially permitted and in demand by a large enough number of individuals.

It is usual to date the beginnings of mass media from the first recognizably modern newspaper, in the early seventeenth century, which in turn was a new application of the technology of printing, already in use for over 150 years for the multiple reproduction of book manuscripts.

This history of media development is more than a record of technical advance and of increasing scale of operation. It was a social innovation as much as a technological invention, and turning points in media history are marked by major social changes. This history of the newspapers, as the first mass medium, illustrates the point very well. Its development is linked to the emergence of power of the bourgeois class. It became an essential instrument in subsequent economic and political struggles, a necessary condition for economic liberalism, constitutional democracy and, also, revolution and bureaucratic centralism. Its development thus reflects political and economic forces on the one hand and major social and cultural changes on the other.

Early social science views of mass media reflect some of these circumstances. Commentators were struck by the immense popular appeal of the new media and by the power which they might exert in society. Views divided sharply on whether to welcome or regret the new instruments of culture and information.

The first period of scientific investigation of mass media undertaken between the mid- 1930s and the late 1950s resulted in a much more modest estimate of media effects than was previously assumed. Since the 1960s there has been further development in the assessment of mass media effects in the direction of a renewed belief in their potency.

Good newspapers are essential if individuals are to function effectively in an increasingly complex world, and if the democratic system is to prevail. Other media can complement, but not replace newspapers.

Traditionally, the newspaper's basic roles have been to inform, influence, entertain, and foster the development of the nation's economy through advertising; those roles are still important. But changing audiences, and potential audiences, have suggested the addition of a fifth basic function : to serve people and help make their lives better.

Compared with other media like television, radio, magazines, etc., and with the latest technology development it could be said that there are many advantages still enjoyed by newspapers. First, newspapers provide a wider variety of news and information than the other media and they present far more details than the electronic media. A second advantage is that they fit into the consumer's schedule more easily than the broadcast media. In the third place, newspapers, along with other print media, are particularly suited to the communication of what has been described as linear or sequential information. Human beings today must assimilate an astounding amount of information to keep pace with a rapidly changing world.

They do this by continuously programming their brains, which can be compared to highly sophisticated computers. The printed word can be used for more efficiently in such programming than the spoken word. Fourth, newspapers can present certain types of entertainment such as the crossword puzzle much more effectively than the broadcast media. Fifth, newspapers can present certain types of advertising far more effectively. Finally, it can be noted that newspapers are particularly effective in presenting information, developing issues and motivating action at the local level. They can give meaning and perspective to community life not possible through the other media.

A newspaper's responsibilities vary with the size, frequency of publication and intended audience of individual publications. The responsibilities of the metropolitan daily, the country weekly and the college newspapers are not the same. Each must determine its particular functions and perform them as best it can. Nevertheless, there seem to be some common responsibilities that apply to all. Newspapers must:

(i) lead in the search for truth;

(ii) in a democratic society, help make democracy work;

(iii) help individuals and communities adjust to change and improve themselves; and

(iv) remain free, independent and solvent.

The history of the development of newspapers must begin with the first efforts to produce them. But a better perspective may be obtained if newspapers are discussed as a major development in the story of man's efforts to communicate with other men. Communication grew out of a need and became more sophisticated. Symbols and materials for communication were developed, and the information of news concept evolved. At first, men relied on gestures and crude sounds. Then they developed the use of objects such as knotted cords and notched sticks to serve as records and reminders. Later they began to record information and ideas through the use of pictures carved into stone tablets or on the walls of caves.

Egyptians are noted for their sacred writings, or hieroglyphics. The Babylonians and especially the Phoenicians pioneered the development of writing. The Greeks modified the Phoenicians' system somewhat. The Romans, and subsequently the Anglo-Saxons, produced the modern alphabet of 26 letters. These were the symbols of communication.

Meanwhile, improved materials for communication were being developed. At first the stone and clay tablets. Then the Egyptians discovered that the papyrus plant could be used as a writing material. The Greeks and Romans used tablets with wax on them, and the Romans developed the use of animal skins for writing. The Chinese developed a form of paper from cotton, rags, hemp and tree bark by the second century after Christ, and its use gradually moved westward. But it was not until the fourteenth century that paper became common in Europe.

Most information was transferred to paper, skins or tablets by hand until the fifth or sixth century when the Chinese developed a form of block printing. Under this system, images and words were carved into blocks, inked and pressed against the paper or printing material. Block printing became common in Europe by the fifteenth century.

At the same time the concept of disseminating information, or news, was being developed. As the need for communication increased, the symbols, materials and methods of providing it became sophisticated.

Prelude and Growth

Johann Gutenberg provided a major breakthrough about A.D. 1450 when he developed the means to cast and use movable type word, but the idea was not quickly transmitted to Europe. Gutenberg developed brass moulds to cast individual letters, and he developed an improved ink out of lamp black and oil. He printed his communications on a press.

The development of movable type opened the way for the development of mass media. Hundreds of copies could be reproduced in a short period of time. Numerous publications, including some newspapers, were produced in Europe in the sixteenth and seventeenth centuries. But the breakthrough in publication potential was not accompanied by an immediate breakthrough in press freedom. On the contrary, those in power who had sought to monopolize earlier forms of communication sought also to control the development and use of printing. Kings and princes realized the potential of printing and sought to use it for their own purposes. The modern struggle for press freedom was soon joined.

England, which provided the model for American journalism, was ruled by a succession of autocratic monarchs during the early development years of modern printing. The absolutist Tudors came to power shortly after printing was introduced into England and remained in power until early in the seventeenth century. Gradually, they used the new methods to further their own interests.

By 1603, when the last of the Tudors died, the people had a surfeit of autocratic rule and wanted individual freedom, including free speech. The Stuart century, which ended in 1714, was thus one of great conflict and change. Out of this conflict, and in response to the needs it created, developed the first newspapers of the English press, and later magazines. Although neither entirely free nor consistently responsible, the early newspapers did provide a vehicle for wider expression of opposing views as well as a medium for other news and advertising. Similar needs and conflicts later resulted in an American press.

The first publication generally designated as a newspaper was a controlled publication founded in 1665 by the head of the Crown's printing monopoly.

It was first called the *Oxford Gazette* and later, after being moved to London, the *London Gazette.* It was the first English newspaper.

England got its first daily newspaper, the *Daily Courant,* shortly after the turn of the century. England's first magazine, *The Review,* was started about the same time by Daniel Defoe, a writer better known for his story of Robinson Crusoe.

The best known publications of the early eighteenth century were the *Tattler* and the *Spectator* of Joseph Addison and Richard Steele. Other English writers also produced models for their American counterparts or provided them with arguments to use in their own battles for press freedom and representative government.

The Press in England remained severely restricted throughout most of the eighteenth century. Parliament enacted a tax in 1712, sometimes called the Tax on Knowledge that hampered Press growth for a century and a half. It was not until late in the century that the Press got some protection against libel and greater freedom to cover the activities of Parliament.

The first colonies developed in the South, but the first newspapers were started in New England because people there had a need for them sooner. Newspapers were not developed sooner in the colonies because they were not needed. Most persons knew already what was going on in their small communities. They received other news from the English papers that were shipped to the colonies periodically, and there was little business or commerce in the early years to support local publications.

The need for better communication was growing in the late seventeenth century when Benjamin Harris decided to start a newspaper in Boston. He was stopped because he sought to publish without the approval of the government and indirectly offended the government. After the suppression of Harris' paper, no one tried to start another for almost 15 years.

The first successful effort to publish a newspaper without permission in the colonies came in Boston in the early 1720s. The paper was called the *New England Courant,* and it was published by James Franklin, elder brother of Benjamin Franklin.

James Franklin's younger brother, Ben, also made a substantial contribution to colonial journalism. He was the most successful, financially and otherwise, of all the colonial journalists. Franklin did everything well and became publisher of the principal newspaper in Philadelphia. He made that newspaper, the *Pennsylvania Gazette,* into one of the colonies' best publications, carrying both news and literary comment. His success can be measured in terms of advertising, circulation, number of pages published, and similar figures as well as in influence.

Franklin was also instrumental in the development of many other newspaper ventures, including a number of foreign language newspapers. Above all, he demonstrated that a printer journalist could serve his community and earn a good livelihood at the same time. John Peter Zenger started his *New York Weekly Journal* in the early 1730s in part to provide a voice for the rising merchant class in New York.

Through their advocacies and their reporting of opinions and events, newspapers helped to create a new government in America. During the revolution itself they helped rally Americans to the cause and helped them sustain their purpose through difficult times. The newspapers did a remarkable job of reporting events and unifying the patriots.

Newspapers continued to play a vital role after the fighting ceased. They grew and developed with the nation they helped create and sustain. The first daily newspapers were started in Philadelphia in the middle of 1780s, and others were begun in other major cities in subsequent years.

The Constitution as amended almost immediately by the Bill of Rights (First ten Amendments) outlined at least in a general way the path that the new nation should follow. The continuing value of newspapers was recognized in the First Amendment, which reads in part, "Congress shall make no law... abridging the freedom of speech or of the press..."

President Thomas Jefferson's view of the press, its roles and responsibilities, are particularly noteworthy. He is generally regarded as one of the great champions of a free press. Said Jefferson : ' "The basis of our governments being the opinion of the people, the very first object should be to keep that right; and were it left to me to decide whether we should have a government without newspapers, or newspapers without a government, 1 should not hesitate a moment to prefer the latter. But I should mean that every man should receive these papers and be capable of reading them."

Benjamin Day founded the first of the penny papers in the fall of 1833. He called it the *New York Sun.* James Gordon Bennett started the *New York Herald* a year or so later. The *Herald* became the nation's leading paper in circulation, and perhaps in influence. Better known than Bennett was Horace

Greeley, who founded the *New York Tribune* in 1841. The daily edition never attained the circulation of the *Herald,* but the weekly edition by the 1850s was reaching 20,000 readers through the East and Middle West

Henry J. Raymond made a major contribution in founding the *New York Times* in 1851. The *Baltimore Sun* became famous for its coverage of the nation's capital, and the *Chicago Tribune* was a leader in the development of Middle West. The *New York Herald* provided the most extensive coverage of the war presumably the Civil War, and it probably caused President Lincoln some sleepless nights. The *Herald* was read by most persons in England and other foreign countries for news about the United States.

Newspapers experienced a second revolution in the latter decades of the nineteenth century. They did not alter their basic function, established in the 1830s and continued to emphasize news. But their methods of collecting, processing and presenting it were changed substantially. Many of the changes came as a response to the rapid expansion of business, industry, government and population. More persons needed more information, and they needed it more rapidly.

Some of the key developments included the Linotype, the half-tone engraving, the stereotype, the web-fed rotary press, colour printing techniques and wood pulp paper used in the mechanical department, and the type-writer and telephone used in the news and advertising departments. Technological development made the rapid expansion of newspapers in the late nineteenth century possible.

Pulitzer was one of a number of editors in the late nineteenth century who pulled together the new techniques in reporting and editing and the new technology to relate bigger and better newspapers to serve an increasing number of persons. Pulitzer at the *St. Louis Post-Dispatch* and especially at the *New York World* showed what amounted to new journalism. He bought the *New York World* in the 1880s and made it the USA's most successful newspaper.

One regrettable extension of the new approach suggested by Pulitzer was the yellow journalism that evolved in the 1890s. Yellow journalism is a term used to describe extreme sensationalism. The term itself evolved from the struggle between Hearst and Pulitzer over a comic strip featuring a character called the Yellow Kid. Hearst hired away the cartoonist who drew the strip for *Pulitzer's World*. Pulitzer then hired another cartoonist to draw a similar strip. Some of the other newspapers thought this struggle typified the unfortunate practice of the time, and dubbed the two offending newspapers "yellow journals" and much of their content "yellow journalism".

The most important development of the early twentieth century newspapers was the introduction of a more responsible journalism in the founding of the *Christian Science Monitor* and the rejuvenation of the *New York Times*. Of the other New York newspapers, *The World* and *The Tribune* probably were the most successful in the early twentieth century.

Some of the larger newspapers could afford correspondents of their own in Washington and in some of the major capitals around the world. But an increasing number of newspapers came to rely on one or more of the wire services and syndicates which developed in the early twentieth century for coverage of distant events and a wide variety of features. Wire services such as Associated Press, United Press and International News Service provided immediate coverage of the news. Syndicates such as King Features and United Features, and others provided a wide variety of news, features and other materials, including the increasingly popular comic strips.

After World War I a new type of newspaper, the tabloid, was born. The tabloids symbolized the era and were characterized by a smaller format than most newspapers, displayed big pictures and big headlines, and laid emphasis on sensational stories.

The first and most successful of the tabloids was the *New*

York Illustrated Daily News. The *Daily News* received tabloid competition in the middle 1920s from the *Daily Mirror* and the *Daily Graphic.* Newspapers achieved new significance and influence in the 1930s with an increasing emphasis on interpretative reporting. Some newspapers employed specialists of their own to explain government, business and other developments. Others relied on the syndicated columnists who rose to prominence in the 1930s.

Many newspapers joined with other newspapers, wire services, magazines and radio to provide extensive coverage of the events involved in World War II. Coverage of the War was extensive and generally impressive. Many correspondents were cited for their efforts. Ernie Pyle particularly effective in reporting the human side of the war, was killed while covering the action in the Pacific. President Truman said : "The nation is saddened again by the death of Ernie Pyle. No man in this war has so well told the story of the American fighting man as American fighting men wanted it told. He deserves the gratitude of all his countrymen. "But also in peaceful time, journalism has claimed its victims.

Another major breakthrough in newspaper operation was the improved and expanded use of offset printing. Since offset usually involves cold type and photography, it fits in nicely with the new photo-composition devices.

The press itself became the subject of criticism, sometimes deserved, often not. Newsmen were accused of stirring up trouble by their very presence at events and demonstrations. Newspapers were criticised for biased reporting, particularly by young reporters who felt they should join the marchers as well as report the march.

In late 1969 Vice-President Spiro Agnew launched an attack on both broadcast media and newspapers for abusing their powers. He charged that too much power over public opinion was concentrated in the hands of the television networks and a few large Eastern newspapers such as the *Washington Post* and *New York Times.*

There are about as many types of newspapers today as there are newspapers. No two are exactly alike, even though they may be part of the same group or one of two owned newspapers in the same city. Most will differ primarily because their purposes and audiences are different. Even group-owned newspapers will have different cities, especially if those cities are in different parts of the country, and jointly owned newspapers in the same city will have morning and evening editions. Newspapers will differ to some extent simply because the persons who publish them are different. Each newspaper has its own functions and its own staff to perform those functions.

Many groupings can be employed to place newspapers into better perspective. They may be grouped according to purpose, such as general and specialised; according to frequency of publication, such as daily, weekly, semiweekly and biweekly; according to time of publication, such as morning and evening; according to circulation, such as large, medium and small; according to geography such as national, regional, metropolitan, suburban and rural; according to method of production, such as letter press and offset: according to format such as standard and tabloid; according to achievement such as good, fair, poor and bad. Other groupings could be suggested and most newspapers obviously could be placed in several of them. Newspapers are most easily categorized by frequency of publication. The two broad groupings are dailies and non-dailies.

The Newspaper is a Business Institution. Today's newspaper owner is constantly challenged by his publication's dual role as quasi-public institution with special privileges and responsibilities and free enterprise operation with a need to pay expenses and show a profit. The newspaper must serve the needs of the public for facts and opinion in an unselfish way if it is to justify its special status; yet it must succeed as a business enterprise in the information field if it is to exist and serve the public in any way.

The organisation and operation of newspapers will vary somewhat with their size and historical development. But certain basic functions are common to all. The jobs could be: owner(s) and corporate officers, publisher or general manager, business, production and news and opinion (editorial and editors). Business will include office activities, advertising, circulation and distribution, personnel and promotion.

The editorial section is vital to the development of a good newspaper. Someone has suggested that the news section is the heart of the newspapers and the editorial section is its soul. The editorial page sets the tone of the newspaper and expresses its character on a continuing basis. Basically, the editorial section performs two functions. First, it provides a continuous expression of the newspaper's opinions on important issues. Secondly, it provides a form for the expression of opinion by others on these issues.

Newspapers have contributed, through their search for truth, to more honest behaviour from government officials and to ethics not only in the USA, but in many other countries where the press could be considered free. The Watergate story unfolded in 1974 and the Iran-contra affair in 1986-87 are cases where this can be seen. Another case was the NASA contracts investigation. It is true also of Peru and many other countries of the new world.

Journalists have asserted with some success that the right to publish without prior restraints, and the right to obtain information about government are essential to the success of the democratic system. Both rights are asserted on behalf of the public at large. Anyone should be able to publish without prior restraint, provided he is responsible for what he publishes; anyone should have broad access to information about his government.

Disagreements have arisen over the specific procedures to follow in administering the rights and the extent to which reports concerning crimes, persons accused of crimes, and judicial procedures can prejudice juries and make fair trials impossible. Newspapers and citizens generally have a great deal of freedom today to provide information and commentary about public officials, public figures, and other persons involved in matters of public interest. Libel laws vary from country to country and even within the same country. This is an area of great discussion and disagreement as well as complication because of definitions of terms like: actual malice, privacy, fair use, etc.

The continuing success of newspapers will depend to a great extent on their ability and willingess to develop and adopt new technology to carry out their information functions. The use of new methods and new technology is essential to their success if not their survival. Newspapers that change with the times can continue to be an important source of printed information and vital participants in the continuing human story.

There is much that newspapers can do in today's complex world. They can still influence, entertain and foster the development of the nation's free enterprise system through advertising. But their opportunities and responsibilities for service go far beyond their basic functions. The life of the nation itself depends on the continued development of a free and responsible press.

Print Media

The printed word is no longer regarded by the educators as "non-communicative" or ineffective. In the words of Holmberg, "By far the most important medium in distance education courses is the printed word. This applies to conventional correspondence study, as well as to highly sophisticated multi-media presentations like courses of the open university." Though we said earlier that the choice of media depends on the subject matter to be covered, the value associated with the print medium seems largely objective and independent of the nature of the subject-matter. Print medium has proved largely effective in cognitive, affective and psychomotor domains, and there will hardly be any educator who wants to belittle or ignore the place of this medium. As Charles Zuber of the University of South Pacific said : "Any medium ... can generally be regarded to a greater or lesser degree as support for course material in the form of print care must always be taken that this existing and fundamental medium should not be overlooked."

In my opinion, the words of Zuber are representative. Yet there are occasions when experiments show that the printed word is more effective in certain domains than in another. In Nashif's opnion, "... if the objective is cognitive, involving analysis as a philosophy, the printed word will probably be more effective."

Secondly, accepting the indispensable value the printed word carries cannot ignore two evident shortcomings of the print media. Print media lack the personal touch and secondly are not flexible or open enough to allow for dialogue. This makes us state the need for supporting the printed word with the non-print media.

Electronic Media : The world appears to be in the midst of an information explosion, A recent advertisement for IBM said that we are living in "The Age of Communications." And, indeed this seems to be the case, even to a casual observer. Satellites relay television signals around the globe. Magazines, newspapers, books, and radio bombard us with facts and opinions. Films offer both information and entertainment. Together, then, the mass media provide us with information more easily and quickly and in greater quantities than ever before. But what are the mass media ?

First, the mass media are the instruments of communication that I have just mentioned : books, such as the one you are reading now; magazines and journals of opinion, like the *Illustrated Weekly of India* or *India Today;* newspapers, like *The Hindu, The Times of India, The Statesman;* television and radio, like Doordarshan and All India Radio; and films from the Films Division of the Government of India and private films producers which are generally distributed in many parts of the world. In essence, these are tools that extend our ability to talk to one another. A conversation between one another serves as a model of communication; someone sends a message, and someone else receives it. Because messages the media disseminate reach thousands and even millions of persons, the media are instruments of mass communication.

But obviously, these "instruments" or "tools" are not at all like the tools we are accustomed to. In the art of painting, for example, the word "medium" (the singular of "media") refers to the liquid substance in which pigment is suspended as well as the liquid used in applying paint. Depending upon the characteristics of the medium — whether it is oil, water, egg tempera, or a cry the artist will achieve different effects.

The first surge in modern communication began about 1440 when Johannes Gutenberg, a craftsman and inventor in Mainz, Germany, developed movable type. Sometimes before 1455, Gutenberg printed his greatest work, the Gutenberg Bible, on a renovated wine press. The method of printing that Gutenberg devised — printing from movable type — was used without any major changes until the 20th century.

The invention of the telegraph and telephone in the 19th century marked the start of a second major surge in communication —the rise of electronic media. By 1835, a painter, Samuel F.B. Morse, had made the first working model of an electric telegraph. By 1838, he had developed the system of dots and dashes known today as the Morse Code, and by 1839, the first telegraph line in the United States came into being.

Radio started as a medium of entertainment but soon became an important source of information. By the 1930s, bulletins broadcast by radio stations had begun to displace newspaper "extras". Radio, however, was soon overtaken by television, which rapidly became the most satisfying source of entertainment.

Functional Aspects

The primary role and responsibility of the "press" is to report what is going on as honestly and as accurately as possible, to inform the public of the good, the bad, the interesting as well as the not-too-interesting and, by doing so, to play a definite and constructive role in bringing about a better informed and more alert, interested citizenry.

The mass media try to persuade as well as inform. The media's power to persuade, however, is generally exaggerated. People are more likely to be influenced by their friends and relatives than by the media. The media cannot easily change deeply rooted opinion.

People also turn to the media for entertainment. The media also stimulate the economy by carrying advertisements for goods and services. To survive, the media must have money. Too often, the public—and even some journalists — forget that most media are private businesses and must earn a reasonable profit in order to remain in business and retain their independence. The media serve as watch-dogs over our society, and journalists believe they have a special responsibility to examine critically the performance of the government. They are often criticized, however, for bias and a lack of credibility. The scepticism towards the media, as towards other entrenched institutions, is healthy in a democratic society.

Inevitably, the media will continue to change. The field of journalism is highly sensitive to changes in its environment: to advance in technology and to changes in the nation's political, economic, and social systems. Media that have become stagnant — that failed to adapt to the times — have been forced out of business.

Journalism is so much a part of the political system that it influences the structure of the system itself. Without mass media, there would be no political system as we know it. And as the source of so much of the information we have about the world around us, including the world of politics, the media have great power to influence what we think about. Some of the older sources of information and influence, such as the school, political party, and religious institutions, seem to be diminishing in importance as politics becomes more media-oriented. But traditional sources of influence such as the family and social environment remain more powerful in influencing political behaviour and voting than exposure to the media.

Fundamental changes in a political system, like revolutions or changes in party dominance, come about slowly and are surely aided by the mass media but hardly caused by them.

Partly because they enjoy more leisure, people are devoting more time to the media. Few media, however, seek a truly mass audience. Individuals differ, and most of the media appeal to specific sub-groups within our society. Newspapers attract better educated and sometimes a wealthier audience than radio and television. Few readers, however, look at every story in a paper. Like restaurants and department stores newspapers offer a wider selection of items.

Relevance in Society

(i) A newspaper should cover government at every level. It would devote special attention to the government agencies in its area — not only by covering meetings but by critically examining the activities of the agencies. Recognizing its role as a check on government, a newspaper should present the views of the critics of government spokesmen.

(ii) A newspaper should go beyond government news and bulletin-board journalism to reveal the equality of people's lives and the human fabric of its community. This can be achieved through several techniques, and stories that provide a local dimension to important national and international issues.

(iii) A newspaper should attempt to publish, as best it can, a complete and balanced presentation of local, state, national, and international news. Obviously a metropolitan paper cannot be judged by the same standard as a small-town paper that prints only four pages a day and is bought for its local news. But papers of all sizes must emphasise the news of continuing importance at all levels — international as well as local.

(iv) In an age when the medium is said to be the message a newspaper must attempt to present its news as effectively and as attractively as possible. Page layouts, photographs, charts, type selection, graphics — all must help guide the reader to the news that is most important and encourage him to read what he otherwise might overlook.

(v) A newspaper should stand for something. Its editorials should take a position on the important local issues. It should clearly, logically explain its point of view. Editorials need not argue forcefully each and every day, but regularly the reader should sense that the editorial writer truly cares about what he is saying. A paper also should encourage diversity of opinion, including letters to the editors that criticize the paper.

(vi) A newspaper's management — as well as its news staff— should operate the paper with integrity; the news columns should be free of bias; employee policies that avoid conflicts of interest should be enforced; pay and working conditions should encourage the professionalism of the staff.

Discussions about the media's responsibilities often overlook two factors of fundamental importance: financial incentives and the related responsibilities of our Indian public. Hope for more responsible media rests not only with journalists, but also with a more informed and discriminating audience — an audience that patronizes the best that the media have to offer.

Most persons including journalists generally agree upon the characteristics that are desirable in news media, but they disagree over questions of who should define the media's responsibilities and whether those responsibilities should be enforced. Journalists reserve the right to determine the standards for themselves. Except for government regulations, there is no clear evidence to indicate that they would succeed. In the broadcasting department, for example, critics contend that the government's efforts to exercise indirect control have stifled the very characteristics which it should encourage.

Because the news media do not have enough time and space to report all the information they receive, they report only the stories that are most important, interesting, timely, and unusual. They also emphasize stories that affect large numbers of persons and that involve their local communities. The media's selection process is also affected by their traditions, sources, and advertisers. Several studies have found that reporters have only a dim or generalized image of the audience they are expected to serve, and that they are more anxious to please themselves, their colleagues, and their editors than the public. Policies — particularly the problem of political bias— are still a factor in the selection process but are declining in importance.

The major services and other prestigious media serve as models for the nation's journalists and often influence their decisions. Many media are becoming steadily candid, but there is still a tendency to avoid material that might offend large segments of their audiences.

The problem of good taste varies from one medium to another. Numerous other variations between the media are also evident. Persons who understand the media and their selection process are able to attract more publicity by manufacturing the types of stories that the media are more likely to report. Only a few of the factors involved in the selection process are acknowledged by conceptions of news.

Because of threats to their credibility, the media try to eliminate conflicts of interest, and many now try to ban the acceptance of favours that used to be common. Even as such issues are resolved, however, new and seemingly more serious issues will inevitably arise. So there will always be problems and reasons to question the media's performance. The issue can play a beneficial role, however, since they force the media to re-examine their traditions and adapt to society's changing needs.

Three different and often contradictory theories attempt to explain the relationship between the media and government: the watch-dog, partnership and participant theories. Even though the watchdog theory does not always predominate, some conflict between the media and government is inevitable because of their different perspectives and different roles in our society. Government officials in other parts of the world attempt to unify their nations and win public support which is vital to the success of their programmes and discuss alternatives suggested by the officials' political rivals. In our country, of late, our political rulers make all-out efforts, first, to entrench themselves in power by hook or by crook so much so that the media with objective and honest traditions find themselves in uneasy situations.

Journalists are concerned about the government's use of publicity and secrecy and its ability to manufacture consent. Nevertheless, journalists appear to rely heavily upon the government's publicity releases. Some additional information comes from leaks and background briefings. Although never specifically authorized by the Constitution, secrecy has become common, particularly in the areas of national defence and foreign policy. Journalists do complain, often times, that the government also uses secrecy to hide its own mistakes.

Best Material : Before evaluating the quality of news coverage, it is essential to consider standards of evaluation. Nothing is good or bad in itself; it is good or bad with respect to some standard. The following are the most important of the many standards that have been proposed and used by the media and media critics :

> The Indian mass media are, for the most part, privately owned and privately financed barring some public limited companies and trusts. Unless they earn a profit, they will fail.

A newspaper, in imminent danger of failure, is unlikely to spend much money improving its news operation. This is generally more common in India than in many other countries of the world. A mass medium that earns a lot of money still does a poor job covering the news. But one that loses money almost always does a poor job.

Like profitability, audience satisfaction is a necessary but not a sufficient condition for media quality. If nobody reads a newspaper article it can accomplish nothing—but many articles are well read and still accomplish nothing.

An inaccurate news story is always, without exception, a poor news story. Most editors and reporters know this, and strive mightily to spell the names right, even if they do not fully understand what their sources are saying.

Nearly all responsible journalists aim at objectivity, and quite often they fail. Words have connotations as well as denotations; they imply more than they say. As long as reporters must work with words, complete objectivity is impossible. And even an "objective" reporter must decide whom to interview, what to ask, and which facts to include in the story. Fairness is a reasonable standard to ask of journalists, literal objectivity is not.

Underground editors and other committed journalists often complain that where one side is right and the other is wrong, objectivity is a false god. Was objectivity a good thing during the declaration of Emergency in India by the then Prime Minister who expected the media to be "fair" to her?

Most editors urge their reporters to find stories that are distinctive, dramatic, or in some way unusual. If overused, this standard becomes more a definition of sensationalism than of news. If the media ignore what is typical and stress what is weird, they inevitably present us with a weird picture of the world. Nonetheless,' 'man bites dog" is still a bigger story than "dog bites man ".

Relevant news is important news. What kind of stories are most relevant ? Those that are local, timely, and directly useful to the audience. This standard, too, is sometimes overemphasized. The most local, timely, and useful stories around, after all, are the supermarket ads.

The Times of India, The Hindu followed by *The Indian Express, The Statesman, The Amrit Bazar Patrika* can be considered to be very near complete newspapers in India. But not for everything — they are somewhat weak in management, science topics and editorial cartoons. And is the most complete medium always the best medium ? A three-hour TV film show is hardly three times as good as a one-hour show, especially if You are waiting for a special feature. When we demand completeness, what we are really asking for is a sample of the show that is adequately large and appropriately varied.

However a medium selects its news, its judgements should be its own, and should not be influenced by outside pressures. If a newspaper kills a story because a big advertiser insists on it, then it is a poor newspaper—not because it killed the story (may be it didn't deserve to run), but because it deferred to the wishes of an advertiser. Independence is absolutely essential for good journalism.

The mass media have an obligation to keep within the bounds of propriety and good taste. But what are those bounds? Some business executives think it is in poor taste to report declining sales figures. Some revolutionaries think it is good taste to report do-it-yourself bomb- making techniques. Most editors disagree on both counts.

As the world grows more complicated, it becomes less and less adequate for reporters to stick to bare facts in their reporting.

Interpretation is essential to put the facts into a meaningful context, to make them comprehensible to the reader or viewer.

Democracy is predicated on the assumption that all kinds of news and opinions are available to the public, competing in the free market of ideas: The trouble with this assumption is that most of the media today are not ideological competitors. They all say pretty much the same things, and that is not healthy. I, therefore, propose the standard of uniqueness.

Any mass medium that is significantly different from its competitors is in this sense "better" than that which is undifferentiated. Calcutta City is better off with both *The Statesman* and *The Amrit Bazar Patrika* as also *Business Standard* than it would be with two papers like *The Statesman.*

The eleven standards listed above are by no means exhaustive. But the broad ones touching the core of the topic have not been overlooked. Standards, like these, can be set in hundreds. The point to be recognized here is that judgements of quality are meaningless without explicit criteria.

You, as public relations persons also involved in journalism to a reasonable degree, can go ahead and criticize the mass media. You are as qualified as anyone else. But make sure you know what your standards are.

It is not uncommon that the owner of a mass medium would like to control news coverage. There are three reasons for doing so. Each reason dictates its own policy. Thus

(i) the economic interests of the company dictate a "business policy ";
(ii) the individual likes and dislikes of the owner dictate a 'personal policy"; and
(iii) the ideological convictions of the owner dictate a "political policy."

Newspapers tend to show their bias in three ways :

(i) They give large headlines to the favoured party.

(ii) They give more prominence to articles by the favoured author.

(iii) They print more quotations from the favoured party, and more remarks praising that party.

For one thing, a newspaper which is not competing against a rival can present news in better balance. There is no need to sensationalise.

Competing newspapers live in fear of each other. They maybe stampeded into excesses by their fear of losing circulation to a competitor less burdened with conscience.

The unopposed newspaper can give its reader relief from the pressures of time. Deadlines no longer loom like avenging angels just this side of the next edition. There is more freedom from financial pressure on the business side. A single ownership newspaper can better afford to take an unpopular stand. It can better absorb the loss of money in support of a principle.

If it is true of natural laws, reasoned the philosophers of the "Enlightenment," it should be true of people's laws as well.

If men were free to inquire about all things to form opinions on the basis of knowledge and evidence, and to utter their opinions freely, the competition of knowledge and opinion in the market of rational discourse would ultimately banish ignorance and superstition, and enable men to shape their conduct and their institutions in conformity with the fundamental invariable laws of nature and the will of God.

An enterprising and result-oriented public relations manager is one who pins faith in the following points with respect to media relationships :

- He loses no opportunities to give them service.
- He answers all questions fully, honestly and promptly.
- He would treat a newsman as he would treat a customer.
- He knows his own organization, its details, its spellings.

- He is never a barrier or obstruction; the public relations professional is not a "suppress" agent.
- He honours a legitimate "exclusive", however much he is tempted to balloon it into a more general break.
- He is impartial between one medium and another.
- He does not bluff, misrepresent, exaggerate or pad.
- He makes every effort to provide a story for a newsman who desires one.
- However much provoked, he is not abrupt with a newsman.
- He is as energetic in helping the media cover an adverse story as any other kind.

First and most important, newspapers should help build the superstructure of democracy—an informed electorate. Thomas Jefferson said "... and were it left to me to decide whether we should have a government without newspapers or newspapers without government, I should not hesitate a moment to prefer the latter."

No ordinary mortal can attend every city council, local government, and zonal meeting and still have time to brush his teeth, much less hold a job and rear a family. The newspapers and their broadcast cohorts must cover for us. Day in and day out newspaper reading should tell us whether health and sanitation codes are enforced, whether the State Government is firm in dealing with unreasonable demands on the Public Transport Undertakings, and so forth.

If a community problem is festering on a side street somewhere, the newspapers should tell us about it long before the lid blows off and disrupts the town.

In short, newspapers should not only tell us *What is Happening*, but must undertake the much more difficult task of giving us a picture of the community itself, a picture of the changing background against which things happen.

This is a rough assignment. Rougher still when you consider the covering of newspaper problems.

Since the advent of radio and television, newspapers have resembled a graying matron vying for her fair share of attention at a dinner party full of movie starlets.

Rising costs and burgeoning competition for advertising revenue have the tendency to squeeze the "news" publication.

In a world that seems more complicated every morning, newspapers must daily report and interpret everything from railway accidents to archaeological digs and do it fast, be objective, make it clear.

If we agree with Thomas Jefferson that newspapers are an essential ingredient in democracy, it follows that we should support our local newspaper.

Here are three good ways to do so :

1. Read it carefully.
2. Honour its best efforts.
3. Criticize it fairly.

Most state and national news comes into the local newspaper office from wire services. Metre after metre of it (without headlines) rattle off the teleprinter and into the desk of the wire editor who must decide what to discard and what to print. Then the news editor looks at dummy sheets showing the day's advertising and decides where to put major stories.

Next, the copy editor writes the headline to fit the number of columns the story should run.

If an important story carries a misleading headline in the newspaper, it is due to a local news judgement error. If it happens often, you have a legitimate complaint.

Important stories are buried in the back of the newspaper. Any newsman will tell you, newspapers don't place stories in descending order of importance throughout the newspapers. In a newsman's eyes, the story on page 7 may be every bit as important as the one on page 9. Don't forget, newspapers sell ads throughout their paper on the basis that you will read every page.

Newspapers invariably try to have a balanced front page to draw people into the newspaper. People are enticed this way to read the paper before they can tell newspapers what they need to know.

The argument is that the masses in general look for such news to read through over their morning cup of tea served by the tea shop.

Standard papers with a national reputation will not be swayed by the "advertiser" influence on their additional content — that is a basic tenet of journalism; advertising revenue supports newspapers, and some newspapers have more integrity than others when it comes to backing a disgruntled advertiser.

The press should take care to see that reporting on incidents do not turn into riots.

Complete objectivity is almost impossible, In the facts newsman select stories, and reporters are subjective. They should announce their position in the beginning and promote it rather than preserve the fiction of objectivity.

Perfect objectivity is impossible; perfect anything is impossible. But a reporter would think he has done a pretty good job if he has given the reader the facts he needs to disagree with him.

Freedom of the Press never rested on the idea that a single reporter could write ten columns of universal truth every time he sat down at the typewriter. It rested on the idea that he was supposed to try... and that out of free and honest discussion, the truth would emerge.

Getting criticism from all sides is perhaps the surest sign that newspapers are doing a good job. But it will certainly worry them if people criticize them for the wrong reasons.

Perhaps criticizing for the right reasons is the citizenship skill that can help our democracy most...and the best way we can support our local newspaper.

" A free Press is the unsleeping guardian of every other right that free men prize"— Sir Winston Churchill.

"News is the statement of freshly ascertained facts about something of interest that has happened, is happening, is about to happen, or that, contrary to expectation, has not happened, is not happening, and probably will not happen."

— Paul White, in his book, "News on the Air", page 171.

"News is an accurate and timely report of some event, situation, condition or opinion... a report which will interest the particular persons for whom it is intended."

— Dowing Leatherwood, in his book, "Journalism on the Air", page 171.

"News may be defined as an accurate unbiased account of the significant facts of timely happening that is of interest to the readers of the newspaper that prints the account."

— William S. Maulsby, in his book, "Getting the News".

News can be read with greater interest if the news stories are written effectively. To make stories effective, attention must be given to the form of lead used with them. The lead is the first part of the news story; it gives the gist of the entire account. In short, it is the first unit of the news story in an epitomized form.

A good lead not only indicates the tone and temper of the story, but also answers questions likely to arise in a reader's mind on learning of a certain event. It is attractive and observes the principles of good news writing. There are numerous types of leads. The most important of that uses the 5 W's and the H. Here are examples :

Smt. Indira Gandhi has been declared the leader of

Congress (I) party to head the National Government this morning...

The murder of the housewife at Indira Nagar, Madras, remained a mystery. So too the tracing of the murderers while the victim was buried today at....

To save his mother's life Appukuttan Nair left his bank job in Madras yesterday and flew to Trivandrum just in time to give her a successful blood transfusion.

Not until Monday or Tuesday will new applicants be able to enrol at the Bhavan's College of Mass Communication, Madras, as the Honorary Principal is faced with piles of applications, notably for the Diploma Course in Public Relations, the Registrar of the College announced here today.

In the Guruvayur temple in Kerala State, Smt. Indira Gandhi, the Prime Minister of India, was weighed in sugar today to respect the vow taken by the party leader who had prayed to the presiding deity for her success as the Prime Minister.

Mr. Devraj Urs's prompt action in stepping down from the Chief Minister's post in Bangalore has not only created a favourable image of him but also precluded the possibility of being ousted from the post by the newly elected political party, Congress (I).

Once the lead is selected, the building of the rest of the story develops naturally if the news writer remembers to put first what is more important. A convenient way to remember the proper structure of a news account is to arrange the facts to be reported in the form of a triangle standing on its point.

In writing a feature one has to depend on the eye and the ear, sentiments, feelings, emotions and observation. The difference between "News Writing" and "Feature Writing" lies in approach rather than in subject matter.

A newspaper man writing on the beggar problem in India,

especially on the life of the pavement dwellers in Bombay and Calcutta, will have to dig facts from records, relate them to each other, marshall them and draw his own conclusions. But if he were to describe the tragedy of the beggar and pavement dwellers of all sorts, he must spend some time with the beggar and pavement dweller, interview him, his friends, his wife and children if any. At the same time, the feature writer cannot dispense with study.

Feature writing has yet to develop fully in India for many reasons. Illiteracy is greatly responsible for this. Demand creates supply. There is not very much demand for features, because 80 per cent of the people cannot read newspapers. Furthermore, feature writers need to get more guidance to compete with their counterparts in the West. We have yet to establish traditions in feature writing. Whatever ideas feature writers have about their craft have been gathered from reading British and American papers.

Even language papers are now showing keen interest in features. They run women's pages, children's pages and the like, but miss the spirit of feature writing.

While writing a feature one should try to write a striking introduction which may arouse the reader's curiosity and interest. How to end a feature is as important as how to begin it. Sometimes the technique of short story writing may be successfully employed to write a feature.

A study of what is called product publicity will help to show the difference between news and puffers.

In the 1920's and 1930's when early newspaper advertising for commodities and services was better known as "puffing", it was hard to tell editorials from advertisements because in the art of displaying advertisements, sophistication was yet to come. It belonged to the day when the space broker found it was easier and more profitably to sell space if he also had creative talent and especially a gift for writing slogans.

In the early 19th century advertisement copywriters were famous authors and poets like Charles Lamb. Puffery was the available aid to marketing although much despised by men like Carlyle who could not understand that a trader or manufacturer must make known in order to sell, and that newspaper advertising was our economic means of broadcasting a sales message to buyers distant from the mill or factory.

To the newspaperman, puffers have continued to mean literary advertisement, and the attempt to present advertising as news has incurred the wrath of editors who were convinced that their editorial columns were being invaded and misused, although a great many things advertised are also of news value.

A puff or a free puff, as it is more often described, means an unmistakable advertisement appearance in the editorial columns. It is the term used by an alert editor when he thinks that somebody is trying to gain from a reference in his columns. It is also used less specifically by advertisement managers responsible for selling space who regard editorial mention as announcements improperly occupying space which they could or should have sold. For these reasons we frequently see the absurdity of a legitimate news story from which all commercial names have been obviously deleted, usually to appease the advertisement manager.

The Press is regrettably inclined to be dominated by the advertisement side rather than the editorial, for the simple reason that many publications exist very largely on their advertisement revenue. However, with competition from TV and radio, high production costs and reduction in advertisement revenue due to economic crisis, income from cover prices is becoming more important, thus encouraging greater editorial independence. And unless the editorial secures adequate sales, the advertisement manager will be unable to sell his space. A good editor may well rely on good officers providing him with materials which help him to achieve a successful journal.

6

Stages in Publishing

One of the great advantages of democracy is that it provides for peaceful voluntary adjustment of disputes through negotiation as an alternative to their settlement by force or fiat. Democracy has accordingly been described as institutionalised peaceful settlement of disputes, making provision for ballots instead of bullets and for counting of heads instead of cracking them Peaceful settlement of controversies being an essential ingredient of democracy, it would follow that *bandhs*, agitations and street demonstrations have not much relevance in a true democracy. As things, however, are, we find that they have become a permanent feature of our public life. Not only that, they create problems of law and order and consume at good part of the time of our law enforcement agencies.

Democracy is a delicate form of government which rests for its successful functioning on conditions which are rather precarious but all the same vital. It postulates that despite difference son matters of detail, emphasis and degree, there should be a broad consensus on major national issues like the fundamental structure of society and form of government. Where, however, the differences and animosities between the winning party and the losing party reach such a point that the losing party entertains apprehensions about its political and physical survival, there arises real danger to democracy. Likewise, democratic structure faces a serious threat when the party defeated at the polls does not reconcile itself to the verdict of the electorate and refuses peaceably to lose.

In either event there arises a grave risk of constitutional barriers being brushed aside. It, therefore, becomes imperative in a living democracy that the victors and the vanquished at the polls should both abide by the rules of the game. Democracy can indeed work properly upon the assumption that the minority will accept the rule of the majority and will not take matters to the streets and the majority in turn will not rule too oppressively and pay due attention to the view of the minority even though it ultimately does not accept it. In other words, both the majority and the minority have rights as well as obligations.

The History

Tolerance of criticism and dissent is the most essential attribute of democracy. In fact democracy is so conceived that criticism of the ruling party, instead of being a weapon of destruction, becomes an instrument of better government. Despite that ideological basis of democratic polity, we find that there is increasing allergy to criticism and every attempt is made to hush it. Democracy postulates an open society. It rests upon accountability of those in power for their doings and conduct to the public. This is possible only if there is no attempt to put an official cloak of secrecy on the acts of those in power, and to whittle down freedom of information.

As things are, there persists a strong impression that an official cloak of secrecy is being used to cover the lapses, bunglings and even misconduct of those in power. This is most unfortunate. Undoubtedly a country can have some national secrets. There can also be no doubt that in certain spheres of government, we have to maintain secrecy. It would, however, be wrong to extend the cloak of secrecy to cover and hide the lapses of those in power. The best safeguard for protection of legitimate official secrets is the credibility of those in power. Secrecy can be maintained, if credibility is preserved.

Excessive adulation amounting almost to deification of the individual in power is another danger, which we have to guard against, for inevitably it degenerates into a personality cult which, whatever its relevance in dictatorship, is the antithesis of democracy. Democracy postulates that the nation is greater than the party, and the party is greater than the individual. Excessive adulation of the individual paves the way to dictatorship and an authoritarian regime. We must beware of warning that no nation can be grateful at the cost of its honour in the same way as no man can be grateful at the cost of his honour, and no woman can be grateful at the cost of her chastity.

Democracy and liberty are twin sisters. In fact the trinity of democracy, liberty and the rule of law is the presiding deity of all liberal societies. Certain basic rights and civil liberties are an essential part of democracy. We have indeed enshrined them in Part III of the Constitution under the head

"Fundamental Rights". We legitimately take pride that our Constitution provides for them. It has, however, to be realised that rights postulate corresponding obligations. Awareness of obligations is the *sine qua non* of all progress.

Democracy makes some assumptions about the capacity of the people, and it presumes the presence of certain material and intellectual conditions favourable to the exercise of that capacity. Where large sections of the population have perpetually to think of the means of bare subsistence, they would not have much interest in political issues. For starving people, as also for people in dire poverty, discussion of general political issues and democratic values is often teasing dilettantism and a luxurious exercise. The danger of money power having sway in such an atmosphere and of polluting the purity of the electoral process is also immense. For the ultimate success, long life and durability of the democratic process, it is essential that the economic conditions of the people should be improved. Economic betterment of the bulk of the population, in the ultimate analysis, is the factor upon which the reality of democracy depends. A few cases of affluence and luxury in a vast desert of poverty and privation constitute dangerous irritants for the health and even survival of democracy. When a sense of class exploitation reaches deep into the masses of the population, democratic institutions are put to severe strain.

Democracy postulates adherence to the norms of democratic behaviour. Recent happenings in legislative chambers with rowdy scenes, physical assaults and even grossly indecent behaviour will not go with the democratic temper. Another disturbing feature is that individuals and their lapses and weaknesses, rather than policies, consume most of the time of the legislatures in India.

It has to be emphasised in this context that the nation has to spend a huge amount for every minute during which the legislature is in session. Disruptions of the legislative session, because of unparliamentary behaviour and conduct, result in an unnecessary drain and undue strain on the public exchequer. Still another disturbing feature is that the debating skill and reasoned arguments are at a discount, while lung practice, theatrical gimmicks and intemperate language are being increasingly looked upon as hallmarks of success.

Democracy also contemplates that the forum for testing whether the leader of the party in power enjoys the confidence and support of the majority of legislators should be the floor of the legislature itself. It would be wholly wrong for the constitutional head of the State, as has been done by some Governors, to usurp that function and make himself the arbiter in the matter. He can assume this role only in the contingency of the head of the government declining to test his majority support on the floor of the legislature at an early date. This apart, any attempt by the constitutional head to do so would be an unwarranted encroachment on the power and function of the legislature.

The State was also ordained by the Directive Principles to regard the raising of the level of nutrition and the standard of living of the people and the improvement of public health, as among its primary duties. The fact that in certain areas of the country the people have still to walk for miles together to procure drinking water, and that because of lack of proper nourishment and want of adequate medical facilities, we come across sunken cheeks and lusterless eyes is a sad reflection on that solemn pledge.

One of our failures lies in the insufficient attention paid to improving the living conditions of people in rural areas. As long as there is a big disparity in living standards of people in rural and urban areas, this exodus from rural to urban areas is bound to continue. Such an exodus can only be checked, if we provide gainful employment to people in rural areas throughout the year.

The Directive Principles enjoined upon the State a duty within the limits of its economic capacity and development to make effective provision for securing the right to work. As against that we find that there has been a sharp increase in the number of unemployed since the coming into force of the Constitution. The tragedy is that amongst those unemployed, we have a large number of engineers, technicians and others possessing technical qualifications.

It is also necessary to strike a note of caution against any tendency to allow ideological affinity for socialism being used as a masquerade for diversion of State funds to public sector undertaking yielding no profit and causing a financial drain. Large-scale nationalisation must justify itself in economic terms and the long-term interests of the public. By no means can it avoid the rigour of financial discipline and demands of accountability.

Needed Material

Newspaper means any material or document other than a book on which the words are written or printed. A paper printed daily or weekly. According to the Press and Registration of Books Act, 1867, newspaper means any printed periodical work containing public news or comments on public news. A newspaper is classified into three categories such as big newspaper, medium newspaper and small newspaper. According to explanation given for the purpose of clause (b) Section 5 of the Press Council Act, 1978, a newspaper shall be deemed to be:

(1) *Big newspaper,* if the total circulation of all its editions exceeds 50,000 copies for each issue;

(2) *Medium newspaper,* if the total circulation of all its editions exceeds 15,000 copies but does not exceed 50,000 copies for each issue;

(3) *Small newspaper,* if the total circulation of all its editions does not exceed 15,000 copies for each issue.

Newsletter : A newsletter is a publication in letter-size format usually issued periodically. It is a sheet containing news issued to members of a group or organisation.

For instance, a newsletter from the cricket association, the consumer association etc.

Editor : In the press the word editor is frequently used. The editor is a person who edits a newspaper. He prepares a manuscript or newspaper for publication. According to the Press and Registration of Books Act, 1867, the editor means the person who controls the selection of the matter published in a newspaper. Accordingly paper news, *i.e.,* any document including a newspaper other than a book. It further provided that book includes every volume, part or division of a volume and pamphlet in any language and every sheet of music, map, chart or plan separately printed.

Editorial : The matter or news in a newspaper written by an editor or belonging to editors. The editorial is a leading article in a newspaper. It consists of comment on the news, and opinion expressed by the news organisation.

Edition : Newspapers containing the same matter; printed during one press run. In other words, the number of copies of a newspaper printed at a time.

Publication : Publication means:

(a) in the case of a literary, dramatic, musical or artistic work, the issue of copies of the work to the public in sufficient quantities;

(b) in the case of a cinematograph film, the sale or hire or offer for sale or hire of the film or copies thereof to the public;

(c) in the case of a record, the issue of records to the public in sufficient quantities;

but does not, except as otherwise expressly provided in the Copyright Act, include:

(i) in the case of literary, dramatic or musical work, the issue of any records recording such work;

(ii) in the case of a work of sculpture or an architectural work of art, the issue of photographs and engravings of such work. (Section 3 of the Copyright Act, 1957).

Publication of Newspaper : Publication of newspapers should be strictly in accordance with the rules laid down for the purpose. Section 5 of the Press and Registration of Books Act, 1867, lays down rules concerning publication of newspapers. The relevant rules under this section as to publication of newspapers are as under :

(1) Without prejudice to the provisions of section 3, every copy of every such newspaper shall contain the names of the owner and editor thereof printed clearly on such copy and also the date of its publication.

(2) The printer and the publisher of every such newspaper shall appear in person or by agent authorised in this

behalf in accordance with rules made before a District, Presidency or Sub-Divisional Magistrate within whose local jurisdiction such newspaper shall be printed or published, and shall make and subscribe, in duplicate, the following declaration:

"I. A.B., declare that I am the printer (or publisher or printer and publisher) of the newspaper entitled... and to be printed or published, or to be printed and published, as the case may be at..."

And the last blank in this form of declaration shall be filled up with a true and precise account of the premises where the printing or publication is conducted.

(a) Every declaration under rule (2) shall specify the title of the newspaper, the language in which it is to be published and the periodicity of its publication and shall contain such other particulars as may be prescribed.

(b) Where the printer or publisher of a newspaper making a declaration under rule 2 is not the owner thereof, the declaration shall specify the name of the owner and shall also be accompanied by an authority in writing from the owner authorising such person to make and subscribe such declaration.

(c) A declaration in respect of a newspaper made under rule (2) and authenticated under section 6 shall be necessary before the newspaper can be published.

(d) Where the title of any newspaper or its language or the periodicity of its publication is changed, the declaration shall cease to have effect and a new declaration shall be necessary before the publication of the newspaper can be continued.

(e) As often as the ownership of a newspaper is changed, a new declaration shall be necessary.

(3) As often as the place of printing of publication is changed, a new declaration shall be necessary:

Provided that where the change is for a period not exceeding thirty days and the place of printing or publication after the change is within the local jurisdiction of the Magistrate referred to in rule (2), no new declaration shall be necessary if :

(a) a statement relating to the change is furnished to the said Magistrate within twenty-four hours thereof; and

(b) the printer or publisher or the printer and publisher of the newspaper continues to be the same.

(4) As often as the printer or the publisher who shall have made such declaration as is aforesaid shall leave India for a period exceeding ninety days or where such printer or publisher is by infirmity or otherwise rendered incapable of carrying out his duties for a period exceeding ninety days in circumstances not involving the vacation of his appointment, a new declaration shall be necessary.

(5) Every declaration made in respect of newspaper shall be void, where the newspaper does not commence publication:

(a) Within six weeks of the authentication of the declaration, in the case of a newspaper to be published once a week or oftener;

(b) Within three months of the authentication of the declaration, in the case of any other newspaper; and

(c) In every such case, a new declaration shall be necessary before the newspaper can be published.

(6) Where, in any period of three months, any daily, tri-weekly, biweekly, weekly or fortnightly newspaper publishes issues the number of which is less than half of what should have been published in accordance with the declaration made in respect thereof, the declaration shall cease to have effect and a new declaration shall be necessary before the publication of the newspaper can be continued.

(7) Where any other newspaper has ceased publication for a period exceeding twelve months, every declaration made in respect thereof shall cease to have effect, and a new declaration shall be necessary before the newspaper can be republished.

(8) Every existing declaration in respect of a newspaper shall be cancelled by the Magistrate before whom a new declaration is made and subscribed in respect of the same.

Provided that no person who does not ordinarily reside in India, or who has not attained majority in accordance with the provisions of the Indian Majority Act, 1875, or of the law to which he is subject in respect of the attainment of majority, shall be permitted to make the declaration prescribed by this section, nor shall any such person edit a newspaper.

Registrar and his Role

There is a Registrar of Newspapers for India called a Press Registrar. The Central Government appoints a Press Registrar under the Press and Registration of Books Act, 1867. Every publisher of every newspaper has :

(a) to furnish to the Press Registrar an annual statement in respect of the newspaper at such time and containing such prescribed particulars;

(b) to publish in the newspaper at such times and such of the particulars relating to the newspaper as may be specified by the Press Registrar.

The Press Registrar has right of access to any relevant record or a document relating to the newspaper in the possession of the publisher. He may also enter at any reasonable time, any premises where he believes such record or a document to be and may inspect or take copies of the relevant records or documents or ask any question necessary for obtaining any information required. The publisher of every newspaper has to furnish to the Press Registrar such returns, statistics and other information as the Press Registrar may from time to time require. The Press Registrar has in turn to prepare an annual report containing a summary of information obtained by him in respect of newspapers in India and giving an account of the working of such newspapers and copies should be forwarded to the Central Government. The Press Registrar is a public servant within the meaning of section 21 of the Indian Penal Code.

The Press Registrar maintains a separate register called the Register of Newspapers. It contains the following particulars about every newspaper published in India:

(a) the title of the newspaper;
(b) the language in which the newspaper is published;
(c) periodicity of the publication of the newspaper;
(d) the name of the editor, printer and publisher of the newspaper;
(e) the place of printing and publication;
(f) the average number of pages per week;
(g) the number of days of publication in the year;
(h) the average number of copies printed, the average number of copies sold to the public and the average number of copies distributed free to the public, the average being calculated with reference to such period as may be prescribed;
(i) retail selling price per copy;
(j) the names and addresses of the owners of the newspaper and such other particulars relating to ownership as may be prescribed;
(k) any other particulars which may be prescribed.

The State Government and the Central Government have power to make rules governing newspapers and the press. The rules made by the State Government should not be inconsistent with the rules made by the Central Government. Section 20 A of the Press and Registration of Books Act, 1867, gives power to the Central Government to make rules covering:

(a) Prescribing the particulars which a declaration made and subscribed may contain and the form and manner in which the names of the printer, publisher, owner and editor of a newspaper and the place of its printing and publication may be printed on every copy of such newspaper;

(b) prescribing the manner in which copies of any declaration attested by the official seal of a Magistrate or copies of any order refusing to authenticate any declaration may be forwarded to the person making and subscribing the declaration and to the Press Registrar;

(c) prescribing the manner in which copies of any newspaper may be sent to the Press Registrar;

(d) prescribing the manner in which a Register may be maintained and the particulars which it may contain;

(e) prescribing the particulars which an annual statement to be furnished by the publisher of a newspaper to the Press Registrar may contain;

(f) prescribing the form and manner in which an annual statement or any returns, statistics or other information may be furnished to the Press Registrar;

(g) prescribing the fees for furnishing copies extracts from the Registrar and the manner in which such copies may be furnished;

(h) prescribing the manner in which a certificate of registration may be issued in respect of a newspaper;

(i) prescribing the form in which, and the time within which, annual reports may be prepared by the Press Registrar and forwarded to the Central Government.

Every rule made under this section shall be laid as soon as may be after it is made before each House of Parliament while it is in session for a total period of thirty days which may be comprised in one session or in two or more successive sessions, and if, before the expiry of the session immediately following the session or the successive sessions aforesaid both Houses agree in making any modification in the rule or both Houses agree that the rule should not be made, the rule shall thereafter have effect only in such modified form or be of no effect, as the case may be; so, however, that any such modification or annulment shall be without prejudice to the validity of anything previously done under that rule.

The Press and Registration of Books Act, 1867 (Act 25 of 1867) has been enacted in India for the regulation of printing presses and newspapers for the preservation of office of books and newspapers printed in India and for the Registration of such books and newspapers. The press laws enquiry committee which was set up by the Government to enquire into the press laws made certain recommendations in 1948 for amending the Press and Registration of Books Act, 1867. Subsequently the Press and Registration of Books (Amendment) Bill 1952 was introduced in Parliament and the amending Act 55 of 1955 came into force and amending Act 26 of 1960.

National Responsibility

"A free press is responsible to its readers and to them alone. It cannot be either the slave or the lackey of Government."

"One of the best tests of professionalism is the ability to present objectively a story about someone or some event with which the writer or newspaper is in strong agreement."

No country can make law abridging the freedom of speech, or of the press.

(1) Bill of Rights derives what is to be perhaps the most basic ethical tenet of journalism. The press is independent of government.

(2) The Founding Fathers of the then infant Indian nation were suspicious of the tendency of Government, even

the best-intentioned government, to become tyrannical at times. Governments are composed of human beings, and human beings can and do commit wrongs. Thus the authors of our Constitution envisaged the press as a kind of social critic with a role apart and distinct from that of government.

Journalists are as patriotic as the next person in pursuing a national interest, and nothing in our bill of rights says that newspapers and government cannot cooperate on occasion. But the clear intent of the founder was that the press and government should not be in bed together. They are natural adversaries with different functions and each must respect the role of the other. Sometimes a free press can be a distinct annoyance and embarrassment to a particular government, but that is one of the prices of liberty. A free press is responsible to its readers and to them alone. It cannot be either the slave or the lackey of Government.

(3) Independence is at the heart of any statement of ethical principles respecting the conduct of the press. A newspaper's proprietor may choose to ally it with a particular political party or interest, but journals in our country are trying to be politically independent as well as independent of Government. This means not that they refrain from endorsing an individual party or candidate, but that they owe no prior allegiance and make the endorsement as an exercise of their independence. The decision is voluntary on the part of the proprietors and editors.

From this it follows that an independent press must cherish that role by resisting pressures of all kinds— from local as well as national governments, from special interest groups in the community, from powerful individuals, from advertisers. This is a noble standard that is sometimes more difficult to follow in a small, community than in a large one. It may be relatively easy for a large and well financed newspaper to risk the displeasure of a particular interest group or advertisers; but for a small paper, where the support of such an advertiser or interest has a direct bearing on management's ability to meet the payroll, it takes courage to resist pressure. Some papers exhibit more courage than others, but respect for the principles is one of the responsibilities the press owes its special constitutional role. Refusal to be intimated by any source ought to be a badge of the journalist's profession.

From this also follows the point that the newspaper and its staff should exemplify independence in their own actions. Not only should they be independent in fact, but, as the British Say of justice, they must be seen to be independent. A newspaper that rewards its friends with an unwarranted puff story of fawning editorials will not long be respected. A newspaper whose reporters also are on the payroll of a special interest or accept free trips or lavish gifts will find it hard to be convincing in its criticisms of corruption or other ethical practices in government.

Occasionally newspapers attempt to justify the acceptance of gifts or services. A conscientious reporter will hardly be corrupted, so the argument goes, by a free meal or ticket to a sports event or the theatre. Perhaps not, but appearances are important. Newspapers ought to pay their own way.

Admittedly, in small communities, journalists sometimes may encounter problems in maintaining a completely independent role. There are pressures to participate in volunteer services or in clubs and business associations or even in local government. Conflicts of interest may arise frequently. Journalists cannot expect to be monks walled apart from the community. But neither can they serve two masters with opposing interests. A conscientious editor or reporter will at least be aware of the conflicts and keep his professional responsibilities foremost in mind. Not surprisingly, the independent journalist may find himself in a lonely position with few or no close friends in the community where he works. Sometimes his best friends inevitably must be other journalists.

But that is one of the prices he must pay for the career and challenge he has chosen.

What special responsibilities does the press incur in return for the protected status its freedom enjoys ? None that is explicitly spelled out. A newspaper has the right to be captious or partisan or untruthful or bigoted or whatever else its conscience allows it to be. And, although newspapers are answerable to the laws of treason, sedition and libel, still within a very large compass they set their own responsibilities. The idea behind this is that from the clash of opinions and ideas presented by a free Press, ultimately something resembling truth emerges. "Though all the winds of doctrine were let loose to play upon the earth", wrote John Milton in his *Aeropagitica,* "so Truth be in the field, we do injuriously be licensing and prohibiting to misdoubt her strength. Let her and Falsehood grapple; who ever know Truth to the worse in a free and open encounter"?

That may be impressive as a philosophical doctrine, but you and I know that things do not always work that way in practice. Truth does not always emerge unless someone digs it out; and there is no single patented version of what constitutes truth. In a community where only one newspaper services — and this is increasingly the pattern in the United States — a reader may not encounter differing opinions unless the newspaper chooses to present them. Radio and television are not always an effective substitute.

But this is not such a calamity as it once would have seemed, for the reason that there is more and more sense of professionalism among our journalists. This means recognition of the importance of fair and balanced reporting in which opinions that may differ from those of the writer, or the newspaper, or a government official, are nevertheless accurately portrayed. In fact, one of the best tests of professionalism, is the ability to present objectively a story about someone or some event with which the writer or newspapers is in strong disagreement.

A good newspaper does not deliberately separate its own opinions from the objective presentation of facts. News stories and analysis are presented on the news pages, with the regions and sources identified wherever possible. The newspaper's own opinions are presented on the editorial page, which also may carry signed columns from syndicated writers or staff members of the newspaper itself.

Indian newspapers today are beginning to recognise the responsibility to open their letters' columns and opposite-editorial pages to views of every perception. Many newspapers receive far more letters than they can publish and, therefore, must choose what they regard as a fair representation; editing for libel, decency and germaneness. Some newspapers are the employee's ombudsmen, whose duty is to be a sort of public advocate in listening to complaints, offering remedies and appraising the performance of the paper. Most newspapers also recognise the responsibility to correct errors promptly, often in a box that appears in the same place in each issue.

Of course a newspaper may endorse the highest standards of ethical behaviour and still have its reputation sullied by the behaviour of its staff members. Arrogance and contempt for the rights of others are one of the surest ways to bring this about. Newspapers need to guard very carefully against undue intrusions on the privacy of persons about whom they are reporting. A photograph of a person jumping off a building or plunging into a fire may be dramatic, but editors ought to debate long and hard over whether they are violating someone's rights or dignity by publishing it. Does the publication serve a defensible purpose, one that will be understood by readers ? Or is it using an indignity to pander to curiosity ?

Reporters enjoy no special rights beyond those of other citizens. They must be forcible in pursuing facts. Indeed, one of the most important functions of a free press is to serve as a watchdog. But its staff members have no dispensation to be rude or discourteous. Television has many sins of its own, but one thing it purveys very quickly to viewers is whether reporters at a news conference are behaving arrogantly or with unnecessary brusqueness. Some, lamentably, seem to have become actors who view their function as making the news, not merely reporting it.

Apart from idiosyncratic behaviour, newspapers may also be affected by a phenomenon that I call "prizemanship"—the presentation of a story either on the part of the reporter or by a broader decision of newspaper management in a fashion calculated to win one of the prizes now offered to newspapers or individual journalists. A few years ago *The Washington Post* won a Pulitzer Prize for a story about an eight-year narcotics addict. Subsequent investigation by others led to an acknowledgement by the reporter, that she had made up the story in order to illustrate a situation. She resigned, and the newspaper returned the prize in embarrassment. I have no doubt that there are other similar fictional stories unidentified. Even if you don't invent "facts" it is relatively easy to present them in such a way as to make a dramatic impression upon prize judges.

Prizes are not bad, but the best ones are those that are conferred by the action of outsiders without the knowledge or participation of the individual journalist or newspaper. Conscientious journalists and newspapers must resist the temptation to display or doctor the story in such a way as to advance a purpose not directly related to the news.

There is one further precept in my own code of journalistic conduct—beyond independence, non-involvement, objectivity, fairness and willingness to correct errors. That is a recognition of our own fallibility. Journalists have no special mandate from God, and a little humility on our part is much in order. The truth sometimes has many sides. No one has a monopoly on it. Even in the dedicated pursuit of truth, error is frequent and innocent persons may suffer. A cardinal journalistic sin, in my view, is that journalists may tend to take themselves too seriously and have an inflated view of their own importance.

Therefore, I should like to see posted above the desk of every member of the press the advice Oliver Cromwell gave the General Assembly of the Church of Scotland in 1650 : "I beseech you, in the bowels of Christ, think it possible you may be mistaken."

The role of the Press in a democracy is that of a watchdog for the interests of the people. But if this powerful watchdog is not reasonably restrained or disciplined, it might run berserk to bite the people, whom it is supposed to serve. Barring occasional lapses, well-established newspapers in India have generally maintained standards of professional rectitude even in the face of coercive and corruptive influences. However, unfortunately, there is a section of the Press, known as Yellow Journalism, which frequently indulges in smut and slime games, smear campaigns, scurrilous, sensational, baseless and graceless writings.

The abuse of this Press freedom by a few delinquents tends to undermine the credibility and confidence of the Press, as a whole, in the public mind. The problem is how to curb or deal with this evil ? Should it be controlled from without, or by law through a governmental agency or other external mechanism with a plentitude of punitive powers, derived from a plethora of restrictive legislation ? It so, would not such external control involving excessive interference by the government or its agencies, in effect, negate the freedom itself ? Another factor which has to be taken into consideration is that the range and terrain of moral restrictions on the freedom of the Press are not always co-terminus with those prescribed by law.

Indeed, the range of ethics in its application to particular cases, is often wider than that of law. The observance of the professional ethics, therefore, is the subjective duty of the Press itself. In the performance of this ethical duty, it is imperative that the Press should be inspired by the consciousness that abuse of this freedom, even if not legally punishable, tarnishes the fair name of the Press, and, therefore, deserves to be censured by fellow journalists.

Views of Gandhi

The whole problem, with its parameters and a key to its solution was pithily put in a nutshell by Mahatma Gandhi—who was an eminent journalist in his own right—in these words: "The sole aim of journalism should be service. The newspaper Press is a great power, but just as unchained torrent of waste submerges the whole countryside and devastates crops, even so an uncontrolled pen serves but to destroy. If the control is from without, it proves more poisonous than want of control. It can be profitable only when exercised from within."

The first British Royal Commission on the Press (1949) also felt that the best way, consistent with the freedom of the press, or maintaining a proper relationship between the press and society, was self-regulation by the press itself. This is the basis of the concept of a Press Council.

The first Press Council or Court of Honour was set up in Sweden, in 1916. It is a voluntary body composed of the representatives of the press. There is also an Ombudsman of the press who is generally a professional judge. All complaints against the press are first screened by him, and if they are found worth inquiry, are forwarded to the Press Council for consideration. By 1980, there were 50 Press and Media Councils in the various countries of the world. A few of them, including the Press Councils of India, Italy and Turkey have been set up under statutes.

Council Act, 1965, was enacted, and under it, the first Press Council was set up in 1966. The Act was, however, repealed in 1975 during the Emergency, and the Press Council was abolished. The Act was re-enacted substantially on the same terms, in 1978, and the Press Council was re-established under it, in 1979. The Council is a body corporate having perpetual succession and a common seal and shall by the said name sue and be sued.

The twin objects of the Press Council of India are embodied in the Press Council Act, 1978. Section 13 of the Act of 1978 states that the objects of the Press Council are to preserve the freedom of the press and to maintain and improve the standards of newspapers and the news agencies in India.

(1) The Council shall consist of a chairman and twenty-eight other members.

(2) The Chairman shall be a person nominated by a Committee consisting of the Chairman of the Council of States (Rajya Sabha), the Speaker of the House of the People (Lok Sabha) and a person elected by the members of the Council under sub-section (6) and the nomination so made shall take effect from the date on which it is notified by the Central Government in the Official Gazette.

(3) Of the other members:

(a) Thirteen shall be nominated in accordance with such procedure as may be prescribed from among the working journalists, of whom six shall be editors of newspapers and the remaining seven shall be working journalists other than editors, so, however, that the number of such editors and working journalists other than editors in relation to newspapers published in Indian languages shall be not less than three and four respectively;

(b) six shall be nominated in accordance with such procedure as may be prescribed from among persons who own or carry on the business of management of newspapers, so, however, that there shall be two representatives from each of the categories of big newspapers, medium newspapers and small newspapers;

(c) one shall be nominated in accordance with such procedures as may be prescribed from among persons who manage news agencies;

(d) there shall be persons having special knowledge or practical experience in education and science, law, and literature and culture of whom respectively one shall be nominated by the University Grants Commission, one by the Bar Council of India and one by the Sahitya Academy;

(e) five shall be members of Parliament of whom three shall be nominated by the Speaker from among the members of the House of the People (Lok Sabha) and two shall be nominated by the Chairman of the Council of the States (Rajya Sabha) from among its members; Provided that no working journalist who owns, or carries on the business of management of any newspaper shall be eligible for nomination under clause (a); Provided further that the nominations under clause (a), and clause (b) shall be so made that among the persons nominated there is not more than one person interested in any newspaper or group of newspapers under the same control or management.

(4) Before making any nomination under clause (a), clause (b) or clause (c) of sub-section (3), the Central Government in the case of the first Council and the retiring Chairman of the previous Council in the case of any subsequent Council shall, in the prescribed manner, invite panels of names comprising twice the number of members to be nominated from such associations of persons of the categories referred to in the said clause (a), clause (b) or clause (c) as may be notified in this behalf by the Central Government in the case of the first Council and by the Council itself in the case of subsequent Councils;

Provided that where there is no association of persons of the category referred to in the said clause (c), the panels of name's shall be invited from such news agencies as may be notified as aforesaid.

(5) The Central Government shall notify the names of persons nominated as members under sub-section.

(a) In the Official Gazette and every such nomination shall take effect from the date on which it is notified.

(b) The members of the Council notified under sub-section (5) shall elect from among themselves in accordance with such procedure as may be prescribed, a person to be a member of the committee referred to in sub-section (2) and a meeting of the members of the Council for the purpose of such election shall be presided over by a person chosen from among themselves. (Section 5 of the Press Council Act 1978).

Term of Office

(1) Save as otherwise provided in this Section 6 the Chairman and other members shall hold office for a period of three years; Provided that the Chairman shall continue to hold such office until the Council is reconstituted in accordance with the provision of Section 5 or for a period of six months whichever is earlier.

(2) Where a person nominated as a member under clause (a), clause (b) or clause (c) of sub-section (3) of Section 5, is censured under the provisions of sub-section (1) of Section 14, he shall cease to be a member of the Council.

(3) The term of office of a member nominated under clause (e) of sub-section (3) of Section 5 shall come to an end as soon as he ceases to be a member of the House from which he was nominated.

(4) A member shall be deemed to have vacated his seat if he is absent without excuse, sufficient in the opinion of the Council, from three consecutive meetings of the Council.

(5) The Chairman may resign his office by giving notice in writing to the Central Government, and any other member may resign his office by giving notice in writing

to the Chairman, and upon such resignation being accepted by the Central Government, or as the case may be, the Chairman or the member shall be deemed to have vacated his office.

(6) Any vacancy arising under sub-section (2), sub-section (3), sub-section (4) or sub-section (5) or otherwise shall be filled, as soon as may be, nomination in the same manner in which the member vacating office was nominated and the member so nominated shall hold office for the remaining period in which the member in whose place he is nominated would have held office.

(7) A retiring member shall be eligible for re-nomination for not more than one term. (Section 6 of the Press Council Act, 1978).

The Council may, in furtherance of its objects, perform the following functions, namely:

(a) to help newspapers and news agencies to maintain their independence;

(b) to build up a code of conduct for newspapers, news agencies and journalists in accordance with high professional standards;

(c) to ensure on the part of newspapers, news agencies and journalists, the maintenance of high standards of public taste and foster a due sense of both the rights and responsibilities of citizenship;

(d) to encourage the growth of a sense of responsibility among all those engaged in the profession of journalism;

(e) to keep under review any development likely to restrict the supply and dissemination of news of public interest and importance;

(f) to keep under review cases of assistance received by any newspaper or news agency in India from any foreign source including such cases as are referred to it by the Central Government or are brought to its notice by any individual, association of persons or any other organisation;

Provided that nothing in this clause shall preclude the Central Government from dealing with any case of assistance received by a newspaper or news agency in India from any foreign source in any other manner it thinks fit;

(g) to undertake studies of foreign newspapers, including those brought out by any embassy or other representative in India of a foreign state, their circulation and impact.

Explanation—For the purposes of this clause, the expression "foreign State" has the meaning assigned to it in Section 87 A of the Code of Civil Procedure, 1908;

(h) to promote a proper functional relationship among all classes of persons engaged in the production or publication of newspapers or in news agencies;

Provided that nothing in this clause shall be deemed to confer on the council any functions in regard to dispute to which the Industrial Disputes Act, 1947, applies;

(i) to concern itself with developments such as concentration of or other aspects of ownership of newspaper and news agencies which may affect the independence of the press;

(j) to undertake such studies as may be entrusted to the Council and to express its opinion in regard to any matter referred to it by the Central Government;

(k) to do such other acts as may be incidental or conducive to the discharge of the above function.

This apart, the Act also confers an advisory role on the Council which can undertake studies and express its opinion in regard to any Bill, Legislation, Law or other matter touching the Press and convey its opinion to the Government or the persons concerned.

The Council is entitled to entertain and deal with complaints against the Press or by the Press. Ordinarily, it takes cognizance on a complaint filed by the person aggrieved. But it has authority to take cognizance *suo moto* also. The complaint is first processed by the Council's secretariat, and if the Chairman is of the opinion that a particular complaint does not disclose sufficient grounds for conducting an inquiry, the Council may not take cognizance of it.

If the Chairman finds that there are sufficient grounds for holding an inquiry, a show-cause notice is issued to the respondent—whether he be the editor or publisher of the newspaper, or the Government or its agency. If the subject matter of the complaint is sub judice in a court of law, the Council ceases to have jurisdiction to hold an inquiry into the matter.

The complaints, after initial processing by the Secretariat, are entrusted to either of the two Inquiry Committees of the Council. Representatives of the parties are also heard. Lawyers engaged by the parties are also allowed to act on behalf of their clients. The hearings before the Inquiry Committees and the Council are open to the public; the decisions are taken, after the public have withdrawn from the meeting room. The decisions of the Inquiry Committee are in the form of recommendations, which are not announced unless approved, with or without modification, by the Council. The decisions of the Council are published in its Quarterly Review and Annual Reports.

The Press Council of India is vested with certain powers of a Civil Court. Section 15 of the Press Council Act, 1978, gives the council the same powers throughout India as are vested in a Civil Court while trying a suit under the Code of Civil Procedure, 1908. The general powers of the Council under the section are:

(1) For the purpose of performing its functions or holding any enquiry under the Press Council Act, 1978, the council shall have the same powers throughout India as are vested in a Civil Court while trying a suit under the Code of Civil Procedure, 1908, in respect of the following matters, namely:

(a) summoning and enforcing the attendance of persons and examining them on oath;

(b) requiring the discovery and inspection of documents;

(c) receiving evidence on affidavits;

(d) requisitioning any public records or copies thereof from any court or office;

(e) issuing commissions for the examination of witnesses or documents; and

(f) any other matter, which may be prescribed.

(2) Nothing in sub-section (1) shall be deemed to compel any newspaper, news agency, editor or journalist to disclose the source of any news or information published by that newspaper or received or reported by that news agency, editor or journalist.

(3) Every inquiry held by the Council shall be deemed to be a judicial proceeding within the meaning of sections 193 and 228 of the Indian Penal Code.

(4) The Council may, if it considers it necessary for the purpose of carrying out its objects or for the performance of any of its functions under this Act make such observations, as it may think fit, in any of its decisions or reports, respecting the conduct of any authority, including Government.

The powers and procedure of the Press Council are exercisable not only in respect of enquiries against the newspapers as studied under the functions of the council but also in respect of enquiries held at the "instance of the newspapers against the Government or against any other person. AIR: 1975 Delhi 79(82); 1974 Rajdhani LR 632. The power to censure is given under section 14 of the Press Council Act, 1978. Accordingly:

(1) Where, on receipt of a complaint made to it or otherwise, the council has reason to believe that a newspaper or news agency has offended against the standards of journalistic ethics or public taste or that an editor or a working journalist has committed any professional misconduct, the Council may, after giving the newspaper, or news agency, the editor or journalist concerned an opportunity of being heard, hold an inquiry in such manner as may be prescribed by regulations made under the Press Council Act, 1978 and, if it is satisfied that it is necessary so to do, it may, for reasons to be recorded in writing, warn, admonish or censure the newspaper, the news agency, the editor or the journalist or disapprove the conduct of the editor or the journalist, as the case may be:

Provided that the council may not take cognizance of a complaint if, in the opinion of the chairman, there is no sufficient ground for holding an inquiry.

(2) If the council is of the opinion that it is necessary or expedient in the public interest so to do, it may require any newspaper to publish therein in such manner as the council thinks fit, any particulars, relating to any inquiry under this section against a newspaper or news agency, an editor or a journalist working therein, including the name of such newspaper, news agency, editor or journalist.

(3) Nothing in sub-section (1) shall be deemed to empower the council to hold an inquiry into any matter in respect of which any proceeding is pending in a court of law.

(4) The decision of the council under sub-section (1) or sub-section (2), as the case may be, shall be final and shall not be questioned in any court of law.

The council is empowered to make regulations, with the prior approval of the Central Government. The Regulations may be for:

(a) Regulating the meetings of the council or any committee and the procedure for conducting the business.

(b) Specifying the terms and conditions of services of the employees appointed by the council.

(c) Regulating the manner of holding any enquiry under the Press Council Act, 1978.

(d) Delegating to the Chairman or the Secretary of the Council any of its powers.

(e) Any other matter for which provision may be made by regulation.

The Central Government shall cause every regulation made under the Press Council Act to be laid, as soon as may be after it is made, before each House of Parliament, while it is in session, for a total period of thirty days which may be comprised in one session or in two or more successive sessions, and if, before the expiry of the session immediately following the session or successive sessions aforesaid, both Houses agree in making any modification in the regulation or both Houses agree that the regulation should not be made, the regulation shall thereafter have effect only in such modified form or be of no effect, as the case may be; so, however, that any modification or annulment shall be without prejudice to the validity of anything previously done under that regulation.

The Central Government is empowered to make rules to carry out the purposes of the council. The Government makes rules consulting the council. Section 25 of the Press Council Act, 1978, gives power to the Central Government in particular, and without prejudice to the generality of the foregoing powers, such rules may provide for all or any of the following matters, namely:

(a) the procedure for nomination of member of the council;

(b) the manner in which panels of names may be invited;

(c) the procedure for election of a member of the committee;

(d) the allowances or fees to be paid to the members of the council for attending the meetings of the council, and other conditions of services of such members;

(e) the appointment of the Secretary and other employees of the council;

(f) the matters referred to in clause (f) of under paragraph of Civil Court Powers referred to above;

(g) the rates at which fees may be levied by the council;

(h) the forms in which, and the time within which the budget and annual report are to be prepared by the council;

(i) the manner in which the accounts of the council are to be maintained and audited.

Every rule made under this section shall be laid, as soon as may be after it is made, before each House of Parliament, while it is in session, for a total period of thirty days which may be comprised in one session or in two or more successive sessions, and if, before the expiry of the session immediately following the session or the successive sessions aforesaid, both Houses agree in making any modification in the rule or both Houses agree that the rule should not be made, the rule shall thereafter have effect only in such modified form or be of no effect, as the case may be; so, however, that any such modification or annulment shall be without prejudice to the validity of anything previously done under that rule.

Code's Formulation

"The question, whether or not, the Council should formulate code of conduct for journalists, has repeatedly cropped up. But, on each occasion, successive Press Councils, after due consideration of the question and its implications have consistently taken the view that it is neither feasible nor desirable or necessary to formulate a comprehensive rigid code of this kind. Because of their elusive nature these moral principles cannot be imprisoned in the strait jacket of rigid definition or formulas; nor do these notions of right or wrong, good or bad prevailing in the society at large, remain immutable or statics for ever. Forces unleashed by rapid social and technological changes are having an inexorable impact on the tastes and attitudes of the people and their expectations from the Press. This makes the problem more complex. These ethical norms are not absolute. They have relativity not only to other dynamic social factors involving a multitude of imponderables but also to the subject-matter, the situation, the facts and the circumstances of each case. For all these reasons, the Indian Press Council Act advisedly leaves it to the Council to "build up" this ethical code over a period of time on case-by-case basis.

The precedents set by the Council through adjudications apart the Act affords great latitude to the Council to improve upon the standards of journalism, through innovation or by articulating general guidelines for this purpose even without reference to specific case pending before it. Such broad guidelines have been articulated by the Council with respect to certain matters including coverage of communication disputes by the Press.

International Principles : Ten International Principles of Professional Ethics in Journalism formulated by the International and Regional Organization of Professional Journalists are:

1. People's RIGHT TO TRUE INFORMATION
2. The journalist's DEDICATION TO OBJECTIVE AND REALITY
3. The journalist's SOCIAL RESPONSIBILITY
4. The journalist's PROFESSIONAL INTEGRITY
5. Public ACCESS AND PARTICIPATION
6. Respect of PRIVACY AND HUMAN DIGNITY

7. Respect for PUBLIC INTEREST
8. Respect of UNIVERSAL VALUES AND DIVERSITY OF CULTURES
9. Elimination of WAR and other great EVILS CONFRONTING HUMANITY
10. Promotion of a NEW WORLD INFORMATION AND COMMUNICATION ORDER

Adaptation in relation to a literary work means any abridgement of the work. Adaptation under the Copyright Act, 1957 means:

(i) in relation to a dramatic work, the conversion of the work into a non-dramatic work;

(ii) in relation to a literary work or an artistic work, the conversion of the work into a dramatic work by way of performance in public or otherwise;

(iii) in relation to a literary or dramatic work; any abridgement of the work or any version of the work in which the story or action is conveyed, wholly or mainly by means of pictures in a form suitable for reproduction in a book, or in a newspaper, magazine or similar periodical; and

(iv) in relation to a musical work, any arrangement or transcription of the work. (Section 2 of the Copyright Act, 1957).

Meaning of Copyright : For the purpose of the Copyright Act, 1957, copyright means the exclusive right, by virtue of and subject to the provisions:

(a) in the case of a literary, dramatic or musical work, to do and authorise the doing of any of the following acts, namely:

  (i) to reproduce the work in any material form;

  (ii) to publish the work;

  (iii) to perform the work in public;

(iv) to produce, reproduce, perform or publish any translation of the work;

(v) to make any cinematograph film or a record in respect of the work;

(vi) to communicate the work by radio-diffusion or to communicate to the public by a loudspeaker or any other similar instrument the radio diffusion of the work;

(vii) to make any adaptation of the work;

(viii) to do in relation to a translation or an adaptation of the work any of the acts specified in relation to the work in clauses (i) to (vi);

(b) in the case of an artistic work, to do or authorise the doing of any of the following acts, namely:

(i) to reproduce the work in any material form;

(ii) to publish the work;

(iii) to include the work in any cinematograph film;

(iv) to make any adaptation of the work;

(v) to do in relation to an adaptation of the work any of the acts specified in relation to the work in clauses (i) to (iii);

(c) in the case of a cinematograph film, to do or authorise the doing of any of the following acts, namely:

(i) to make a copy of the film;

(ii) to cause the film, in so far as it consists of visual images, to be seen in public and, in so far as it consists of sounds, to be heard in public;

(iii) to make any record embodying the recording in any part of the sound track associated with the film by utilising such sound track:

(iv) to communicate the film by radio-diffusion;

(d) in the case of a record, to do or authorise the doing of any of the following acts by utilising the record, namely:

(i) to make any other record embodying the same recording;

(ii) to cause the recording embodied in the record to be heard in public;

(iii) to communicate the recording embodied in the record by radio-diffusion.

Any reference in subsection (1) to the doing of any act in relation to work for a translation or an adaptation thereof shall include a reference to the doing of that act in relation to a substantial part thereof. (Section 14 of the Copyright Act, 1957).

Period of Copyright

Copyright shall subsist in any literary, dramatic, musical or artistic work other than a photograph published within the life time of the author until 50 years from the beginning of the calendar year next following the year in which the author dies. (Section 22).

A copyright shall subsist until 50 years from the beginning of the calendar year next following the year in which the work is published in the case of literary, dramatic, musical or artistic work other than a photograph. (Section 23).

Term of copyright in case of posthumous work is also fixed. Copyright exists in the case of literary, dramatic or musical work or an engraving in which copyright subsist at the date of the death of the author or in the case of any such work of joint authorship are immediately before the date of the death of the author who dies last, but which or any adaptation of which has not been published before that date. In these cases copyright shall subsist until 50 years from the beginning of the calendar next following the year in which the work is first published or where an adaptation of the work is published in any earlier year. (Section 24).

The term of copyright in photographs shall subsist until 50 years from the beginning of the calendar year next following the year in which the photograph is published. (Section 25).

The period for which copyright shall subsist in the case of cinematograph films until 50 years from the beginning of calendar year next following the year in which the film is published. (Section 26).

Copyright shall subsist in the case of a record for a period of 50 years from the beginning of the calendar year next following the year in which the record is published. (Section 27).

Where Government is the first owner of the copyright, copyright Shall subsist until 50 years from the beginning of the calendar year next following the year in which the work is first published. (Section 28).

Copyright shall subsist in the case of a work of an international organisation until 50 years from the beginning of the calendar year next following the year in which the work is first published. (Section 29).

Chapter XIII of the Copyright Act describes various offences and penalties. Sections 63-70 of the Act provide for offences. The following are the various offences :

> Infringement of copyright or other rights conferred by the Copyright Act is an offence. It shall be punishable with imprisonment which may extend to one year or with fine or with both. Any person who knowingly infringes or abets the infringement of:

(a) The copyright in a work; or

(b) Any other right conferred by the Act. (Section 63)

The police is empowered to seize infringing copies. Where a Magistrate takes cognizance of any offence of infringement of copyright in any work, it shall be lawful for any police officer not below the rank of sub-inspector to seize all copies wherever found without any warrant from the Magistrate. All the copies so seized shall be produced before Magistrate. If any person having an interest in any copies of a work seized may make an application to the Magistrate within fifteen days of such seizure for such copies to restore him. The Magistrate after hearing the applicant and the complainant and after making such further inquiry he may make such order as he deems fit. (Section 64).

The Act also imposes penalty by way of punishment with imprisonment which may extend to one year or with fine or with both. The offence attracts penalty if any person who knowingly makes or has in his possession any plate for the purpose of making infringing copies of any work in which copyright subsists. (Section 65).

There is a provision for disposal of infringing copies or plates for the purpose of making infringing copies. The court may order that all copies of work or all plates in the possession of the offender to be delivered up to the owner of the copyright. This is whether the alleged offender is convicted or not. (Section 66).

An offence of making false entries in the register or producing or rendering false entries attracts penalty. The offender shall be punishable with imprisonment which may extend to one year or with fine or with both, if any person who :

(a) makes or causes to be made a false entry in the Register of Copyrights kept under this Act; or

(b) makes or causes to be made a writing falsely purporting to be a copy of any entry in such register; or

(c) produces or tenders or causes to be produced or tendered as evidence any such entry or writing knowing the same to be false. (Section 67).

The Act imposes a penalty for making false statements for the purpose of deceiving or influencing any authority or officer. Any person who :

(a) with a view to deceiving any authority or officer in the execution of the provisions of the Act; or

(b) with a view to procuring or influencing the doing or omission of anything in relation to the Act, 1957, or any matter thereunder, makes a false statement or representation knowing the same to be false shall be punishable with imprisonment which may extend to one year or with fine or with both. (Section 68).

Where an offence has been committed by a company every person who is incharge and responsible to the company for the conduct of the business the person and the company shall be deemed to be guilty of such offence. He is not liable if he proves that the offence was committed without his knowledge or he exercised due diligence to prevent the commission of such offence. Where it is proved that the offence was committed with the consent or connivance or is attributable to any negligence on the part of any director, manager, secretary or other officer of the company, they shall be deemed to be guilty of that offence and shall be liable to be proceeded and punished. (Section 69).

Only Presidency Magistrate or a Magistrate of the first class shall try any offence under the Copyright Act, 1957. (Section 70).

A separate chapter is provided for appeals. Sections 71-73 of the Act deals with appeals against orders and procedure. Section 71 permits appeal against certain orders of the Magistrate under Sub-section (2) of Section 64 or Section 66. Sub-section (2) of Section 64 deals with the order of the Magistrate regarding against the application for infringing copies to be restored to him. Section 66 deals about disposal of infringing copies or plates for the purpose of making infringing copies. Under these sections any person aggrieved by the order may go on appeal within thirty days of the order. The appellate court may direct the execution of the order be stayed pending disposal of the appeal. (Section 71).

Section 72 deals with appeals against the orders of the Registrar of Copyrights and the Copyright Board. The aggrieved person may go on appeal to the Copyright Board against the final decision or order of the Registrar of the Copyrights within three months from the date of the order. Similarly, any aggrieved person may go on appeal to the High Court against the final decision or order of the Copyright Board within three months.

There shall be no appeal against a decision of the Copyright Board in respect of certain disputes to be decided by the Copyright Board alone. The High Court makes rules as to the procedure to be followed in respect of appeals.

Infringing Copy

(i) in relation to a literary, dramatic, musical or artistic work, a reproduction thereof otherwise than in the form of a cinematograph film;

(ii) in relation to a cinematograph film a copy of the film or a record embodying the recording in any part of the sound track associated with the film;

(iii) in relation to record, any such record embodying the same recording: and

(iv) in relation to a programme in which a broadcast reproduction right subsists, a record recording the programme, if such reproduction, copy or record is made or imprinted in contravention of the provisions of this Act. [Section 2(m) of the Copyright Act, 1957].

The following are the circumstances as to when copyright in a work shall be deemed to be infringed:

(a) When any person, without a licence granted by the owner of the copyright or the Registrar of Copyrights under the Copyright Act or in contravention of the conditions of a licence so granted or of any condition imposed by a competent authority under the Copyright Act :

(i) does anything, the exclusive right to do which is

by this Act conferred upon the owner of the copy right or

(ii) permits for profit any place to be used for the performance of the work in public where such performance constitutes an infringement of the copyright in the work unless he was not aware and has no reasonable ground for believing that such performance would be in infringement of copyright, or

(b) When any person :

(i) makes for sale or hire, or sells or lets for hire, or by way of trade displays or offers for sale or hire, or

(ii) distributes either for the purpose of trade or to such an extent as to affect prejudicially the owner of the copyright, or

(iii) by way of trade exhibits in public, or

(iv) imports (except for the private and domestic use of the importer) into India.

any infringing copies of the work.

Explanation : For the purposes of this section, the reproduction of a literary, dramatic, musical or artistic work in the form of a cinematograph film shall be deemed to be an "infringing copy".

Broadcast reproduction right

(1) Where any programme is broadcast by radio diffusion by the Government or any other broadcasting authority, a special right to be known as "broadcast reproduction right" shall subsist in such programme.

(2) The Government or other broadcasting authority as the case may be shall be the owner of the broadcast reproduction right and such right shall subsist until twenty-five years from the beginning of the calendar

year next following the year in which the programme is first broadcast.

(3) During the continuance of a broadcast reproduction right in relation to any programme, any person who,

(a) without the licence of the owner of the right:

(i) rebroadcasts the programme in question or any substantial part thereof; or

(ii) cause the programme in question or any substantial part thereof to

be heard in public; or

(b) without the licence of the owner of the right to utilise the broadcast for the purpose of making a record recording the programme in question or any substantial part thereof, makes any such record, shall be deemed to infringe that broadcast reproduction right.

7

International Scene

There is now an enormous amount of communication about communication-a literature which relates *inter alia* to cybernetics, neurology, linguistics, psychology, social anthropology, physics, group dynamics, semantics and the sociology of culture. We must also add library studies and documentation. The librarian is indirectly concerned with communication because his collections of material need to be organised for use, and until they are so organised an important agency in the communication process breaks down. The information role of the librarian involves him in the world of communications, and that is why students should study methods and types of communication. What follows is an outline of some communication problems, but I have been particularly concerned to make clear that the sphere of information is a limited one, whereas communication is basic to our culture in a different and more fundamental sense.

Global Perspective

The ability to communicate is a key element in culture, and most living things have developed rudimentary methods of communication which include sound as well as visual display. The communications of animals include cries, gestures and thumps which express simple responses to stimuli such as the mating call, or the alarm signal, or the warning display. The purpose has apparently gone beyond this stage of development and uses a language which linguists are trying to decipher. Claims are even made for the domestic fowl, which according to one authority, possesses an international 'language' made up of thirty basic sentences. The social insects such as the ants have communications systems, and the bees do their 'dance' to indicate the locations of a new source of nectar.

But non-human creatures have not evolved a formal language in the true sense, and it is this which in this context distinguishes them from humanity- In the beginning was the word. Apes possess several characteristics which are necessary for culture, such as the ability to walk and to use thumbs and vocal cords. In addition, their children mature slowly and they share with man the dubious blessing of a continuous sex urge. Indeed, sexual activity may well be the most basic of all forms of communication. The vast literature of sex probably owes its origins to the fact that sex relations represent an attempt at total communication, and an escape from isolation. Further more, sexual union exhibits one important characteristic of true communication insofar as it is, or should be, a two way process: to use the current jargon, feed-back occurs.

Hence the only valid objection to solitary masturbation as a practice is presumably that it excludes communication with others. McLuhan's otherwise dubious dictum that the medium is the massage is perhaps most applicable in this sphere. But to return to the animals, they cannot be said to possess true culture because they cannot symbolise, and the essence of human culture is accumulation-the retention and passing on of cultural manifestations from one generation to another. The extraordinary cries of birds, for example, can be recorded and even preserved in libraries, but this, of course, is for our benefit, not theirs.

Differnet Sources

It is established, then, that when homosapiens uttered his first words human culture really began, just as the child enters the cultural heritage when it begins to speak. But the original ,cause of spoken language is not known. Conflicting theories have been advanced and they are commonly and seriously known by fanciful names. The 'bow-wow' theory claims that men learnt speech by imitating animal cries. The 'Pooh-Pooh' adherents believe that language developed as a result of involuntary noises provoked by violent stimuli, in contrast to the 'ding dong' people who propose that men must have imitated all kinds of noises in an onomatopoeic fashion. The 'yo-ho-ho' explanation is that men acquired speech to assist in cooperative labour, just as songs are used in the same manner today. Finally, other linguists have suggested that the first words were used to accompany gestures which must have long preceded speech.

Whatever the origins, we know that the languages of the world can be classified into families which were produced by the wandering of tribes and peoples. The resultant babble of tongues is one of the most obvious barriers to communication, when our earliest fore-fathers built the city and the tower of Babel, the people had one language and were therefore building a true community wherein 'nothing will be restrained from them which they have imagined to do'. But in developing their isolated city culture they were neglecting their global responsibilities as laid down, which required that they should be scattered abroad upon the face of all the earth. Accordingly, the Lord said "Go to, let us go down and there confound their language that they may not understand one another's speech." So the Lord scattered them abroad.

That was long ago, yet we are still confounded and are likely to remain so. The proposals for an international language (such as Esperanto) ignore cultural realities, particularly the fact that languages are not artificial creations but reflections of a way of life in time and place. The foreign language barrier is, of course, a great obstacle to all forms of international communication, and is felt so particularly in the field of scientific research where speed of communication is important.

There is in consequence a bibilographical problem with which we are not concerned here. What is more-relevant to our theme is the fact that obvious foreign language barriers may be less dangerous than the other divisive elements in culture mentioned elsewhere. In most countries people officially speak to write the same language as each other, but the use of language may vary so much that communication fails. Groups in one country often have more in common with groups in another country than with their own compatriots, in spite of the language complications.

After the invention of language the next step was the development of the ability to produce pictures to correspond with a thing described in words. Those symbols which literally represented things pictorially are called pictograms, whereas what is called ideogrammatic writing used symbols which indicate by association. The ancient Egyptian hieroglyphic contained both forms, and the Chinese language to this day is based on the dual principle. Such methods of writing have the advantage that they are 'international', in the sense that algebra or chemical formulae or musical scores are, but the corresponding disadvantage is that there is no link with words.

It is an entirely visual medium-and those who used it had to learn two 'languages' which were not at all related. Modern scholars can decipher early pictorial languages, but they do not knew what they sounded like when 'read' aloud. If visual communication had remained pictorial, written languages would have remained separate from spoken languages and the latter would have succumbed to a proliferation of dialect and jargon. That is what happened in China.

The Egyptians hieroglyphics included some signs which represented sounds, but they did not develop a phonetic linear alphabet. This was the achievement of the Phoenicians, who produced a practical alphabet, the main limitation of which was that it contained no vowels. Modern sematic languages such as Hebrew also have this characteristic. The final development-that of providing vowels-was carried out by the 'Greeks, and the alphabet had by that time become substantially what it is now. Usage in the Western world was fixed by the Romans, who wrote horizontally from left to right in descending lines and used the letters which we still use.

Update Technology

The fourth stage in the evolution of media was the invention in the fifteenth century of printing from movable type. It has remained the main medium of visual communication for the last 500 years. Its significance is too well known to warrant description. It is because of printing that the repository role of the library became so important, since libraries were able thus to accumulate culture. The role of the librarian is to make communication possible. In our time the mass media of communication are to some extent modifying the role of print.

So far we have been discussing what is mainly rational communication involving the conscious levels of the mind. There remain those regions where people communicate by means which involve other faculties and other types of perception. Some of these are still a matter for conjecture and dispute, so that I shall omit telepathic communication or psychic phenomena such as messages from beyond the grave or from supernatural beings.

In any event, these are not normally considered to be part of a librarian's responsibility. It is however impossible to ignore the fact that, even though language or print may be used, messages are sometimes conveyed by indirect means, often in order to try to express the inexpressible. Thus the literary artist will use words to reflect a multiplicity of human experiences which has many levels and many meanings. This incorporates both the aesthetic sphere and the technique of suggestion used by the advertiser and the propagandist.

Social Problems Ahead

Pre-literate communications were oral, and when human memory is the cultural connecting link we invariably find it impossible to distinguish between history and legend. Indeed history without written records it myth (unless it can be substantiated by precise archaeological research); who knows whether King Arthur ever did ride to Camelot? Having noted this it should be added that many myths have been explained in other ways without reference to history; they have been variously described as parables, allegories and early scientific theories.

Fraud, basing his theory on the remarkable similarity of content in the myths and folk tales of the world, and on his analysis of individuals, claimed that myths are thinly disguised representations of unconscious fantasies common to all mankind, Lung carried this theory further with his concept of the collective or racial unconscious, which lies below the personal unconscious, and beyond this yet again the deepest levels common to all humanity. For him the collective unconscious is the deposit of ancestral experience for millions of years, and he calls certain themes which recur in dreams and in mythology 'archetypes'.

The postulation of a collective unconscious seems to suggest that certain 'ideas' may be inherited, and it is not one which scientists will normally accept, but Lung's work has been influential and much of his terminology has passed into our culture.

The Preacher, then, apparently overstated his case when he asserted that 'There is no remembrance of the former generations, neither shall there be any remembrance of the latter generations that are to come, among those that shall come after'. But his words serve to remind us that those, who invented the alphabet also invented Time, which eventually became fully mechanised with the arrival of printing and with the invention of the clock. When this happened the old organic cycle of generation, birth, development and death lost its full meaning. Non -literate cultures do not have this impatient sense of time as duration.

As soon as we consider language as a medium of communication it becomes apparent that language and reality are not the same thing. Language is not a mirror of experience, not even a destroying mirror, because it exists in its own right, and interacts with other social realities. A word is in fact a thing-in addition to being a symbol of some other thing. As Jesse Shera says (in Documentation, p. 66) 'We do not know the effect of the symbolic structure that is language upon the behaviour patterns of society'.

We do know, however, that language can be used consciously or unconsciously to conceal objective truth. This is obvious enough in the case of detectable untruths, and psychoanalysis has made us all familiar with the processes of rationalisation by which individuals deceive others and, make particularly, themselves. If people are unable to communicate with one another, it emerges at once that language (or the thinking based upon it) serves many other purposes than external communication, and many of these purposes are either evil or supersitions.

The word itself, as Ogden and Richards emphasised in 'The meaning of meaning, may gather round itself occult powers and the aura of taboos.' There have been many deities whose names are held to be unmentionable, and so on. As a thing the word is inevitably a conservative force, and produces a kind of cultural lags, because it reflects (insofar as it reflects at all) a reality which no longer exists. In a time-of rapid change, such as the present, this is one reason why the middle aged (*i.e.*, anyone over thirty) cannot understand the young-and why the young try to invent a new language.

It follows, therefore, that words are not labels but social tools, whose use and meaning depend on conventions which differ according to the class and group affiliations of individuals.

If this relates to education at all it only does so insofar as the education structure may reflect (or modify) diverse social backgrounds. In fragmented societies there are various partially separate groups or subcultures who use language in a way which may not be comprehensible to other groups. For complete understanding, a community of experience and thought is required, and when this is absent we state literally that people 'are not speaking the same language', even though their vocabularies may be identical.

It is the understanding which is lacking, and this is nothing to do with language as such. This is commonly appreciated with regard to conversation: many people, particularly those past middle age, either do not talk at all, or else rarely finish their sentences, because they have lost faith in language as a means of communication.

The other groups have gone beyond the pale-and one group, or one individual (the 'outsider') or one class becomes culturally alienated. This overworked term (alienated) expresses a variety of meanings, but the common factor in all of them is a psychological condition produced by social isolation. Where no real community exists there can be (by definition) no communication, and alienation is therefore very relevant to communication problems.

The concept of cultural alienation as originally used by Marx, and before him by Hegel, Schiller and other German philosophical idealists, is worth a further note, since it is a part of Marxism which has become relevant at the present time and one which has brought about an attempt by some European Christian thinkers to continue a 'dialogue' with Marxism. According to Marx, man has become self-estranged, or dehumanised, or alienated, because what he produces becomes objectified-turned into a 'thing' or 'reified' as something separate from him which he can no longer control. Marx, at least in his early work, blamed Christianity for this process, because of its 'other worldly' nature and because of the emphasis on the individual which meant that collective social life was ignored. But ultimately and more particularly in his later work he regarded alienation as fundamentally economic in nature, "So that it could only be healed by political revolution.

These ideas have been developed and modified in Sartre's influential Critique of dialectical reason, 1960, and, like many American writers also, Sartre automatically supports the 'anti-social' alienated individual (such as Genet), which the English tradition, as exemplified in Leavis, does not Raymond Williams, for example, has always stressed social values and his belief that alienation need not occur even now, and will be overcome in a return to a true socialist community.

It will be seen that the term 'alienation' as commonly used at present means something much less precise than this, and may simply refer to cultural or social fragmentation which results in separate sub-cultures, such as those of the teenagers, or the black Americans, or the very-poor-or, in another sense, that of the intellectuals.

The use of language, then, rests on assumptions which are shared these are present in all of the members of a particular group. Since everyone belongs to some types of in-group, how can the influence of closed groups be modified or destroyed? Aranguren, in Human communication, p 140, suggests that this is the special social function of the intellectual: 'A intellectual is someone who is capable either of emerging from the social group to which he belongs or else of criticising it from within', This is way intellectuals are usually only partially integrated in society. At a further extreme, this is why, in Aldous Huxley's words in Literature and science, p 13. The elements of experience which are unique, aberrant, other than average remain outside the pale of common language.

It remains to note that in open or pluralistic, societies these groups are partly an abstraction, since individuals may belong to several different ones. But the result in cultural terms is the same, and from the point of view of the individual, conflicts between groups will naturally be reflected in his mind-which is not necessarily a bad thing, since it helps to ensure social progress.

Scientific Development : Meredith, in Instruments of communication, stresses the social elements in scientific information work: 'Social communication among scientists is an essential condition of their work'. He claims further that because of the limitations of the printed word, it is more important in science to talk to people than to read books. Noting the traditional classical concept of oratorical argument where, because uncertainty prevails, emotive techniques can be used, he points out that there are not only depths of emotion which traditional rhetoric recognised, but also depths understanding which it failed to distinguish.

It follows that communication problems are rooted in social and technical changes which go far beyond the realm of language studies. From the more narrow point of view of librarianship, the implications have been recognised by many of those engaged in the retrieval of scientific information. A number of investigations have indicated that scientists use information retrieval systems and library information service far less than might be expected, and that social factors are largely responsible.

There are, therefore, or there should be, as many types of spoken and written language as there are types of readers, and bad writing is simply that which is inappropriate for its purpose, and which fails in the full sharing of understanding. When one considers that the most effective means of communication in modern physics, for example, is often the use of mathematical symbols alone, but that the results of its researches must also be presented to the understanding of the layman; the extent of the problem becomes apparent. Kapp, in 'The presentation of technical information' has indicated the main difference between functional and other kinds of writing, by noting that a good functional style maintains receptivity in the reader: it should not be 'creative', since receptivity cannot be stored. But as far as scientific research or discovery is concerned, there is obviously a 'creative' element, which means that scientific activity is by no means as wholly objective as sometimes alleged.

The creative aspect in science includes subjective insights, and in consequence there are often accidental features in research and discovery. The information scientists have also had to recognise this element, hence the increasing attention which has been paid to 'serendipity', or random selection.

Apart from these factors, language in itself often fails as an instrument of communication because of the rapidity of change. There is in fact a language crisis now, because the old association been words and the things they represent becomes impossible. The older use of language was much more rhetorical, in the sense of the word used above: this rhetoric may now hinder contact with 'reality', which, at least as far as the material world is concerned, is increasingly scientific.

Within the field of linguistics itself, a number of authorities have studied the fact that our thinking is determined by the structure of particular languages. This work has been particularly associated with the theories of B L Whorf, who, in Language, thought and reality, claims that language actually organises reality. According to Whorf, the world is presented in a kaleidoscope flux of impressions which has to be mentally organised-and this is done not by classification systems, but largely by the linguistic structures in our minds. The pattern of our language imposes an obligatory codification.

The Dark Phase : Increasing concern has been expressed in many quarters that an outstanding defect in modern cultures is a failure in communication. The proliferating literature on communication studies exhibits the same use of specialists' jargon, incomprehensible to the layman, which characterizes other specialist topics: the communicators are talking to themselves. Seligman's Encyclopedia of the social sciences defines communication as a 'network of partial or complete understandings' one might equally well substitute the word 'misunderstandings'. What follow is a discussion of some of the possible reasons for this relative failure.

Information Network : The increase in the quantity of information (and the speed with which it appears) is the factor which most librarians think of which considering how to control the flood of publications by bibliographical and library means. The first problem is to ensure that relevant information gets to users at the right time. As is indicated in my book 'Bibliography and the provision of books,' these matters are fundamental to library and bibliographic organisation. The same figures are constantly repeated for the quantity of publications, with particular reference to science and its exponential rate of growth. One authority (Professor Price of Yale University) has pointed out there if the present rate continues, there will soon be more scientists than people; another has calculated that there are more scientists alive today than in the sum total of the past.

The answers to the explosion lie in the field of social and bibliographic organisation. Yet even if solutions on this level were to be found, there is no evidence that real communication would be achieved. The fact that information is emitted or disseminated, and even received, is no guarantee that communication occurs. The transmission in itself has no meaning, and the information has to be deciphered and interpreted, and as a result it is frequently not understood. There are, in fact, more fundamental barriers to communication, some of which we have already noted in relation to language.

Within the field of information flow as a social process it is evident that a modern society requires a far-ranging network of communications in order to function at all. It is only to be expected, therefore, that information often fails to circulate. The apparatus of the welfare state, for example, is so complex that many citizens (particularly those who need the services most) are not aware what actual benefits they might receive.

State agencies, and all organisations within the state, organise information services, and this is an essential element in management technique. As a social process the free flow of information is wholly dependent on the existence of free democratic (*i.e.*, politically unrestricted) institutions at all levels, and on the absence of censorship or authoritarian suppressions.

It is possible to have a free flow of some types of information within particular organisations and still not have a free society, because there is some overall control. The growth in size of modern organisations, particularly those engaged in scientific research, may also produce, and indeed is producing, a situation where individuals work on a specialised job without knowing for what purpose their particular operation is intended, or what the complete venture is. This is a further example of the dehumanisation which can occur. It follows that a man may be working, could be working on some totally anti-human form of research without even being aware of the fact.

One response to this and similar problems is the current demand for 'participation' in all forms of social, political and economic life. This amounts to a claim that information itself is not enough and a consideration of it would take us beyond information as such, and into politics.

It was suggested above that the use of language is often inadequate because it no longer describes reality. This seems to be part of a trend which has many facets. In Kafka's nightmares, the main protagonists never discover what is happening or why. The 'theatre of the absurd' is truly absurd on one level at least, because nobody can communicate at all, and Becket's clowns and tramps are primarily studies in the manners of non communication. The key factor in modern developed society, as Herbert Marcuse constantly proclaims, is that social structures seem to be wholly rational but rebellious individuals instinctively feel that this rationality does not satisfy human needs. As Daniel Bell states in Technology and social change, edited by Eli Ginzberg, p 59, 'The whole breakdown of the rational cosmology is imminent and will ultimately create the most serious problems for society because of an alienation of the modes of perception about the world'. Society is unable to find cultural terms for expressing what is happening-and twentieth country thought lacks confidence in the rational solution of social and cultural problems.

The implication can only be that the 'rational solutions' are inadequate. Many radical critics would dispose of the matter in the traditional Marxist manner by pointing out that capitalist ideology inevitably obscures the real nature of society. (It should not be forgotten that the word 'ideology' means, or originally meant, a system of beliefs which does not explain, but explains away reality, just as rationalisation obscures reality for the individual.) If this is the case, as it certainly is in the USA, it is probably true in the USSR also, where the official ideology corresponds even less with life as it is experienced-and furthermore any attempts to modify radically this discrepancy cannot appear above ground.

There is therefore a blockage in the communication of ideas. Traditional political or religious faiths provided an analysis of social reality which *inter alia* explained how society (and the universe) was believed to work. At one time the Christians, and the Marxists, explained everything to the satisfaction of millions of adherents. Up to the end of the country even the scientists provided answers whose implications could be understood by everybody.

The gods have failed now because their analysis is irrelevant, and in consequence their panaceas do not help. As McLuhan has claimed, the overworked concept that God is dead really refers to the Newtonian universe that has passed away, and the ground rule upon which so much of the Western World is built is dissolved. Because of this we cannot control events, and 'nobody knows what is happening.' (Harrington deals with this at length and that is why he calls his book on our times the accidental century.) In many spheres where ideas are important, few people have anything valid to say, and for this and other reasons we stop listening to the message and there is a widespread growth of disbelief, scepticism and negative criticism but leaders seem to be more in the dark than anybody else, illustrating in a new guise Acton's dictum that power corrupts. A Bob Dylan has it, 'Something is happening but you don't know what it is-do you Mr. Jones?'

It is most noticeable in the case of the revolting young that they tend to use terminology-for example anti-capitalist slogans-which does not really express what they are trying to say. They are grouping towards a new language-a true communication-but, meanwhile, in adequate slogans from the past must serve. The millions of young people who stick a poster of the Guevera on their wall do not share either his beliefs or his language. Most of them are aware of this circumstance: they are also very conscious that there is this need for true communication, and the leaders of the pop world like the Beatles have frequently said so. This is why the trends in clothes and long hair are to them so important: they are fundamentally methods of communication. There is a Beatles song called 'All you need is love', which on the face of it is a banal and puerile statement, but they are not simply referring to the usual commercial concept at all. Sex as a basic form of communication was discussed above.

On another level it is beyond doubt that without love, in the sense used by most of the great religious leaders, true human communication is impossible. If society as it exists does not allow for this act of communication, either because the structure is wrong or because of social injustice or because there is no freedom to express opinions, then the social consequences will be revolutionary.

The trumpet calls for human solidarity are based on a recognition of this, but what usually happens in practice is that the kind of solidarity which is based on human love only occurs temporarily within small groups (opposed to other groups), or where societies are at war or in times of revolution and crisis. Or else these human needs are perverted and rendered evil by false prophets like Hitler, who must base their movements on error. This brings us back to those radical opposition movements which fundamentally reject modern societies, since what they are fighting is hypocrisy in all its forms: where untruth prevails, communication breaks down. That is why this chapter is not about technical processes such as 'positive and negative feedback loops'. All the loops in the world cannot obliterate fabrication.

An Exclusive Case : The history of the press is at the same time a reflection of political history. Journalists are the chroniclers of their age and the results of their labours, the newspapers, reveal what problems confronted the different epochs in a nation's history.

Germany is the mother country of the modern press. It is true that other countries made attempts to provide information for the' population by means of periodic announcements on the part of the state or the state authorities. This was the case for instance in ancient China, where an official journal was published, being printed by the woodcut method. The official journal appeared from the ninth century onwards under the name of King-Po, and in the course of centuries, with a succession of titles, it developed into the precursor of the later official imperial gazette in the Celestial Empire.

Before the Chinese however the Romans had also found ways and means of providing the population with information on the affairs of state in a kind of prejournalistic publication. This was the daily gazette which was published by Caesar under the title of Acta Diurna making public the decrees of the Roman authorities around about the middle of the first century before Christ.

Press in Germany : The modern press, which originated in Germany, could not really have been created anywhere else than in the land of Gutenberg.

Gutenberg was the first person in Europe to invent movable type and is thus the father of the modern art of printing, the black art, the art which is concerned with the colour black which has become the symbol not only of journalism but of the entire modern age. Gutenberg might however also justifiably be called the father of journalism. His efforts to create an instrument for circulating news rapidly and simultaneously in many areas corresponded even in those days to the journalistic flair which in Gutenberg was combined with the boldness of the inventor and the precision of the scientist. Gutenberg's name is closely connected with the German city of Mainz. "Golden Mainz" (the name which the first arcbishopric of the Holy Roman Empire bore for centuries, just as Cologne for instance was known as "Holy Cologne" was Gutenberg's birthplace.

Gutenberg's real name was Henne Gausfleisc zu Laden, but he became more well-known under the name of Johannes Gutenberg. In the year 1854 his 42-line Bible appeared for the first time. Many copies of the Holy Scriptures, previously written out laboriously by hand on parchment by the monks, could now be circulated among the people. The art of printing with movable type, invented and perfected by Gutenberg in the space of about a decade, began its triumphant progress throughout the world.

The man whose invention of printing gave the entire 'population access to learning and knowledge, which bad hitherto been confined to the privileged wealthy few, did not however get any thanks for his invention. In order to perfect his printing machine he was forced to borrow money from a wealthy citizen of Mainz, Fust by name. Round about 1447 appeared the first Gutenberg publication, period at his parents' house, the name of which was "zum Gutenberg", and it was by this name that Henne or Johanes Gansfleisch was later known. This publication was a minor epic work by some contemporary, known as the Weltgerichts-gedicht (The poem of the universal court). A year later appeared the "Calender for 1448". But people did not yet display much interest for the new technique.

This did not happen until the printer came out with the idea of publishing the Bible. Now people in Mainz began to prick up their ears. The above-mentioned Fust lent Gutenberg so much money that after the publication of the work, on which Gutenberg had laboured for two years or so, that entire inventory of the Gutenberg printing works belonged to him. Fust later went into partnership with another wealthy burgher and created the Fust-Schoffersche Press. The inventor of printing however lived a hand-to-mouth existence. Relatives supported him and enabled him later to bring out smaller publications now and again. Thus the Catholicon which appeared in 1465, was probably printed in his workshop. Today no one knows where this was situated. The Bible was printed in living quarters where Gutenberg had some time before established a workshop, in the house "zum Humbrecht", a building which today in Number 18/20 in the "Schustergasse".

The Archbishop Adolf von completely impoverished inventor gave Gutenberg a place in his him by means of this board death. Nassau took pity on the in his old age. In 1465 he household, thus preserving and lodging from certain.

Later generations desired to make good the neglect which Gutenberg suffered at the hands of his contemporaries in Mainz. In 1837 Maim; erected a fine Gutenberg Memorial, designed by Thorwaldsen. The inscription-on the memorial reads:

> Artem quae Graecos latuit latuitque Latinos Germani sollers extudit ingenium. Nunc quidquid veteres sapiunt sapiuntque recentes, Non sibi, sed populis omnibus id sapiunt. (The art which remained concealed from the Greeks and Romans Was brought to light by the inventive genius of a German. Now the knowledge of ancients and moderns is not confined to Them alone, but known to all the nations of the world.)

The Gutenberg Museum established at Mainz in 1900 and the Gutenberg Society set up in 1901 have kept alive the memory of one of the greatest inventors of all time.

The man who received such honour at the hand; of later generations died in 1467 or 1468; the exact date is not known. He was buried in the Franciscan Church, which was demolished in 1742. There is nothing to recall the last resting place of this great citizen of Mainz. With his invention he heralded the dawn of a modern age, and set in motion the mechanism that was to cause an intellectual awakening. In the same period, by some strange whim of fate an unknown man in far-away Korea was using movable copper type for making reproductions. In the Far East no one took any notice of this invention. Within a century however it altered the entire social and intellectual face of Europe, making education and culture the common property of all men.

One of the historians of the German press, Robertrot who published his Geschichte des deutschen Journalismus (History of German Journalism) in 1845, rapturously described journalism as the highest form of Gutenberg's art Journalism is the most perfect use to which Gutenberg's invention could be put; it is, so to speak, the press in its, most concentrated form the energetic quintessence and embodiment of all the effects produced by the art of printing.

The newspaper which appears regularly every day with the daily news have various names in different languages, which point to its characteristic features. In German the daily paper is called "Zeitung". In the fourteenth century this word was written as "Zitunge", a form which originated in Central and South Germany. The word "Zeitung" originally meant nothing else than "news". Thus the first journals, flysheets and pamphlets, which were only produced in connection with some specific event, were called "Neue Zeitungen" (or "Newe Zytungen" in the spelling of that period), meaning the "Latest news". The oldest printed work still in existence is a Newe

Zytung von orient und auff gange (Latest News from the Orient and the East), from the year 1502. Pamphlets of this kind were however already appearing in Germany in the last decades of the fifteenth century.

In time there also appeared what were known as serial issues of newspapers, dealing with a major political event in two or three issues. This scheme was also frequently employed for announcing some military event or other, an imperial proclamation or an event of religious and political significance.

As well as these serial issues there were also the so-called Messrelationen, published quarterly or monthly at the time of the Spring and Autumn Trade Fairs in Frankfurt-on-Main by the historian Michael von Aitzing at Cologne. These Messrelationen, journals which gave information about the trade fairs, may be described as the precursors of economic periodicals and also of political journals. Experts on the history of the press are not absolutely certain of the publication date of the first newspaper to conform more or less with the modern definition of "mass medium". Some take the view that it was the Historische Relation, printed by Samuel Dilbaum of Augsburg, and published by Leonhard Straub at Rorschach. A complete annual volume of this monthly journal from the year 1597 is still in existence.

At that time, however, several journals must already have been appearing regularly. In 1587 for instance there was already a periodical with the following title: Newe Zeittung/ Warhafftiger Bericht aus Nurnberg an einen guten Freundt geschrieben/was sich im Monat April dieses 1587. Jahrs zugetragen und begeben (Latest news/Accurate report from Nuremberg, written to a good friend of the events and happenings in the month of April in this year of 1587.) Some German researchers cautiously describe these monthly journals as the forerunners of the weekly periodicals. The newspaper expert Professor Hans A Munster for instance has the following to say in an article entitled "The oldest Periodical Newspaper and Review" (Die alteste periodische Zeitung and Schrift), which appeared in the monthly Die Deutsche Zeitung, Bielefeld, July 1953:

> 'There is thus nothing new in describing the old monthly reviews as the "oldest periodicals", and certainly there are good grounds for this assumption. For the longer gap between dates of publication in the case of monthlies as compared with weeklies is after all not a fundamental difference but only a relative one. The step forward from the "Newe Zytungen", which did not appear regularly, to the periodicals was taken by the publication of either the monthly reviews (in 1587 and 1597 respectively, or the "Messrelationen" (in 1588).

Most historians of press history however hold the opinion ,that the year 1609 is of special significance for the development of the press and that it was in this year that really modern newspapers came into existence. In 1609, for the first time, there appeared two weekly papers, and the complete annual volumes of them both are still in existence. These two papers were called Relation and Aviso respectively.

It is likely that the Relation was published at Strassbourg. It is a rather more Protestant journal, which made available information on political and economic affairs to readers in the former German imperial city. The full title of the journal was as follows: Aller Furnemmen und gedenckwurdigen Historien/ so sich hin und wider in Hoch und Nieder Teutschland/auch in Franckreich/ftalian/Scbott and England/Hispanien/ Hungern/Polen/Siebenburgen/Wallachey/Moldaw/ Turckeyetc. Inn diesem 1609. Jahr verlauffen und zugetragen mochte. Alles auf das trewlichs wie ich solche bekommen und zu wegen bringen magjln Truck verfertigen will. (An account of all undertakings and noteworthy events/occurring in Upper and Lower Germany/as well as France/Italy/Scotland and

England/Spain/Hungary/Poland Transylvania/Wallachia/ Moldavia/Turkey/etc., in the year 1609. Everything having been edited and printed exactly in accordance with the news items as they came in.)

The geograpbical origin of the news items printed in the second newspaper, the Aviso, already reveals a bias towards American and Asiatic countries. The name of this periodical with the characteristic heading and long-winded title corresponding to the fashion of the time reveal the still close relationship of the periodical with the book. The full title was as follows: Relation oder Zeitung. Was sich begeben and zugetragen hat/in Deutsch: und Welschland/Spanien/Nieder landtjEngelland/Franckreich, Ungern, Oesterreich, Schweden, Polen und in allen Provintzen/in Ost: und West Indian etc. So aIlhie den... angelangt. Gedruckt im Jahre 1609. (Journal or newspaper. The events and happenings in Germany and Italy/ Spain/The Neitherlands/England/France/Hungary/Austria/ Sweden/Poland/and in all the provinces/in the East and West Indies etc. All items printed as they arrived, in the year 1609).

It has still not been definitely established where the journal was printed. It might have been Augsburg, but Nuremberg is also a possibility, while there are various reasons that would appear to suggest Wolfenbuttel as its source.

The significant thing about these newspapers was not that they attracted a large circle of readers but that were read by a small class of politically and economically important persons who now suddenly received regular information from a news paper. This then was the birth of the political press, i.e. the press of modern times.

Between 1618 and 1648 there appeared various new pamphlets, which for the next few years proved something of an obstacle to the development of periodicals. All the same, it was precisely in this early period that well-known publishers such as Andreas Aperger of Augsburg developed into prominent newspaper publishers.

Newspaper history reveals that the towns where there newspapers originated were not the political centres but the' famous merchants cities of the Holy Roman Empire. Thus an important weekly paper was published at Frankfurt-on-Main as early as 1615, while by 1617 this city already had two weekly competitors.

During the Thirty Years War a forerunner of the press in our own century appeared at Magdeburg; it was published in, 1664 by what afterwards became the Muller-Faber publishing house, later developing into the Magdeburger Zeitung which is published in the Federal Republic of Germany today; this newspaper is read in exile by the citizens of Magdeburg who have fled from the Soviet Zone.

During the sixteenth century a number of German book printers emigrated to other countries and, just as they had already been doing in isolated places for a century, disseminated the art of Gutenberg to an ever growing extent beyond the boundaries of the Holy Roman Empire. The first forerunners of the French newspapers developed as early as 163 Land some time later the first papers were also published in England. From the very beginning the English papers differed considerably from the continental ones in that they revealed differences of opinion, whereas the French government had some control over newspaper policy right from the start. The German press however reflected the attitude of the various German princedoms.

One of the old trade centres was Leipzig, the city where the traditional Leipzig Trade Fair is held. This city can claim to have published the first daily newspaper of modern times. The Leipzig daily newspaper appeared on I January 1660 with the following title: Neu einlauffende Nachbricht van Kriegs- und Welt-Handeln, (The latest news of events from the military and commercial sphers.)

A feature of the seventeenth century is the establishment of various prominent newspapers and journals, for instance the Frankische Kurier in 1673, or the Jenaische zeitung in 1674. The first German learned periodical appeared in 1682, entitled Acta Eruditorum. Six years later there also appeared the first learned periodical printed in German: Schertz-und ernsthaffter Gedanken uber allerband nutzliche Bucher und Fragen... (Humorous and serious thoughts on diverse books and questions, both amusing and instructive).

In 1693 we find a monthly journal appearing in Jena with the following title: Monatlich mutzspielende Lustfragen zu Gelehrter und Ungelehrter sonderbarer Ergetzung. (A monthly review of useful humorous matters for the amusement of scholars and others. This journal is a forerunner of the type known as "moralist weeklies", established for the political and moral instruction and enlightenment of society, which originated in Germany in the year 1713. The first genuine moralist weekly to appear in Germany was Der Vernunfller (The Sophist) in Hamburg.

In 1725, with the publication of the weekly journal Die vernunfligen Tadlerinnen (The judicious-Faultfinders) which appeared in various places, such as Halle Leipzig and finally Humburg, the writer Gottsched bestowed a certain measure of fame on these moralist weeklies in Germany and the rest of the world. The journals themselves are based on English models, Defoe, Steele and Addison having become models for German journalists. Already the press was growing aware of its international significance.

The beginning of the eighteenth century also saw the birth of the intellectual reviews which were to have such a stimulating effect on intellectual life in Germany. In the year 1703 the famous Wiennerische Diarium appeared, a review which still appears today under the same title, and is the doyen of all publications of this nature in the German-speaking world.

Another new type of publication were the so-called' "privileged journals". In 1740 the Koniglich privilegierte Nachrichten von Staats und Gelehrtensachen (Journal of affairs of state and scholarship, under royal patronage) appeared in Prussia. The King himself, Frederick the Great, was responsible for its publication. Later, as the Haude Spenersche Zeitung, this newspaper was to represent the old middle classes of Berlin. There was however an even earlier forerunner of these "privileged journals". A weekly periodical published in Berlin from 1691 onwards, called Allergnadigst privilegierte Curiosen Natur-, Kunst-, Staats und Sittenprasenten erster Jahrgang durch R. Oelven zum Nutzen und Ergotzen. (The first and annual volume of curious events from the realms of science, art, politics, and morals, published by R. Oelpen for the instruction and amusement of all).

In this period Frederick the Great, who was rebelling against the Empress Maria Theresia, founded the forerunner of what was later called the Schlesische Zeitung; it appeared in 1741 in the German city of Breslau, entitled Schlesisch privillegierte Staats- Kriegs- and Friendenszeitung (Silesia, journal of state, war and peace, under royal patronage). Today the Schlesische Zeitung is read by all the German Silesians who were expelled from their homeland and do not forget Breslau or other towns in the territory of Eastern Germany.

One could compile a long chronological table giving the most important dates of foundation for German newspapers.

The most significant names to appear are the forerunners of the Bremer Nachrichten (1743), the Braunschweigische Zeitung (1744), the Saarbrucker Zeitung (1761), the Anhalter Anzeiger (1763), the Kolnische Zeitung (1763), the Elbinger Zeitung (1789), the Vogtlandische Anzeiger and Tagesblatt (1789) and the Geraer Zeitung (1795).

The seventeenth and eighteenth centuries thus displayed a welcome degree of initiative in the sphere of the press. At the same time however the newspapers were not without their critics. At Leipzig, as for back as 1672, Professor Otto Mencke had introduced a kind of historical and political study of the press into the university syllabus.

Some years later Ahasver Fritsch published the first learned work on the press: Discursus de Novellarum quas vacant Neue Zeitunge Hodierno usu et abusu (Discourse on the Present Day Uses and Abuses of the Publications Known as Newspapers), which appeared at Jena in 1676. In the same year Christian Weise followed with a similar work. In 1679 Johann Ludwig Hartmann had a book published under the title of Unzeitige Neue Zeitungssucht. (Untimely Passion for Newspapers). This look is the first learned work on the press published in German.

Leipzig was also to be the place where the first treatise of the press was published. It was written by Tobias Beucer in 1698 and entitled De Relationibus Novellis (On Newspapers). Hamburg followed in 1695 with Kasper Stieler's Zeitungs Lust und Nutz (Amusement and Instruction from Newspapers), while in the same year the first treatise on press law, entitled Jus Novellarum was published by Friedrich Hagen at the University of Kiel. Thus the outlines for newspaper and press research were marked out. When Johnn Peter von Leipzig began to lecture on "The uses and abuses of newspapers" at the newly founded University of Halle in the year 1698, the study of the press bad already become a field of research taken for granted at the universities. It is astonishing bow the world of learning subjected the mass media to critical scrutiny during the seventeenth century revealing an admirable and instinctive awareness of the danger and advantages of the press.

During the reign of Frederick the Great, the government of Prussia as it was then was liberal and tolerant in its treatment of the press. This factor also had a decisive influence on neighbouring regions. Until the seventeenth and eighteenth centuries German journalism, that is to say the press in German speaking countries, had been the province of anonymous writers. Of course, as has already been mentioned there were a number of prominent writers contributing to journals of a high standard. But the type of journalist able to achieve a certain amount of power and consequently exercise a considerable influence on public opinion does not appear until later on in the eighteenth century.

Mention should be made here in particular of the statesman and writer Justus Moser (1720-1794), who published a journal called the Wochentlicbe Osnabruckische Anzeigen (1766-1782), which represented a note-worthy achievement in the field of journalism. Another scholar who combined a statesman like insight with a flair for journalism was August Ludwig von Schlozer (1735-1809), who was active in the field of journalism as Gottingen, his more important publication being the Staats-anzeigen (1783-1794), which provided information on events in Europe at that time and the rest of the world.

The journalist Friedrich Karl Freiherr von Moser (I723-1798) was active during the same period. In annual volumes entitled Patriotisches Archiv fur Deutschland, published from 1784 to 1790 and from 1792 to 1794, he created a unique documentation worthy to rank alongside the periodical documentary works of our time.

Similar to the link with politics, journalism was also even more intimately connected with art. The great writer Gottfried Ephraim Lessing, the German herald of tolerance, was for a period .of hour years literary editor of the Vossische Zeitung (1751-1755). During this time he created a critical journal that betrays the pen of the gifted writer that he was. Another writer Matthias Claudius (1740-1745), the editor of the Wandsbecker Boten (from 1751 to 1755), published a critical journal whose attractive style and responsible tone earned it a reputation that extended far beyond the local region and gained it subscribers all over Germany.

Another of these prominent journalists was Wieland (1733-1813), who published a journal chiefly devoted to literary matters, whose political significance however cannot be overestimated; this was the Teutsche Merkur (1773-1810). The gifted but ill-starred Heinrich von Kleist (1777-1811) was publisher and editor of the Berliner Abendblatter (1810-1811).

At the moment when Napoleon was taking steps to crush the press, Kleist was bold enough to show the nation, cautiously and cleverly, that national dignity and national aims were still possible. He was one of the German who fought against dictatorship and oppression. The Swabian Christian Friedrich Daniel Schubart (1739-1791) founded the Deutsche Chcronik (which appeared in Augsburg in 1794, in Vim from 1774 to 1777 and in Stuttgart from 1787 to 1791). In these journals we find over and over again a harmonious blend of revolutionary poetic enthusiasm and the prudence of journalists with a critical turn of mind. Other great journalists of the period were Ludwig Weckherlin (1739 to 1792), Moritz Flavius Trenck von Tonder 1746-1810) and Arnold M allinckrodt (1767-1825). It was the latter's dream, even in those days, that one day there might be a united Europe.

Apart from art, the book trade too now tried to establish -closer links with press. Particular mention should be made ,here of Johann Friedrich Cotta (1764-1832) and Friedrich Perthes (1772-1843). During the period of Napoleon's despotism Johann Josef Gones (1776-1848) was the most prominent ;figure in German journalism to join in the national struggle, with his outstanding periodical the Rheinischer Merkur (1814-1816). The Rheinischer Merkur's contribution to the resistance against Napoleon and to the efforts at reviving the Empire was so substantial that the mighty despot regarded it as a kind of fifth columnist movement.

After Napoleon, Europe was the realm of experiment for journalists who either on a national or a European basis proclaimed their desire for one great state of Europe united in the brotherhood of nations. Here one should note the journalistic efforts of Johann Georg August Wirth (I798-1898), the publisher of the Deutsche Tribune (1 July-18 December 1831 at Munich, and until 18 March 1832 at Homburg).

In the struggle against Napoleon and in the post Napoleonic era there appeared a new phenomenon in the world of journalism: the party press. Journals advocating a particular idea or policy were founded in that period, and the birth of the party press represents at the same time the birth of public opinion in the party political sense. The newspapers claimed to be liberal, but had a general moral, Catholic or Protestant bias, so that their readers were always groups linked by denominational or political connections. These newspapers in the first half of the nineteenth century are regarded by the German political press of today as their legitimate predecessors.

The nineteenth century however also witnessed another phenomenon in the sphere of journalism the birth of the popular press. Even in those days the popular press employed telegraphic communications, receiving news from the telegrafic agencies and news services. In the year 1849 the Wolff Telegraphic Agency was established in Berlin. This is the oldest modern news agency in the world.

It was in Germany, the traditional home of the "Relationen" and trade fair journals, that one of the largest and most important news agencies in the world commenced its activities: Reuter's was set up two years after the establishment of the Wolff Telegraphic Agency. We know the exact dates of its foundation On 22 April 1850 the newspaper correspondent Julius Reuter arrived at Aachen, where he was met by the brewery and distillery owner Heinrich Geller. This Heinrich Geller owned one of the largest earlier-pigeon lofts in the old imperial city of Aachen. The two men diliberated for two days, and then, on the 24 April, they signed a contract providing for Reuter to establish a carrier-pigeon post for the conveyance of all kinds of news. This contract of 24 April represents the birth of a world enterprise which became a by word in the field of journalism.

The first carrier-pigeons were dispatched on 27 April. Important items of news-particularly stock exchange quotations -were often reported in other places one or two days quicker than by conventional methods. A year later the great firm of Reuter's as Aachen, with its first branch at Verviers and connections with of the chief cities of Europe, had achieved such a reputation that it transferred its headquarters to London, the capital of the British Empire. There is 1865, Reuter's Institute, which had meanwhile expanded into an international undertaking, was converted into a limited company. Paul Julius Reuter, born at Kassel in 1821, died at Nice in 1899, having been created a baron by the Duke of Coburg-Gotha in the year 1871. Possessing German and British nationality, and at home too in France and Italy Reuter represented a considerable section of European thinking in the nineteenth century.

The nineteenth century was equally mindful of technical progress as well as intellectual activity. Thus in the year 1811 Friedrich Konig patented his invention of the mecbanical press. In 1814 this mechanical press was employed for the first time in the printing of a newspaper: The Times of London. The first newspaper on the European continuant to introduce the new invention in its printing house was the Haude-Spenersche Zeitung in Berlin, but this was not until 1823.

The result was that in 1824 the Haude-Spenersche Zeitung and the Vossische Zeitung in Berlin began to appear daily. Stereotype offset was invented in the year 1829, and this invention acquired particular significance in 1872 with the construction of the first German rotary press at Augsburg. Then, in 1852, the German teacher Philipp Reis demonstrated the first telephone, an invention which was just as important as that of Daguerre, who invented the process of photography in the years 1837-38.

The circulation of the popular press received a further impetus through the reduction in price that resulted from a new paper manufacturing process. Then, in 1880, Georg Meisenbach made it possible for photographs to be reproduced on newspapers with the aid of autotype. In 1884 the type-setting machine was invented by Ottmar Mergenthaler, who how had just emigrated to America, but such machines were not constructed and employed in Germany until 1896.

The 1920's saw the development of radio as a rival to the press. The first German radio company was established in 1923. A few years later Herman Tolle broadcast from Cologne the first spoken radio commentary and the first leading article on German radio. The first radio pictures appeared in 1927.

The popular press is noncommittal in tone. It does not represent any definite political point of view, but is for the most part only interested in increasing its readership by pandering to the popular taste. A typical example of a nonpolitical newspaper of this kind was the Tagliche Rundschau in Berlin. This publication was strictly non-party. It made its first appearance on September 1881, presenting itself as a "newspaper for non-politicians, as well as a supplement to the political organs of all the parties." In the year 1884 it described its functions as being a "newspaper for non-political politics". Its slogan, as declared in leading articles and other publications, was to provide happiness and harmonious gritty for all.

To some extent it was a newspaper apart, for unlike other papers it claimed to be political without supporting any particular policy. Later however it modified its point of view a little, tending more in the direction of the National Liberal Party.

It is interesting for historians of the press to know that the first official organ published by the Sovier military authorities in the occupied zone of Central Germany bore the name Tagliche Rundschau. However the former non-political Tagliche Rundschau was published in the early years of the Bismarck state at a time when even a harmless family gossip magazine like the Gartenlaube could appear; whereas the Tagliche Rundschau published by the Soviet authorities commenced an extreme policy of communist indoctrination.

Here we may be permitted to look back for a moment. In the era of the popular press the "General an zeiger" also played a prominent part. This type of newspaper claimed to be more serious than the average popular paper, but still tried rather to gained the non-political section of the population as its readers. The leading promoter of this type of newspaper was Josef La Rouelle, who experimented with publications at Aachen in 1871 and Cologne in 1875, before publishing his Billigste Zeitung fur Arm und Reich (Cheapest newspaper for rich and poor) in 1882, thus producing a genuine type of "Generalanzeiger". Hermann Minjon was active in Frankfurt, while the name of August Scherl is eternally linked with the history of the Berlin press. Other men prominent in the general advertiser press were W. Girardet and August Huck.

German newspapers were particularly active in the political sphere, whatever their political tendencies. Shortly before the First World War there were around 532 Conservative and Free Conservative newspapers, 509 National Liberal and Radical Democratic papers, 419 newspapers supporting the party of the Catholic Centre and 85 Socialist newspapers, plus 61 publications representing the Polish, Danish and other minorities. As opposed to this number there were a total of 1,621 non-party newspapers.

In 1932 the numbers were approximately as follows:

596 newspapers supporting the Centre and Bavarian People's Party,

197 supporting the German Social Democrat Party,

121 supporting the National Socialist German Worker's Party,

81 supporting the German National People's Party,

50 supporting the Communist Party,

14 supporting the People's Party,

11 supporting the Economic Party,

8 supporting the German State Party.

Another analysis presents the following picture: 562 newspapers advocating more conservative views, 363 with progressive middle-class views, 64 with more liberal views, 58 with liberal-democratic views, 19 with progressive republican views, and 9 with general socialist views, while 1,814 papers claimed to be independent; 123 newspapers advocated varying policies, and 337 made no declaration of their views at all.

The long list of newspapers existing at that time, many of which were what was known as "Kopfzeitungen", *i.e.,* the political section on the first two pages was often taken over on matrices from a larger newspaper) presents a colourful and varied mixture a new and decisive event however was soon to compel the German press to take on a more gloomy and monotonous appearance.

On 30 January 1933 Hitler book office as Chancellor, and it did not take long before he usurped sole power in his position as Fuhrer and Chancellor, brusquely ignoring the promises he had given to the nation about allowing it the opportunity to criticise his policies at regular intervals. Dictatorship and dictators always proceed in accordance with a similar scheme. This period when the German press was in fetters has recently been the subject of particular study in quite a number of publications. General surveys have appeared of the process of concentration, throwing light on the National Socialists' control of the press. By the end of the Third Reich this process had led to 80 per cent of the newspapers and journals which appeared in Germany being in the possession of the party-owed Eranz Eher- Verlag at Munich.

Today it requires considerable effort to get a clear picture of the mass of legislative and other measures taken by the National Socialists against the independent press in Germany. The result however was plain: the elimination of serious criticism. Apart from the Minister of Propaganda, Goebbels, the leading figure in the campaign to bring the press into line was Max Amann, director of the Eber- Verlag; in his capacity as representative of his party he brutally expropriated leading publishing firms and brought them under the control of his own giant publishing house.

The press policy commenced in 1934, when the Ullstein house was transferred into the hands of the National Socialists, and continued until 1944, when Hugenberg's Scherlverlag was taken over. The National Socialists' Pravda was the Volkischer Beobachter. This newspaper had its origin in the Munchener Beobachter, founded in 1887, appearing for the first time under its title Volkischer Beobachter on 9 August 1919. This was the beginning of a troubled period of German history.

This period of German history has however been consistently continued in one part of Germany which is not yet free. This is the case in the Soviet-occupied Zone of Germany, which with a conscious debasement of political terminology has given itself the title of "German Democratic Republic".

The Communist and National Socialist ideologies, based on the same intellectual source, *viz.*, a false interpretation of Hegelian philosophy, pursued the same policy in regard to the press, just as they also seized power in the same way. Their newspaper often bear epithets such as "free" or "national", or have titles like "die Wahrheit" ("The Truth"). But their newspapers are not intended to serve any human values, but simply and solely the aims of one party, a despotism represented by a minority in control of the state. The press in the Soviet Zone following Lenin's oft-quoted dictum, which applies today as much as it ever did, gave itself the task of "being not only a collective propagandist and a collective agitator, but also a collective organizer." True to this formula the Soviet Zone press has agitated, organized and spread party propaganda in accordance with the example of the Soviet press.

It praised Stalin extravagantly. And the same men and the same pens were just as indignant in their criticism of Stalin when the Party came out wita its condemnation of the men without whom three decades of Communist history would be unthinkable. It also criticized Krushchev in exactly the same way, in accordance with its instructions.

The only criticism against measures taken by the authorities and the Party in a communist state is found in "readers" letters'. The situation is exactly the same in the Soviet Zone as in other communist countries, as the London Times wrote of Isvestia on 24 February 1965 in a series of articles entitled "Newspapers of the World":

> "In a communist country a letter to the editor is one of the few channels open to the individual to appeal against injustice and bureaucracy."

In the postwar period the press has experienced a great change in what is today the Federal Republic of Germany. After the end of the Second World War the press, which until then had been controlled by the National Socialists, virtually ceased to exist. At first the occupying powers published their own newspapers, and later gave certain persons licenses to publish newspapers and magazines. In the American and French Zones members of the different parties combined to publish independent newspapers, whereas in the British Zone the preference was given to a definite party press system.

In the same way the Soviets favoured a party press system in their zone of occupation-the communist press and the so-called "middle-class press", which is subject to communist pressure. The existence of the latter is intended to lead the rest of the world to believe that the press supports different political parties in the Sovietoccupied Zone. The licensed press continued until 1 September 1949; after which it was no longer necessary to hold a licence in order to publish a newspaper. As from this date, a large number of newspapers again began to appear under their former titles.

In some cases there was a struggle, even carried out in public (for instance in the case of the newspaper Die-Welt), between these old papers, which called themselves local German papers ("Hdmatzeitungen") and the licensed press. Many of the old publishers' newspapers, which reappeared after 1 September 1940 suddenly failed to arouse the echo which they had hoped for, or they were unable to adapt themselves to changed conditions.

The flood of expellers from the eastern territories of Germany, now under Polish and Russian Administration, and the flight of inhabitants of the Soviet occupied Zone to the Federal Republic of Germany also had a particular effect in that they wrought a considerable change in the composition (If the population. This change did not however make any difference for some of the other old newspapers which boldly took up the struggle against the licensed press and today, with an imposing body of regular readers, are again, playing a leading part in the sphere of the German press.

The monotony of a twelve year long totalitarian regime had thus given way to a press which again reflected public opinion, in accordance with the tradition of the press in the mother country of the press. In addition there are of course also news-, papers, which take no definite political line, adapting them selves to please tastes, or rather the alleged tastes of their readers. In the modern industrial state the popular press plays a prominent part in every field.

As in every state which believes in free competition, there is rivalry among the publishers, who compete for the favour of regular subscribers. By and large the press in the Federal Republic is still supported by regular subscribers, the newspaper being delivered to the reader's house every morning. There are however also a few large popular tabloids which are sold at newspaper stalls and in the streets these are holding their own. With the popular tabloids there also came the illustrated magazines, of which a variety of types are available.

A gratifying large section of the press was concerned with publications for young people, ranging from school magazines to the younger readers' section in the weekend magazines. Many of these publications had a particular political bias, or follow a cultural or religious line. Unlike the totalitarian systems in the Third Reich of the National Socialist and in the communist Soviet Zone there were also a number of denominational newspapers and magazines in the Federal Republic, which commented and criticized as they please and meet with a positive response from their readers. It is true that there were newspapers which call themselves religious in totalitarian states too, but their influence is confined to the affairs of the parish, while the majority of the other papers, on the other hand, were free to attack religion and religious institutions with political means.

Journalists in Germany, have their own local associations and their German Press Association. In some cases they cooperate with the International Journalists' Federation, which endeavours to arrange a regular exchange of ideas on certain matters affecting the journalists' profession; it also investigates the position of journalists in all the countries of the world, considers salaries and wages, examines the development of radio and television and their effect on the printed press, organises international conferences on the subjects of vocational training and measures for the protection of journalists in the exercise of their profession, and generally deals with all matters connected with journalistic activity and the relationship among one another of journalists from different nations.

It is also fosters good relations among journalists' and journalists organisations, and among the newspapers and publishers of different countries, as well as devoting itself to the struggle for the geniun internal freedom of the press.

In the early days of printing Gutenberg's new invention rapidly conquered the world. The most imaginative offspring of his invention was the regular periodical, the newspaper or magazine, .read by millions every day. Millions of people who arc prevented from reading themselves, by reason of their age or their youth or other adverse circumstances, get others to read aloud to them. The newspaper is the link between events all over the world and the individual, and for this reason its task is considerable.

The most essential function of all newspapers however should be the eternal theme-to ensure that the nations of the world live in peace and harmony, to try to educate people in freedom and respect for other people's views, though rejecting totalitarian and ideological one-sidedness; the press should help to build such a world along the path of peace. The newspaper serves the printed world.

In the Holy Scriptures of the civilized nations and the great religions, both Christian and non-Christian, in the Bible and in the ancient Veda scriptures of the Indians, the World has become a concept of a divine power which can reach the height of perfection. Christians speak of the World, the logos, which brought the world salvation. Christians and non-Christians understand the power of the Word: "And the World was made flesh..." The true Word is wedded to true reality, not the slogan or the political phrase. Let us repeat once again the Christian Word, the truth liberates, and the words from the Upanishad, which became the motto of the Republic of India-and there is no finer motto imaginable Satyameva jayate "Truth will conquer".

Journalists and pressmen from every era who have defended the nations right to freedom ought not to forget that every form of freedom begins with the freedom of the Word, the honourable Word uttered without haste or taint of propaganda.

8

Error Free Functioning

In journalism nothing can be taken for granted. There arise situations that put not just the reporter or sub-editor concerned, but prestigious publications and sometimes the entire profession to shame just because somebody in the profession has just not been careful enough.

If a reader is careful enough he can easily find lapses which result in repetition of stories in the same edition of a newspaper. It could be because of several reasons. One sub-editor may edit the agency copy and send it for printing and when newspaper's own correspondent files the same story, it is also sent for printing by another sub-editor, maybe on a different shift. Different versions of the same story may appear in the same edition, on different pages and, sometimes more embarrassingly, on the same page.

It could also happen that two different agencies file the same story with different leads and both may be carried in the same edition leading to an embarrassing situation. Chances of this kind of lapse increase if the time gap of report coming from different sources is more, even more if the shift has changed in between. There is another way to add to this type of trouble when material ready for printing of one edition is being selected from the material used for the earlier edition. In this case sometimes the same story could get printed the next day also with all possible variations mentioned above.

Such mistakes are avoided by careful copy sorting and dividing subjects among sub-editors, careful change-over of shift and better overall supervision and coordination. Care has to be taken in these areas even on feature pages. *The Times of India,* New Delhi, made such a major lapse on January 4, 1990. The paper used the article sent by its London-based correspondent, L.K. Sharma, on the edit page (page 6) and repeated it on the facing Agenda page (page 7). However, the headlines were different and so were the editing teams.

Presentation of the Main Page

LONDON: Britain in the 70s seemed reluctant towards change but in the 80s it went in pursuit of the free market Utopia, thus gaining political dynamism and an economic recovery that brought material benefits to large sections. The powerful trade unions were tamed and collectivism was discarded for economic competitiveness, private enterprise and individual liberty. In the process, Britain also improved its standing in the international community.

It was Mrs Margaret Thatcher's decade. She released market forces and a new version of *laissez faire* against the welfare state and public intervention in the economy. She began her prime ministerial career in 1979 with a determination to kill socialism and rejuvenate the terminally sick British industry and a paralysed polity.

Mrs Thatcher's sense of purpose and strategic political design was a change from the frivolity of the Wilson years. She had a set of objectives. Like Indira Gandhi, she displayed a superb political instinct and showed her contempt for some of the established institutions. Military is one institution that Mrs

Thatcher did believe in and she bolstered national pride by waging and winning the Falklands war.

The previous Callaghan government had departed in a winter of discontent. At the end of the 70s, Britain was looking for a nanny and Mrs Thatcher fitted the role eminently. It is another matter that after a measure of economic and diplomatic recovery, it is now yearning for a caring companion to heal the scars of achievement and comfort those who failed to achieve. It is now looking for a leader who will not ignore the social costs of change.

This, in brief, is the history of the British decade which was dominated by Mrs Thatcher, still determined to go on and on, by creating a new mutation of Thatcherism. She has after all won three successive general elections, attracting new segments of society to her Conservative Party and making the opposition Labour Party appear anachronistic.

She inspired changes in attitude and instilled a new sense of confidence after a spell of despondency. She mobilised public support for curbing trade union power, once unthinkable but now demonstrated as done. She kicked overmanned and uncompetitive industry into action and made it recognise that Britain was part of an international economy and an insular enclave. In another miracle, she turned even Labour supporters into first-time buyers of houses and shares. A new class of individual entrepreneurs arose. Mrs Thatcher modified the value system to glorify money and justify greed. The emergence of hippies was applauded. Few would deny that Britons are, as a result, materially better off today.

The discovery of oil in the North Sea was lucky both for Britain and Mrs Thatcher as it enhanced the impression of growing prosperity. There followed flogging of council houses and of assets of public undertakings which were privatised with diffused ownership. Whatever be the current situation, Mrs Thatcher was long considered to have wrought an economic-miracle. She herself likes to recall publicly now beholden pre-Thatcher used to be to the International Monetary Fund (IMF)—"like a third world country", she adds in contempt.

Mrs Thatcher's battle, however, was won on the intellectual plane than in actual performance. Her championship of individual choice and liberty found a valuable ally in the Soviet premier, Mr. Mikhail Gorbachev. Every development in East Europe has made Mrs. Thatcher ecstatic. She keeps reminding the nation that the torch of freedom that dispelled darkness in East Europe was lit by her in Britain. Mrs Thatcher cannot be faulted for believing that the fall of communism has vindicated her. "We knew it in 1979."

A decade is a long time in the life of a leader of a western democracy and too long for public gratitude to last. To her declaration to carry on by public acclaim, her opponents' reply was to call her the Ceausescu of western Europe. The spotlight now tends to focus less on her achievements and more on her failures. The decline in her party's popularity and its recent electoral reverses have questioned her own invincibility as a leader and the durability of Thatcherism.

Thatcherism, moreover is under attack on its own chosen ground. Was there indeed an economic miracle in the past decade? Britain today is plagued by high inflation, a balance of payment crisis, high interest rates and a steady decline in the exchange rate of the pound sterling. They say that the gross domestic product of Britain grew less than in the previous three decades, that the growth rate was not exceptional, that labour productivity grew less and that industry did not turn more competitive.

And striking workers are back on the streets. Currently, ambulance workers can be seen collecting more sympathy and contributions at street corners. To add to these hostile arguments and statistics are the images on TV of the homeless sleeping on the footpaths in cardboard boxes in sub-zero temperatures and the arrival of an underclass in the British society.

Mrs Thatcher's other card—appeal to moral values and the law-and-order lobby—is lost in the Westland and Rover scandals while the crime rate shows no signs of declining.

Even as the very achievements of the Thatcher decade are being doubted, the costs of change are becoming more obvious. Britons see iniquities growing, and the nation split by two socio-economic systems. The infrastructure is run down and cities are dirtier. Britain today is more divided, economically, socially and racially. The Church keeps deploring the ills of an uncaring society and an uncaring government. There is a yearning for quality of life, social cohesion and community feeling.

In reaction, Mrs Thatcher's staunch supporters advise the prime minister to be more a Thatcherite and not feel constrained by populism. They see no limits to Thatcherism, but the free market fanatics seem to be on the retreat as ecological concerns are growing. In her New Year message, Mrs Thatcher reached out to those in need of help. War widows were given Christmas raise in pension. Will she, or will she not, rearrange her face, the tenor of her voice and also her policies?

Whatever may be in store for Britain in the new decade, some elements of Mrs Thatcher's political legacy will endure. Not even under a Labour government will exchange controls, state ownership or the trade unions return to their past glory. The decade has already reformed the Labour Party sufficiently. It remains to be seen whether the decaying Thatcherite edifice can be reinforced either by her or by some other. Here, as at home, the challenge is to carry the legacy of the 80s forward to meet the imperatives of the 90s.

Please mark how the same copy can be edited differently by another team in the following version that appeared on the Agenda page. While on the edit page it was displayed in two columns, the facing page carried it with a different headline spreading over four columns.

Importance of other Pages

Britain in the seventies seemed reluctant to move towards change but in the eighties, it went in pursuit of the free market utopia, gaining political dynamism and an economic recovery that brought material benefits to large sections of the population. The powerful trade unions were tamed and collectivism was discarded for economic competitiveness, private enterprise and individual liberty. It also improved its standing in the international community.

It was the decade of Mrs Margaret Thatcher who released market forces and a *neo-laissez faire* reaction against the welfare state and public intervention in the economy. She began her prime ministerial career in 1979 with a determination to kill socialism and rejuvenate a moribund British industry and a paralysed polity.

The previous Callaghan government had departed in a winter of discontent. At the end of the seventies Britain was looking for a tough nanny and the iron lady fitted the role eminently. It is another matter that after a measure of economic and diplomatic recovery, it is now yearning for a caring companion to heal the scars of achievement and to comfort even those who failed to achieve and to get anywhere. It is now look in for a leader who will not ignore the social costs of change.

This, in brief, is the history of the British decade which was dominated by Mrs Thatcher who is still determined to "go on and on", if need be, by creating a new mutation of Thatcherism, although earlier, "The lady was not for turning". She had after all won three successive general elections, attracting new segments of society to her, conservative Party and making the opposition Labour Party appear anachronistic.

She inspired changes in attitudes and instilled a new sense of confidence in the British after a spell of despondency. She mobilised public support to rub trade-union power, once unthinkable but now very much a fact. She kicked an uncompetitive industry into action and made it recognise that Britain was part of an international economy and an insular island. Another miracle, she turned even Labour supporters into first-time buyers of houses and shares. A new class of individual entrepreneurs rose.

She and Britain were lucky in the North Sea oil find to enhance the impression of growing prosperity; there followed flogging of council houses and of assets of Public Undertaking which were privatised with diffused ownership. Whatever be the current situation, Mrs Thatcher was long considered to have wrought an economic miracle. She herself likes to recall publicly how beholden pre-Thatcher used to be to the IMF— "Like a third world country", she adds in contempt.

Thatcherism's battle, however, was won easier on the intellectual plane than in actual performance. Her championship of individual choice and liberty found a valuable ally in Gorbachev. Every development in East Europe has made Mrs Thatcher ecstatic. She keeps reminding the nation that the torch of freedom that dispelled darkness in East Europe was lit by her in Britain. Mrs Thatcher cannot be faulted for believing that fall of communism has vindicated her. "We knew it in 1979."

A decade is a long time in the life of a leader of a western democracy and too long for public gratitude to last. To her declared intention of carrying on by public acclaim, her opponents' answer was to call her the Ceausescu of Western Europe. The spotlight now tends to focus less on her achievements and more on her failures. The decline in her party's popularity and its recent electoral reverses have questioned her own invincibility as a leader and the durability of Thatcherism.

Thatcherism, moreover, is under attack on its own chosen ground. Was there indeed an economic miracle in the past decade? Britain today is plagued by high inflation, a balance of payment crisis, high interest rates and a steady decline in the exchange rate of the pound sterling. They say that the Gross Domestic Product of Britain grew less than in the previous three decades, that the growth rate was not exceptional, that labour productivity grew less and that industry did not turn more competitive. Striking workers are back on the streets. Currently, ambulance workers can be seen collecting sympathy and contributions at street corners. To add to these hostile arguments and statistics are the images on TV of the homeless sleeping on the footpaths, in cardboard boxes in sub-zero temperatures. The underclass in the British society has well and truly arrived.

Even as the very achievements of the Thatcherite decade are being doubted, the costs of change are becoming more obvious. Britons see inequities growing, and the nation split by two socio-economic systems. The infrastructure is run down and cities are dirtier. Britain today is more divided, economically, socially and racially. The church keeps deploring the ills of an uncaring society and an uncaring government. There is a yearning for quality of life, social cohesion and community feeling.

Ecological concerns are growing. In her New Year message, Mrs Thatcher called out to those in need of help. War widows were given Christmas pension raise. She has also acquired a tint of green. Will she, or will she not, rearrange her face, the tenor of her voice and also her policies?

One can easily make out the absence of sub-headings and deletion of three paragraphs in the Agenda page version. But there are some stylistic differences which should not be there in such a reputed paper. The 'gross domestic product' on the edit page has become the 'Gross Domestic Product' on the Agenda page. Utopia and IMF should also be seen from this point of view, 70s and 80s are also interesting. The Agenda page version has 'look in for' in place of 'looking for' on the edit page. One should carefully read the two versions and compare both the versions, sentence by sentence to mark the difference. Please do read carefully the last sentence of the first paragraph in both the versions.

Look at the following story put out by the UNI and used by several newspapers:

New Delhi June 28 (UNI) : The Government proposes to increase minimum wage by 11 per cent for minors in 34 employments.

The proposed wages for unskilled workers are Rs 12. 25 per day for work above ground as against Rs 11. 00 earlier. The proposed wages for work below ground will be Rs 14. 75 as against Rs 13. 25 at present, an official spokesman said here today.

The proposal to revise minimum wages has been issued following consumer price index crossing 50 points and touching 592.

According to the notification issued by the Ministry of Labour the concerned persons can send suggestions and improvements within two months for consideration of the Government.

The suggested wages for semi-skilled workers are Rs 15. 25 for work above ground and Rs 18. 25 for work below ground and the new wages for skilled workers will be Rs 19. 00 and Rs 25. 50 respectively.

Can you make out what it means? It has passed through several gatekeepers and has appeared in this form in print. Obviously, the reporter and sub-editors concerned have not tried to understand what the whole thing means, otherwise they would have given some background to help us understand or would have spiked it.

Here is a story from *The Business & Political Observer*, New Delhi which appeared on its front page on November 28, 1990:

> London, Nov 27 John Major, the 47-year-old son of
> a former circus trapeze artiste was tonight elected

prime minister of UK, succeeding Mrs Margaret Thatcher, who resigned last week.

Mr. Major, who was chancellor of the exchequer in the outgoing Thatcher government, won today in the second round, securing just two votes less than what is required for an absolute majority. His rivals, Mr. Heseltine and Mr. Douglas Hurd, quickly conceded defeat, ensuring that Mr. Major was elected leader of the ruling Conservative party unanimously and that a third round was avoided.

Mr. Major, a Thatcherite in his economic and foreign policy and increasingly a Liberal in domestic affairs, has made major concessions including a thorough review of the controversial poll tax to unite the party and face the Labour challenge in the next general election, widely expected to be held in next February or March.

Mr. Major, a former banker, has steered British economic policy in the crucial issues like joining the European monetary system. Like Mrs Thatcher, he is opposed to a single European currency in any haste and has pronounced the "hard ECU" as a second currency for all European countries together with their national coin.

Mr. Major's major task at the moment is to unite the Conservative party which has been deeply divided by the Iron Lady's fight against the challenge by a group of rebels led by Mr. Heseltine. The deep division in Conservative ranks which threaten it with the loss of power for the first time in 11 years is a major task that Mr. John Major faces. The ouster of Mrs Thatcher restored the conservative image last week, making them favourites again.

Mrs Thatcher had enthusiastically supported the candidature of Mr. Major, regarded here as her political heir. She actively sought support from him among the 372 Conservative MPs and yesterday said she would be active as a backseat driver (on government policies of the future). This has been immediately taken up by the Labour and Liberal

Democrat parties as evidence that the Thatcherite era will continue.

Mr. John Major, who entered the prime ministerial race only after Mrs Thatcher announced her resignation, started as a second to the main challenger, Mr. Michael Heseltine, but soon gathered support as the media condemned Mr. Heseltine for the "assassination" of Maggie.

Careless copy and perhaps no editing. Mark the repetitions, unexplained phrases as if directly lifted from London eveningers. Also take note of various qualifications of Mr. Major and the way each successive paragraph begins with his name. The "Major task" of the new prime minister has appeared more than once in a futile attempt to make some literature out of his name. Poor copy, poor editing and there has, been no concern for the Indian audience for which this much talked about paper is published.

Carelessness can create problems even when writing captions for photographs. *The Times of India,* Bombay on July 4, 1990, carried a photograph of Bharat Bhavan, Bhopal with a caption, "Bharat Bhavan designed by Charles Correa, looks across the river at Bhopal town". However, there is no river in Bhopal, the mass of water seen in the photograph belonged to the famous Bhopal Lake. Anybody who visits Bhopal will not miss this fact. Naturally, Manjula Sen, who had sent the story from Bhopal could not commit this blunder. The sub-editor in Bombay tried to be a bit poetic and imagined that the water seen in the photograph should be of some river. If the effort was made to find out the name of the river, the blunder could have been avoided.

At the time of make up carelessness results in a situation which can turn a reader crazy. Sometimes chunks of matter lifted from one place are misplaced in the same copy or in a different copy. Parts of Delhi Diary of *The Times of India,* New Delhi on October 15, 1990 made crazy reading:

> (First column last paragraph) Finally, they claim given the tolerance of all religions, "we can turn the course of history by building a sanctuary of holy names. The walls of such a interfaith sanctuary would have carvings of ver-(Second column) while she would get up to ask whether her "turn" had come. But the leader followed voluble leader and no one called the old lady."

Then we have (Column 4, first paragraph):

> There was this "Romeo" on a two wheeler, who forced her to change the leisurely walk into a breathless one. He saw her walking on the other side and decided to catch her attention. He did without much from the Ramayana and the Bhagwad Gita, the Ayat of the Holy Koran, teaching from the Bible, the Buddhist sutras, Mahaviras teachings and the Zoroastrian scriptures, with translations in Hindi, English and Urdu."

The last para in column four runs into the fifth column making this crazy reading:

> She waited patiently almost until the end of the rally. Once in a effort. He simply stopped and said "hello". The colleague just looked through and walked ahead. He turned and made it look as though he was leaving. But he did not. He came back again and said something incoherently. The same exercise was repeated-back and forth with minutes' gap...

A careful reading discovered the fact that in this Delhi Diary three chunks of matter have been misplaced, resulting in the chaos. No reader would have time and patience to correct such lapses and the natural reaction would be to turn the page.

A bit of carelessness sometimes leads to a major fiasco.

When United Nations Secretary General, Dag Hammarskjold, flew to Ndola, in northern Rhodesia, in 1961 for talks on the Congo crisis, reporters were waiting for him at the airport. An aircraft landed and reporters saw a tall, white man who looked like Hammarskjold walk down the steps and into a limousine. Some of the waiting reporters asked local airport officials, to be certain, if the man was the UN Secretary General and they were assured he was. Dispatches were sent and the correspondents returned to their hotels.

These reporters learnt only later that Hammarskjold was dead in a plane crash in the jungle. The arriving passenger was a British envoy. David Habberstam, then of the *New York Times,* missed covering the arrival by some quirk of fate as he wrote later that if he had been at the airport he most likely would have made the same mistake. Instead of going to Vietnam and a subsequent Pulitzer Prize, he said, he might have ended up back in New York, discredited.

The moral of this internationally famous fiasco is that the reporters should not take things for granted and must check and recheck their information from the right and trustworthy sources. But all journalists do not follow this difficult path and this results in bloomers that reduce the credibility of the media.

There has been a case where very many reporters and sub-editors across the country took things for granted and in fact reinforced each other's misinformation. The result was that newspaper readers throughout the country believe that a dead hangman was involved in the hanging of Satwant Singh and Kehar Singh.

Ever since the hanging of the murderers of the Chopra children, it was known that hangmen Kallu of Meerut and Fakira of Patiala are called to Delhi, whenever such occasion arises, as there was no hangman in Delhi. The Chopra children murder case has been so extensively covered that the names of the hangmen who hanged Billa and Ranga were remembered by Delhi crime reporters and many of them thought that the two hangmen will be called again to hang Satwant Singh and Kehar Singh and so when the black warrants were issued, many reporters took it for granted and used the stuff in the story. A news agency report from Delhi carried this information to all the corners of the country.

A reporter with *The Tribune*, Chandigarh, who had interviewed Fakira earlier perhaps, thought that this was an opportunity for him to get a byline in his paper and so he rehashed the old interview in such way as if he had interviewed him recently. He knew that Fakira had retired and that he put in his story, but he took it for granted that the agency story was correct and did not bother about rechecking the fact. His report said, "Fakira, who retired as a constable from Patiala jail sometime ago, has again been chosen to go to Delhi as one of the hangmen selected to execute Satwant Singh and Kehar Singh."

This interview was published along with a photograph and gave further credence to the earlier story that Fakira had been called for the hanging. Only Patiala jail staff and officials knew that Fakira was long dead. They laughed at the story, talked about it in their circle, but perhaps stopped at that. Local reporters did not bother to check it. And so Fakira kept on appearing in newspapers throughout the country.

On January 7, 1989 people read a graphic description in most newspapers adding colour to the story, "Jail sources later said the executions were carried out by hangmen Kallu and Fakira, who drew the levers to open trapdoors on a signal by jail Superintendent. A Magistrate and the prison doctor were present, they said." This was an agency story. Perhaps the reporter was never told what he wrote and people read and believed or was it disinformation? Perhaps, the jail authorities were inaccessible and they did not want to disclose the names of hangmen for security reasons and reporters took the names for granted. However, Fakira the famous hangman was a warder in Patiala jail. He retired on June 30, 1987 and died on November 25, 1987.

Names of the people being quoted in the story have to be checked carefully. Let me give an instance which involved myself. I participated in the 'Inter-Continental Journalists' Meet' which discussed New World Information and Communication Order. S. Venugopal, a staff reporter of the Patriot reported what I said as, "Dr. J.P. Srivastava felt the absence of 'gatekeepers' in newspapers to encourage NANAR If non-aligned nations cannot work collectively on this issue, then we will continue to be fed by western news agencies, he said."

The reporter did meet me at tea-break and had a chat, but he had taken my name for granted as he had a list of speakers and therefore did not feel like checking. In fact, Dr. J.P. Srivastava did not even attend the session.

Bibliography

Ahuja, B.N. : *Theory and Practice of Journalism*, Surjeet Publications, Delhi, 1979.

Alfred, John : *Mass Communication in the New Millennium*, Prime Publication, New Jersey, 2003.

Apter, Michel : *The New Technology of Education*, MacMillan, London, 1968.

Aronson, James : *The Press and the Cold War*, Beacon Press, Boston, 1970.

Awasthy, G.C. : *Broadcasting in India*, Allied Publishers Private Ltd., Bombay, 1965.

Bard, F. Eraser : *An Introduction to Journalism*, The MacMillan Co., New York, 1958.

Bernard, H. W. : *Principles of Journalism: A Basic Text*, Allied Publishers Private Ltd., New Delhi, 1998.

Bhatia, A. : *Journalism in Modern India*, Asia Publishing House, Bombay, 1964.

Brank, S.M. : *Journalism Characteristics and School Learning*, Harper, New York, 1976.

Carrol, L. : *Occupational Information*, Prentice Hall, New York, 1961.

Cattell, B.B. : *Media Structure, Growth and Action*, Houghton Mifflin Co., Boston, 1999.

Chatterjee, R.K. : *Mass Communication*, National Book Trust, New Delhi, 2002.

Chauhan, S.S. : *A Textbook of Mass Communication*, Sterling Publishers, New Delhi, 2001.

Cottle, W.C. : *Interest and Personality Inventories*, Houghton Miffling Co., New York, 1968.

Cream, David : *Explaining Teaching Machines and Programmes*, Featon, San Fracisco, 1961.

Critchfield, Richard : *The Indian Reporter's Guide*, Allied Pacifiç Pvt. Ltd., Bombay, 1962.

Curfis, D. : *Interpretotive Reporting*, MacMillan Co., New York, 1957.

Dale, Edgare : *Audio-Visual Method in Teaching*, Dryden Rinehart and Winston, New York, 1969.

Das, R.C. : *Educational Technology*, Sterling Publishers, New Delhi, 2000.

Donald, H. : *Developmental Counselling*, The Ronald Press, New York, 1966.

Donald, Mc. : *The Art of Radio*, Faber & Faber, London, 1961.

Emery, Edwin : *The Press and America*, Prentice Hall, New Jersey, 1999.

Eve, A. A. : *Micro-teaching Theory into Practice*, Oxford, New York, 1969.

Frank, H. Krouse : *Media Technique with Youth*, Charles and Mervil, Ohio, 1990.

Gagne, R.M. : *The Conditions of Learning*, Holt Binsort and Winston, New York, 1965.

Gaur, J.S. and Saraswat, R.K. : *Mass Media*, NCERT, New Delhi, 1998.

Ghiselli, Edwin E. : *Personnel and Industrial Media*, McGraw Hill Book Co., New York, 1955.

Gunning, Robert : *The Technique of Clear Writing*, McGraw Hill Book Co., New York.

Haban, F. : *Movies that Teach*, Dryden Press, New York, 1945.

Hancock, Alan : *Planning for Educational Mass Media*, Longmans, London, 1977.

Hercleread, A.V. : *Instruction: Materials and Methods*, Mc Graw Hill Book Co., New York, 1964.

Hoppock, Rebert : *Occupational Information*, McGraw Hill Book Co., New York, 1997.

Hudson, Kenneth : *The Dictionary of Diseased English*, The MacMillan Co., Bombay, 1977.

James, S. : *Audio-Visual Materials and Techniques*, American Book Company, New York, 1959.

John, A. : *The Asian Newspaper's Reluctant Revolution*, The Iowa State University Press, Iowa, 1977.

John, Hohenberg : *The Professional Journalist*, Rinehort and Winston, New York, 1969.

Johnson, Stanley and Julian Harriss : *The Complete Reporter*, The MacMillan Co., New York, 1942.

Joseph and Jospeth : *Idyels Past and Present: An Editor's Wet Copy*, Orient Longman, Bombay, 1979.

Kaul, B.N. : *Studies in Mass Media*, Har Anand, New Delhi, 1998.

Knight, R. : *Intelligence and Intelligence Tests*, Methuen and Co. Ltd. London, 1943.

Kothari, O.S. : *Report of the Indian Education Commission, 1964-66*, Publication Divison, New Delhi, 1966.

Krug, R.E. : *Ability Testing in Developing Countries: A Handbook of Principles and Techniques*, Praeger, New York, 1972.

Laxman, N.J. : *Introduction to Media Technology*, Oxford Publishing Company, New Delhi, 2003.

Lowman, J. : *Mastering Techniques of Media*, Prentice Hall, New York, 1999.

Luhan, Mc : *Understanding Media*, Routludge, London, 1964.

Mahler, C.A. : *Media Counselling in the Schools*, Houghton Mifflin, Boston, 1969.

Matheson, Alastair : *The Communication Materials and Methods*, McGraw Hill Book Company, New Delhi, 1964.

McCully, C.H. : *The Media—Instrument of Change*, National College Record, Bombay, 2001.

Mehta, D.S. : *Mass Communication and Journalism in India*, Allied Publishers Pvt. Ltd., Bombay, 1979.

Menon, Narayan : *The Communication Revolution*, National Book Trust, New Delhi, 1976.

Miller, Care G. : *Modern Journalism*, Rinehart and Winston, New York, 1962.

Miller, Carroll, H. : *Foundations of Guidance*, Harper and Brothers, New York, 1961.

Mitchell, V. : *Reporting*, Rinehart and Winston, New York, 1960.

Mohanty, J. : *Educational Broadcasting: Radio & Television in Education*, Sterling Publishers, New Delhi, 1984.

Mojar, N.F. : *Current Trends in Mass Communication*, Deep & Deep Publications, New Delhi, 2001.

Mokam, K.B. : *Dynamics of Mass Media in India*, Deep & Deep Publications, New Delhi, 2000.

Mosan, N.N. : *Indian Education in the Emerging Society*, Sterling Publishers, New Delhi, 1982.

Moven, Kiran : *Studies in Educational Broadcasting*, Deep & Deep Publications, New Delhi, 1996.

Mujuni, J.P. : *Studies in Media Education*, Deep & Deep Publications, New Delhi, 1995.

Muni, K.W. : *Media Technology*, Deep & Deep Publications, New Delhi, 2003.

Murthy, Nadig Krishna : *Indian Journalism*, University of Mysore, Prasaranga, 1966.

Natrajan, J. : *History of Indian Journalism*, Publications Division, New Delhi, 1999.

Natrajan, S. : *A History of the Press in India*, Asia Publishing House, Bombay, 1962.

Oscar, Krisen : *Encyclopaedia of Mass Media and Journalism*, Oxford, New York, 1998.

Ottaway, A.K.C. : *Press and Society*, Routldge and Kegan Paul, London, 1962.

Oxtoby, J.S. : *Media and Cultural Environment*, Methuen, London, 1969

Page, C.M. : *Society and Media*, MacMillan, London, 1950.

Panda, K.C. : *Role of Mass Media in School Learning*, RCE, Bhubaneswar, 1978.

Parikh, R.D. : *The Press and Society*, Popular Prakashan, Bombay, 1965.

Quirk, A. : *Editor and Editorial Writer*, Rinehart & Co., New York, 1955.

Reston, James : *The Artillery of the Press: Its Influence on American Foreign Policy*, Harper & Row, New York, 1967.

Rewntreu, Desk : *Media Technology in Curriculum Development*, Harper and Row Publishers, London, 2001.

Richder L. : *Handbook of Broadcasting*, McGraw- Hill Book Co., New York, 1957.

Roland, E. : *Exploring Journalism*, Prentice Hall, New Jersey, 1958.

Sadanand, K.R. : *New Media: Memo to Educational Planners*, John, Wiley, London, 2002.

Sahni, J.N. : *Truth About the Indian Press*, Allied Publishers, Bombay, 1974.

Schramm, Wilbur : *Big Media, Little Media*, Edward Arnold, London, 2000.

Sethi, Patanjali : *Professional Journalism*, Orient Longman, Bombay, 1974.

Shaw, David : *Journalism Today*, Harper's College Press, London, 1977.

Shelly, C. : *Fundamentals of Mass Media*, Houghton Miffin Co., Boston, 1976.

Thedore, M. : *Headlines and Deadlines*, Columbia University Press, New York, 1961.

Thorndike, R.L. : *Media Psychology and Education*, Wiley Eastern Pvt. Ltd., New Delhi, 2001.

Ullan, J. : *Technical Reporting*, Rinehart and Winston, New York, 1963.

Vedanayagam, G. : *Media Teaching Technology for College Teachers*, Sterling Publishers, New Delhi, 1989.

Viner, B. : *The Practice of Journalism*, Heinemann, London, 1963.

Warich, D. : *Modular Circula: International Encyclopaedia*, Pergamone Publications, London, 1994.

Whinnie, Donald : *The Art of Broadcasting*, Faber & Faber, London, 1961.

Willian, Charvat : *Handbook for Writers*, Prentice Hall, New Jersey, 1962.

Wolseley, E. : *How to Report and Write the News?*, Prentice Hall, New Jersey, 1961.

Zanda, B. : *Journalism as Guidance*, MacMillan Co., New York, 1998.

Zohar, B. : *Principles and Techniques of Journalism*, Vikas Publishing House, New Delhi, 1982.

Index

❑❑❑